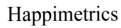

Happimetrics

T0293121

NEW HORIZONS IN MANAGEMENT

Series Editor: Professor Sir Cary Cooper, *50th Anniversary Professor of Organizational Psychology and Health at Alliance Manchester Business School, University of Manchester, UK and President of the Chartered Institute of Personnel and Development and British Academy of Management*

This important series makes a significant contribution to the development of management thought. This field has expanded dramatically in recent years and the series provides an invaluable forum for the publication of high quality work in management science, human resource management, organizational behaviour, marketing, management information systems, operations management, business ethics, strategic management and international management.

The main emphasis of the series is on the development and application of new original ideas. International in its approach, it will include some of the best theoretical and empirical work from both well-established researchers and the new generation of scholars.

Titles in the series include:

Happimetrics
Leveraging AI to Untangle the Surprising
Link Between Ethics, Happiness and Business
Success

Peter A. Gloor

*Research Scientist, MIT Center for Collective Intelligence, USA,
Honorary Professor, University of Cologne, Germany and Chief
Creative Officer, Galaxyadvisors AG*

NEW HORIZONS IN MANAGEMENT

Edward Elgar
PUBLISHING

Cheltenham, UK • Northampton, MA, USA

Cover image: Joscha Eirich

Published by
Edward Elgar Publishing Limited
The Lypiatts
15 Lansdown Road
Cheltenham
Glos GL50 2JA
UK

Edward Elgar Publishing, Inc.
William Pratt House
9 Dewey Court
Northampton
Massachusetts 01060
USA

Paperback edition 2023

A catalogue record for this book
is available from the British Library

Library of Congress Control Number: 2022943071

This book is available electronically in the **Elgar**online
Business subject collection
http://dx.doi.org/10.4337/9781803924021

Printed on elemental chlorine free (ECF)
recycled paper containing 30% Post-Consumer Waste

ISBN 978 1 80392 401 4 (cased)
ISBN 978 1 80392 402 1 (eBook)
ISBN 978 1 0353 1215 3 (paperback)

Printed and bound in the USA

I would like to dedicate this book to my late mentor Thomas J. Allen, who spent his research career as a professor at MIT Sloan studying the flow of knowledge in organizations. When I left Deloitte twenty years ago and came back to MIT as a research scientist at the Center for Collective Intelligence, Tom generously shared his lifelong experience researching the management of technology and taught me the key principles of measuring communication, which have guided my research over the last twenty years. Thank you, Tom!

Contents

Acknowledgments

This book is the product of a collaborative innovation network of 20 years. Without the support and collaboration of my colleagues, it could never have been written. In particular, I would like to thank the director of our center at MIT, Thomas W. Malone, and my colleague Robert Laubacher for their continuous support over the last 20 years in my pursuit of many crazy ideas. I would also like to thank Andrea Fronzetti Colladon and Francesca Grippa; together as a "dream team" we have written dozens of papers about many different research projects. I also thank my children Sarah and David, who were early critics of most of my ideas, greatly sharpening and improving them through their feedback.

I thank Joao Marcos De Oliveira and Matthaeus Zylka for being first-rate creators at Galaxyadvisors, building the tools we use in our happimetrics analysis, and Harry Toukalas for applying his design skills to the beautification of the charts in this book.

But the COIN is much larger than that. Adam Almozlino, David Aloini, Keith Arano, Robin Athey, Linda Bäbler, Matias Barahona, Melina Becker, Tim Boyle, Hans Brechbuhl, Lucas Broennimann, Pascal Budner, John D. Collins, Scott Cooper, Marius Cramer, Patrick DeBoer, Arash Delijani, George Dellal, Marco DeMaggio, Pierre Dorsaz, Lyric Doshi, Scott Dynes, Marc Egger, Joscha Eirich, Eric Esser, Kai Fischbach, Karin Frick, Hauke Führes, Manuel Galbier, Cristobal Garcia, Gianni Giacomelli, Julia Gluesing, Detlef Guertler, Beth Hadley, Michael Henninger, George Herman, Teresa Heyder, Lola Higuera, Takashi Iba, Orr Inbar, Bill Ives, Eric Johnson, Adriaan Jooste, Jermain Kaminsiki, Min-Hyung Kang, Yared Kidane, Reto Kleeb, Jonas Krauss, Dustin Larimer, Casper Lassenius, Rob Laubacher, Jonas Lauener, Charles Leiserson, Hanumateja Maddali, Marton Makai, Fillia Makedon, Tom Malone, Buenyamin Oezkaya, Peter Margolis, Pascal Marmier, Joao Gabriel Silva Marra, Molly McKean, Christine Miller, Leeban Morgan, Stefan Nann, Keiichi Nemoto, Tuomas Niinimäki, Daniel Olguin, Daniel Oster, Maria Paasivaara, Karsten Packmohr, Sandy Pentland, Philipp Peter, Oliver Posegga, Peter Praeder, Shannon Provost, Johannes Putzke, John Quimby, Ornit Raz, Renaud Richardet, Ken Riopelle, Jannik Roessler, Tejasvita Saran, Daniel C. Schmid, Michael Schober, Detlef Schoder, Thomas Schmalberger, Michael Seid, Joao Gabriel Silva Marra, Yang Song, Martin Stangll, Alessandro Stefanini, Marius Stein, Katharina Stolz, Shosta Sulonen, Jiachen Sun, Lirong

Sun, Masamichi Takahashi, David Verrill, Manfred Vogel, Gloria Volkmann, Christoph Von Arb, Ben Waber, Xin Wang, Qi Wen, Andrew Westerdale, Stephanie Woerner, JoAnn Yates, Wayne Yuhasz, Qiaoyun Yun, Maximilian Zeyda, Kang Zhang, Xue Zhang, Yan Zhao, Yuhong Zhou, Antonio Zilli, Kevin Zogg – thank you all for being bees in my COIN.

Abbreviations

AI	artificial intelligence
CEO	chief executive officer
CMU	Colorado Mesa University
COIN	collaborative innovation network
CQ	creative quotient
EQ	emotional quotient
FFI	Five Factor Inventory
IQ	intelligence quotient
MFCC	Mel Frequency Cepstral Coefficient
NLP	natural language processing
OCEAN	openness, conscientiousness, extraversion, agreeableness and neuroticism
PACU	post-anesthesia care unit
SNA	social network analysis
US	United States
YOLO	you only live once

1. Introduction to *Happimetrics*

It was on Saturday evening in the second week of the fall 2021 concert season of the world-renowned Boston Symphony Orchestra, just after the intermission. Symphony Hall was filled with an excited audience, still fully masked because of Covid-19, but euphoric that it was finally possible to indulge again in their shared passion after lonely months of lockdowns and Internet-streamed performances. The piece to be played was Mozart's piano concerto in E-flat for two pianos. The orchestra members already sat on their chairs when conductor Andris Nelsons welcomed the two solo pianists, twins Christina and Michelle Naughton. They sat down behind two grand pianos, facing each other, waiting for the conductor to give them the cue for their entry. And then they started playing, not as two pianists, but as one. As their teacher at the Juilliard School said,[1] "when they play together, they seem to have one mind and one body – it's extraordinary – like one person with two hands playing."

The Naughton twins are fully entangled, to the extent that, in their own words, there are times where they forget they are two people playing together. Since birth, they have spent their lives together, forming a bond so strong they mostly don't need to talk, as they can read each other's mind. If they speak, they typically talk about music, using their own lingo, that others don't understand. According to Christina, "we kind of speak our own language, so if someone were to listen, I don't think they'd know what was going on."[2] When studying at Juilliard, they even attended every single one of each other's piano lessons.

On that evening in Symphony Hall, the listeners were mesmerized, forgetting time and space, only living in the moment, immersed into the music of Mozart created by the Naughton twins together with the musicians of the Boston Symphony Orchestra. They were all in flow, in groupflow, the listeners, the members of the orchestra, the conductor and the two pianists.

Getting into groupflow, the most productive state of creative collaboration, takes an entangled team, an entangled collaborative innovation network (COIN). The secret ingredient is the entanglement among the group members, intensive teamwork without words, where each team member knows what the others are thinking, and spoken words are used only rarely to convey what needs to be done. More important is communicating by other means, through body language, through glances, through the speed with which each other's actions are answered. The knowing smile, the twinkle in the eyes, the little gesture, the shared emotion, best visible when meeting in the same room, but also essential when communicating by video call, are the glue that keeps the team together. This is what the Naughton twins beautifully demonstrated on that evening in Symphony Hall, seamlessly entangled, having spent their entire lives together, operating as one unified team together with the Boston Symphony Orchestra musicians, themselves entangled as they have been playing and practicing together for decades; all communicating through shared thought and feelings, leading to a superb flow experience of their tribe of classical music lovers.

I have been studying COINs for the last 20 years. While it has now been commonly accepted that innovation happens as a collaborative endeavor, it is still far from clear how and why COINs work. I have seen many aspiring COINs where everything seemed right, where people agreed on the goals of the team, team members brought the right skills set, logistics were set up perfectly, all members were passionate about their goals and they still never got off the ground, or the team foundered a few weeks after a promising start. These are the orchestras where the music just does not sound right, where the conductor gets in the way of the orchestra, or players who are not team players spoil the flow experience of the team.

In our research since 2002, we have been exploring COINs at hundreds of organizations, ranging from jazz orchestras, teams of surgeons, open-source communities and startups, to Fortune 500 firms with hundreds of thousands of employees. What we found is that to fully unleash the power of COINs, entanglement among team members is key. They are entangled through a shared context and shared values which allow them to communicate without words, through "honest signals," body language and shared action. In other words, they should be members of the same virtual tribe, sharing the same morals and characteristics. Entangled members of COINs operate in an environment of positive energy. Their humility, kindness and compassion will generate positive emotional energy. They avoid overconfidence, arrogance and egotistical behavior, which would drain energy and create a toxic work environment.

The key to a successful COIN is its members. Obviously, they all need to share the same goal, and be passionate about it. However, that is not enough. Rather, we found that team members all need to speak the same language, in words and in deeds. This shared language can be expressed in face-to-face interaction, but it can also be in emails, slack posts and WhatsApp messages. Language not only consists of substantive words, but also of the honest signals embedded in the interaction, the speed of the response to an email, the use of little filler words besides the ones carrying the main content and the emotions contained in interactions. Language can also be the gestures, the glances, the facial expressions shown when interacting with others. By speaking the same language, COIN members are adherents to the same virtual tribe, living by the same values and ethics. Members choose their tribes by their attributes and symbols, such as their shared love for classical music, or wearing a particular brand, for instance demonstrating that they are "in the business to save our planet" by wearing Patagonia apparel. Individuals also show tribe membership by using certain terms and expressions such as "#MakeAmericaGreatAgain." Being with their tribe makes them happy, as the other tribe members are "just like them," so they don't have to explain themselves; individuals can trust other tribe members as others will trust them.

Choosing the right tribe, whose members all share the same values, is key. When considering joining a particular tribe, how can I know if other people share my values? When buying a specific clothing brand, or going to a classical concert, demonstrating tribal loyalty is straightforward. However, figuring out the value system of a narrowly focused tribe can be demanding. Frequently, a tribe might advertise a set of values but still have other more hidden principles. For instance, Covid-19 vaccine refusers are unified in their rejection of the vaccine; however, their political views are widely divergent, as there are fanatic refusers both at the right and the left end of the political spectrum. Obviously, we can ask tribe members about their values, but words can be misleading, and people might want to hide some of their beliefs in order to join a tribe. Asking their friends is a more reliable way to tease out the personality characteristics, ethics and values of a person than asking the person directly. People usually are sharp judges of others, capable of seeing through self-deceiving illusionary self-perception. However, a person might have no friends, or they might not be around or might be unwilling to answer our questions. Therefore, instead of asking friends, we might ask artificial intelligence (AI).

AI and machine learning give us a novel way to measure the true personality characteristics, morals and values of a person, based on that person's behavior and their honest signals. These honest signals are the little words, the body language, the tone of voice, the glances, the body posture, that a person shows in response to external events. By aggregating the personality characteristics, morals and values of thousands of people, and comparing them with the little words, body language, tone of voice, glances and body posture of these thousands of people, we can create a machine learning model that will predict an individual's moral values more accurately than the individual can by him or herself. This means that instead of asking their friends for their assessment of the personality of a person, we ask the collective wisdom of large groups of people aggregated and made accessible in an AI system.

This book introduces AI-based methods to identify personality, moral values and ethics of individuals based on their body language and interaction with others. The same methods will also be used to measure the degree of entanglement between two individuals and to find entangled COINs, and show how they can be made even more creative, productive and happy by identifying their virtual tribes through their shared values and morals and mirroring these insights back to them. While these methods could be used by managers to assess the (im)morality of their employees, this is absolutely not how they should be used. The key tenet of the "virtual mirroring" approach introduced in later chapters is that these insights are *only* shown to affected individuals, and not their bosses. AI is never 100 percent accurate, in fact the methods introduced in Part II of this book have accuracies ranging from 65 to 90 percent. This means that there is a 10 to 35 percent chance that AI is wrong. For example, in earlier work we have found that the speed with which individuals respond to email is a proxy of their passion, and this metric is part of some of our AI algorithms. However, there could be perfectly legitimate reasons why somebody is slower than usual in answering – they might have to care for a sick child or are on vacation – and then AI, not knowing the context, is wrong! Only the individual knows the full context, and that's why the key principle of virtual mirroring is to only show individual information to the affected individual, and anonymized aggregated information to others. Studying organizations starts with studying individuals. These individuals want to be treated respectfully, as individuals, and not as "human robots" to be pushed around by AI algorithms and zealous bosses.

1.1   AN ALGORITHM FOR HAPPY EMPLOYEES

Knowing what makes you happy will make you happier!

Becoming aware of what and who makes people happy or stressed will increase individual happiness and create blockbuster business performance. Research has clearly shown what creates happy employees – giving them respect, empowering them to make their own decisions and being an empathic, humble leader – but it is awfully hard to actually lead by those principles. This book lays out a proven and tested method for reaching this goal, analyzing individuals' communication patterns, and making them self-aware by mirroring their behavior back to them in a privacy-respecting way. It describes three key steps to building happiness and better performance through entanglement, first how to communicate better to create a sustainably happy workplace, second how to optimize communication to increase happiness and teamwork by mirroring back the measurements to the individual and third how to measure groupflow and happiness as input for virtual mirroring. This method is based on 20 years of research from our MIT COIN project on leadership, creativity, team building and positive psychology published in over 250 peer-reviewed scientific papers. We take insights from hundreds of industry and research projects our team conducted on individual and organizational creativity and performance and distill it into an AI algorithm for building exceptional teams and organizations, improving individual happiness and organizational performance by establishing and nurturing groupflow.

Groupflow extends the flow concept coined by Hungarian-American psychologist Mihaly Csikszentmihalyi to teams. Flow is the highest state of individual productivity, where an individual is fully immersed into an activity just for the joy of doing it, and not by external motivation such as money, power or glory. Groupflow enables teams to reach their highest productive and creative state, cooperating above and beyond what each team member is capable of. Groupflow is the most fruitful mental condition a group of people can achieve, working together to solve a seemingly impossible task. In a state of elation and positive stress, they outperform themselves and the expectations of their peers and deliver a product that is far superior to what each of the team members individually could do.

Figure 1.1   The Rubik cube of happiness

Figure 1.1 shows the "Rubik cube of happiness," illustrating the building blocks of our approach for creating, measuring and increasing groupflow through consciously tracking and steering emotions, entanglement and tribes. As illustrated in the Rubik cube of happiness, the book answers three main questions, as follows.

1.1.1   How Do Emotional Reactions Reflecting Individual Morals Create Entangled Tribes?

Part I lays out the foundations of groupflow and how it creates happy, high-performing teams. Groupflow arises when people unified by the same morals and thus sharing similar emotional reactions get together to work on a seemingly impossibly hard task. Groupflow is based on the theory of flow defined by Mihaly Csikszentmihalyi, extended to groups of creative people who develop radically new ideas. Flow in the sense of Csikszentmihalyi consists of operating in positive stress while being fully immersed in a near impossible task. Groups of people get together in creative swarms, sharing similar ethical and moral values, and establish digital virtual tribes. People in the same virtual tribe show similar emotional responses and thus signal to each other membership of the same tribe. They become "synchronized" in entanglement through shared emotional responses to form the collaborative bond – entanglement – that carries them to groupflow.

1.1.2   How Can Measuring Emotions and Morals Create Happy and Successful Teams?

The key to increasing happiness and groupflow is virtual mirroring, showing individuals how they communicate and how they can do better. Creating groupflow through entanglement happens in COINs, teams of intrinsically motivated people collaborating on a shared creative task to create something radically new. They become part of a virtual organism operating in collective awareness. Their collective consciousness, their entanglement and their group-flow are supported and reinforced through insight gained by virtual mirroring, showing them how much they are already synchronized and what they can do to become even more entangled. As has been shown in our research, giving teams access to their virtual mirror greatly improves their performance, creativity and happiness. This is based on the principle "the best against the rest," showing people how they are doing compared to the anonymized aggregated communication patterns of their peers together with recommendations for more happiness and groupflow. The virtual mirror also exposes individuals to oversight by integrating feedback from others, leading to stress and pain, as they might discover that they are not as popular, fair, ethical or collaborative as they think they are. Accepting potential weaknesses and demonstrating will-ingness to change will be temporarily painful, but will lead to more groupflow, better performance and thus superior results.

1.1.3   How Can Emotions and Morals Be Measured with Artificial Intelligence?

Our work has combined three different approaches to track and mirror human interaction while groups of people collaborate in groupflow: measuring emotions, measuring network structure and measuring interaction dynamics. These methods are enabled through the most recent advances in AI, machine learning and deep learning. Emotions of individuals can be measured through body signals using smartwatches, through image recognition of body language, through image recognition of facial expressions and through voice emotion recognition. Most prominently, emotions can also be recognized through word usage. These different emotion recognition systems use different AI algorithms, for instance deep learning for face emotion recognition and body language recognition, or other machine learning algorithms for natural language processing to calculate emotions from words. Besides recognizing the emotion of individuals, the structure of the interaction network can be tracked using graph algorithms and social network analysis to compute the centrality of individuals in the network and the distribution of centralities among all members of the network. Finally, network dynamics can be calculated by looking at changes in the network structure and position over time. The content of what is being said by whom at what time can also be analyzed: the more the words of an individual in a network differ from the words of the other members of the network, and the faster they are picked up by others, the more influential that individual is. Entanglement measures the rhythm and synchronicity of mutual interaction in the network. The more synchronized the interaction and changes in network position among members of a network, the more entangled are these individuals.

NOTES

1.   www.wsj.com/articles/christina-and-michelle-naughton-twin-pianists-perform -at-naumburg-orchestral-concerts-1407173152.
2.   www.wsj.com/articles/christina-and-michelle-naughton-twin-pianists-perform -at-naumburg-orchestral-concerts-1407173152.

PART I

Principles of groupflow

2.   What is groupflow?

Listening to a live performance of a top-level orchestra is a magical experience. With closed eyes, their bodies swinging in synch, the musicians are in flow with the music and with each other, while their hands fly over their instruments, expressing the emotions flowing through their brains, producing heaven for their audience. Without having to look at each other, simply by listening to each other's playing, they know what comes next and how to respond to new cues. Through decades of training, but also through shared passion, values, empathy and compassion, they have become one. Such an orchestra is an exemplar of an entangled team in groupflow.

Groupflow is not restricted to musicians playing together in a symphony orchestra or a jazz band. The construction workers building two temporary hospitals with 2500 beds for Covid-19 patients in Wuhan in just ten days, or the researchers at the 49 pharmaceutical companies working on a vaccine for Covid-19 at a frenetic pace, are similarly in groupflow. Any team delivering top performance without knowing if it will succeed is in flow.

Members of high-performing organizations are entangled and play together like musicians in a top orchestra. Whether it is programmers in the Linux open-source project or construction workers building a replacement for a collapsed highway bridge in Genoa in less than two years, they are all in flow as a group under huge stress to deliver a product as quickly as possible, highly uncertain if they will succeed in reaching their extremely ambitious goal, but at the same time energized as members of a unique team of creative and creating individuals, giving their best, more than their best, to deliver as a team what they never could achieve as individuals.

In one of his last interviews, Steve Jobs said: "Making great products is hard. But what's really hard is making a great team that will continue to make great products." Ten years after the death of Steve Jobs, Apple is still humming along, cranking out one blockbuster product after another as one of the world's most valuable companies. How can one build such an organization that supports high-performing teams lasting for decades? While a world-class orchestra or Apple are examples of organizations operating in groupflow over decades, the same state can be reached spontaneously, as in the examples of building a hospital in ten days, or a bridge in two years. Groupflow is analogous to the concept of Wu Wei (无为), which originates in ancient Chinese philosophy. Wu Wei means "effortless action," "non-action" and "going with the flow" and

is a key concept of Chinese Taoist philosophy. It describes a state of uncon-
flicting personal harmony, free-flowing spontaneity and passive mindfulness.
"Change is like a river: nothing is the same, even for an instant. Everything is
continually moving through the six stages of change: about to come into being,
beginning, expanding, approaching maximum potential, peaking, and finally,
passing its peak and flowing into its new condition."[1]

Groupflow leverages the "wisdom of swarms" by combining the creative
output of intrinsically motivated people into a final product that is far more
than the sum of its parts. As said beautifully in the *I Ching*, groupflow cannot
be controlled and mandated into action. Just like water flowing down a hill will
find its way autonomously, the only thing that can be done to nurture and foster
groupflow is setting up the dams of the river, and then letting the water flow.
Groupflow is the opposite of the "madness of crowds" engaging in pyramid
schemes or "black tulip bulb crazes." Such collective madness is characterized
by negative entanglement that gets groups of people together as conspiring
mobs. Examples are rogue derivatives traders, or groups of hackers trying to
extort bitcoin ransom from unsuspecting users by hacking into their IT system.

Groupflow can be greatly boosted by AI and machine learning. In two
decades of research at MIT and elsewhere, our team has developed AI-based
algorithms and software to empower individuals to measure their own emotions, their networking structure and their interaction dynamics as individuals
and when working together in teams. The goal is to automatically redirect and
channel emotional energy, to enhance communication within organizations
to create high-performing, happy, resilient, entangled teams collaborating in
groupflow. Small patterns invisible to the naked eye of the individual can
be recognized by the computer and be combined into global insights helping
individuals to become entangled with their team members. For instance, the
way leaves of a plant move in response to somebody passing by will indicate
what emotional state the person is in (we experimented with *mimosa pudica*
and the dancing plant *codariocalyx motorius*). This leaf movement would not
be visible to the naked eye and not recognizable to a computer camera through
a single measurement. Only by combining many measurements of plant leaf
movements triggered by many different people walking by the plant, and then
analyzing the plant reaction through electrical sensors and image recognition
with machine learning and AI, are computers capable of recognizing the leaf
movement pattern to discern in what emotional state the human being passing
by is.

In another example, by combining the hidden email communication patterns
of all members of a department we are able to measure the satisfaction of the
members of the department, and tell them how they can change their communication behavior to become happier and more productive, while at the same
time increasing the satisfaction of their customers. The goal is to create an

AI-enabled environment for groupflow, which has as its prerequisite the state of mutual entanglement, a shared context where participants are aligned in thinking and acting, capable of communicating with few words, just by reading non-verbal and verbal communication signals. This reading of non-verbal communication is augmented by AI, with the computer analyzing the way people interact, and calculating a forecast of how successful, happy and ethical the product of the teamwork will be, thus offering participants the opportunity for corrective action, leading to a better end product. For instance, showing the employees of a company to what extent they are entangled, and what communication pattern has increased the satisfaction of their customers in the past, will significantly increase customer satisfaction in the future. We call this process "virtual mirroring" and it has been employed and tested successfully in many projects. For instance, we have been measuring the happiness of employees with smartwatches through the way they move their bodies, which through virtual mirroring has increased their happiness. We also have been improving ethical behavior, the performance of star employees and reduced dissatisfaction of employees by tracking the hidden signals in their email communication. All of these examples will be discussed in detail later in the book.

2.1 WHAT IS FLOW?

According to Mihaly Csikszentmihalyi:[2]

> Flow denotes the holistic sensation present when we act with total involvement. It is the kind of feeling after which one nostalgically says: "that was fun," or "that was enjoyable"; it is the state in which action follows upon action according to an internal logic which seems to need no conscious intervention on our part. We experience it as a unified flowing from one moment to the next, in which we feel in control of our actions, and in which there is little distinction between self and environment; between stimulus and response; or between past, present, and future. (p. 43)

Csikszentmihalyi describes the elements of flow as follows.

2.1.1 A Challenging Activity That Requires Skills

This activity can be in sports, it can be in work and it can be artistic or literary. A simple way to create a challenging activity is to make it competitive. A soccer team at a match needs to get into flow, or it will have no chance of winning. Computer games are another opportunity to get into flow.

2.1.2   Merging of Action and Awareness

People become so immersed in what they are doing that the action becomes spontaneous and automatic. I am a very mediocre skier, but on a sunny winter day with gorgeous powder snow under a blue sky I forget all my fears and technical limitations, swinging downhill through fresh powder snow. The same is true for a group of musicians oblivious to their environment and fully immersed in the beauty of the melody they are playing together.

2.1.3   Clear Goals and Feedback

For instance, somebody learning to juggle balls will have very clear goals and will get immediate feedback for losing the flow of juggling when the balls fall down. The same is true for a band of musicians who will immediately know when they are getting out of flow if one of them misses a beat or a note, as will a passionate chef working on a complex meal if it is not cooked to perfection.

2.1.4   Concentration on the Task at Hand

When in flow, we focus exclusively on the chosen task, forgetting all the unpleasant aspects of life. This means that we live in the instant, and don't worry about the time before or the time to come. For instance, a musician playing in a band, if her mind is wandering to marital troubles and her upcoming concert tour, will not get into flow.

2.1.5   The Paradox of Control

By this Csikszentmihalyi means that we feel in control of our own destiny and do not worry about failure. To employ again the image of the juggler, the juggler needs to stop worrying about missing a ball and concentrate his mind on catching the balls. Or taking the image of a rock climber, the climber needs to stop worrying about falling down the cliff and single-mindedly focus on the climb ahead and the next grip in the rocks. As Csikszentmihalyi says, almost any enjoyable activity can become addictive, leading to enjoyable activities such as online games having negative aspects as participants can be glued to the screen for days at a time, with adverse consequences for their health.

2.1.6   The Loss of Self-Consciousness

When an activity leads to flow, the affected individuals forget about past and future, including their own self. Because the full attention of individuals is focused on the present flow task, they have no attention left to focus on themselves. As the focus on one's own self is normally a big worry and distraction, this is an essential part of increasing the enjoyment of flow.

2.1.7   The Transformation of Time

In the flow state, time runs differently from the normal state. Time might come to a standstill for a jazz musician while jamming, or time might fly for a passionate sailor sailing for hours on a beautiful day.

2.1.8   The Autotelic Experience

To describe the intrinsic motivation of people to engage in a flow experience, Csikszentmihalyi uses the expression "autotelic," from the Greek "auto" meaning "self" and "telos" meaning "goal." People engage in flow activities not because they are paid or ordered to do them, but because they honestly and intrinsically enjoy them. Whether it is an open-source programmer developing an addition to the Linux operating system or a painter working on a piece of art, they do it not for monetary reward, but because they genuinely enjoy what they are doing.

* * *

Besides studying flow as a psychological phenomenon, flow can also be analyzed and tracked on the physical level, measuring brain waves, and the chemical process probing hormone production in the human body.

What happens in the brain when an individuum is in flow? Measuring the brainwaves of computer gamers in flow[3] through an EEG found increased alpha and beta brainwave activity. Most prominent was the increase in alpha brainwave activity, which is associated with quietly flowing thoughts, meditation and a relaxed state of mind. Depending on the task, also an increase in beta brainwave activity was found, indicating that the observed individuals were engaged in a cognitive task, alert, interacting with the outside world, involved in problem solving, decision making and judgment.

On the hormonal level, a cocktail of hormones such as cortisone, oxytocin, dopamine, anandamide, endorphin and serotonin influence our perception and experience when reaching the flow state. Playing educational computer games leads to a reduction of the stress hormone cortisol in the body.[4] The same happens when a choir is singing together.[5] Singing together also increases the level of oxytocin in the blood.[6] Oxytocin is the happiness hormone, originally associated with mothers when giving birth to increase bonding with their babies. An increase in oxytocin levels in the blood has also been found to lead to increased trust and social bonding. Just listening to relaxing music is enough to increase oxytocin levels.

Dopamine is commonly known as the "pleasure hormone." It is released as a reward when having positive thoughts and experiences and its positive effects can lead to addiction to pleasure-producing sources such as food, sex and drugs. Researchers found that people with more dopamine receptors in their brain are more prone to experiencing flow.[7] Anandamide is the joy hormone, for instance ingested when eating chocolate as the cacao bean contains small amounts of it. Anandamide concentration in the blood increases after strenuous exercise such as a long bike ride,[8] potentially increasing the feeling of "bliss" and joy. Similarly, endorphin creates "runner's high" after a marathon,[9] helping the runner to ignore pain and feel elated. Norepinephrine release mobilizes the body for action, reaching its highest level in so-called "fight or flight" situations, increasing heart rate and blood flow and triggering the release of glucose into the blood. Norepinephrine and dopamine also help people pay attention and focus on a task. Serotonin is essential for regulating emotions and sleep and wake patterns. People with higher levels of serotonin are less impulsive and show less anxiety and depression. There is thus a mix of hormones playing together in triggering the flow state of an individual.

2.2   GETTING INTO GROUPFLOW

How do the flow states of interacting individuals play together to get a group into flow? At the final presentation of my one-semester COINs seminar there were seven teams, each with three to five graduate students. The team members were from three universities in Germany and Switzerland and had worked extremely hard to produce amazing results. They had created hardware and software to measure face-to-face and online human interaction. One team had developed sensors and software to track human–plant interaction. A second team had built a system to measure personality profiles from facial emotional responses when watching a video (see Chapter 15). Another team had created a system for AI-supported matchmaking based on automatic personality extraction from text. Other teams predicted the success of YouTube videos from facial expressions on video thumbnails or studied Covid-19 anti-vaxxers from Twitter behavior. The teams had invested a huge amount of time and effort, at times struggling with overload and not knowing what to do. But in the end, they derived immense satisfaction from their teamwork; in other words, they had been in groupflow – all while working on projects on how to measure and improve groupflow. How did I know they were in groupflow? Looking at the emotions in their faces, in their voices and in their email interactions told me as much. Getting into groupflow was supported by virtual mirroring sessions half-way through the course where they got a mirror of their communication behavior, together with suggestions on how to improve communication to improve their flow experience.

The process through which individuals in an organization reach groupflow is laid out in Figure 2.1. Groupflow is achieved through a confluence of psychological and sociological processes. External stimuli get us to respond with a particular emotion. The way we respond to an external stimulus is similarly influenced through the social network we are embedded in. This interaction can happen over long distances, using online social networks, email and other means of long-distance communication. Alternatively, it can also happen face to face. Through hidden subconscious "honest signals" – body language, word usage and facial cues – individuals signal to each other their emotional state. This means that it is not just the network structure and network dynamics, but also the emotional tone that decide how a social network interaction will play out. In particular, individuals who consciously and correctly perceive their own emotional state as well as the one of their interaction partners will be more effective collaborators, as frequently people are not aware of their own and others' emotions.

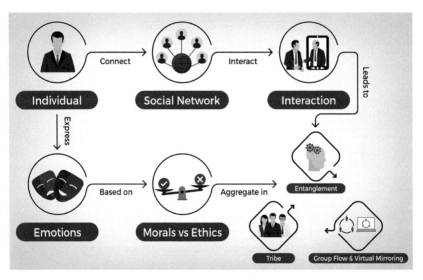

Figure 2.1   Process of getting into groupflow

The more I am with "others like me," the happier and the more easily in flow I will be. In other words, the more like us the company is we keep, the more we feel at home. People will aggregate in "tribes," which can be face-to-face communities, but also virtual tribes, groups of people virtually connected over the Internet based on shared values. People in the same tribe have similar morals and ethics, and respond to the same external stimulus with the same emotion. Aggregating in tribes, they become entangled. Entangled people thus share similar values and interests. The more entangled they are, the higher the likelihood that they will reach the state of groupflow. Collaboration between fully entangled people does not need many words, as entangled people intuitively know what their collaborators are thinking and doing. When collaborating in groupflow, the team will reach a state of collective consciousness where communication and collaboration are innate, without the need for external coordination. When a team reaches the state of groupflow, its members will be in a condition of happiness and elation, immensely enjoying their collaboration while producing superior results. Figure 2.2 describes the key components involved for individuals and teams to reach groupflow.

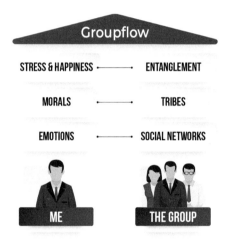

Figure 2.2   Pillars of groupflow

Groupflow starts and ends with emotions, triggered by individuals interacting with each other in social networks. Emotions are shown through tone of voice and facial expressions. For instance, the musician Prince used to say that he would show an "ugly face" when getting "in the zone," which is what he called the flow state when jamming with his bandmates. At the same time, emotions are also expressed by body movements – for instance we can either walk limp and depressed or happy and full of energy. When listening to the music at a jazz concert, the listener's body will start swinging in synch with the other people at the concert, reflecting shared happiness and an upbeat mood. These emotions influence and are influenced by the people that the individual is interacting with – their social network. Emotions are contagious, in positive and negative ways. If listeners come home from the concert in a happy, elated mood, they will infect their family members who stayed home with their joy. Or think how a little child showing his excitement under the Christmas tree infects the sober adults with her innocent joy. The opposite is of course also true, with a depressed person spreading sadness among the people they are interacting with. In particular, the structure of the interaction – if somebody is connected to many people or isolated; the dynamics of the interaction – how quickly others are responding; and the contents of the interaction – if somebody is using emotionally flat or emotionally charged words in their writing, are indicators of the flow of a team. For instance, the more the audience at a jazz concert is energized by the music of the performers, the more the listeners swing their bodies in synch with the musicians, the more the room is packed instead of half-empty, and the more the music is filling the room instead of being barely audible, the more musicians and listeners are in groupflow. The same is true for a project team working frantically under tight deadlines: the more honest they communicate with each other face to face and in their emails by "speaking up," sharing their emotions, responding and deciding quickly and communicating directly, not along managerial hierarchies but between those who need to know, the more they will be entangled.

Moral values and membership in virtual tribes decide if we like somebody or not. People like to be with people like themselves. Soccer fan likes soccer fan, jazz fan likes jazz fan, somebody with deep Christian values wants to spend time with other people sharing their Christian faith – in other words, we like people that are members of the same virtual tribe, and share the same moral values. For instance, Trump supporters all share the same values, they admire authority and tradition and want to MakeAmericaGreatAgain! If we share the same emotions with other members of our organization, because we respond similarly shocked or enraptured by an event, because we all buy into the same goal – for instance building a hospital in ten days, releasing the next version of an open-source software application or performing an opera together – we will be highly positively stressed, but also very happy, and thus fully entangled with the other people collaborating with us in reaching our goal. Measuring the shared emotions of the team members will tell us how entangled the team is. The more entangled the team is, the more it will be in groupflow.

To successfully get into groupflow, we need to care so much about reaching our goal that we will be willing to accept pain to reach it!

2.3   NO PAIN NO GAIN: THE YIN AND YANG OF GROUPFLOW

Certainly, trying to evade pain at all costs can lead to huge pain in the end. Because 51-year-old Darren Wilkinson was afraid of the dentist,[10] he skipped dentist appointments for 27 years. However, by evading the small pain of going to the annual dentist checkup, he paid with huge pain after 27 years. When one morning he discovered blood on his pillow, he finally mustered the courage to go to the dentist. The dentist's X-ray showed a black hole in the middle of his face. Eventually an ameloblastoma was discovered, a rare, benign tumor of the bone, which mostly occurs in the lower jaw. As a consequence, through seven surgical operations, 90 percent of his lower jaw and most of his teeth had to be removed, and for three months Mr. Wilkinson had to be fed through a tube inserted into his nose. After that his jaw had to be rebuilt from bone transplants from his lower leg bones. Had Mr. Wilkinson accepted small pain each year – going to the dentist – he could have avoided this huge pain in the end.

The same is true for achieving high lifetime satisfaction. Accepting small pain now will lead to big gain later! In a famous experiment, the "marshmallow test," researchers offered six-year-old children a marshmallow. If they were able to wait for 15 minutes before eating the marshmallow, they would get a second marshmallow. When the researchers ten years later checked on the metrics of success of the children such as educational achievements, body mass index and the ability to cope with stress, they found that the better children were able to pass the marshmallow test at a young age, going through the small pain of having to wait for 15 minutes until they ate the marshmallow, the higher was their success later in life. This means that if they were resilient in resisting the short-term temptation at six, they were also far more likely to work harder in their school years towards higher educational grades and resist the temptation to overeat. In other words, gaining more lasting happiness – by getting a better education and thus access to better opportunities in life – can mean giving up short-term gratification and reward and accepting pain in the moment to gain happiness and satisfaction in the long run. Although the scientific rigor of the original marshmallow test experiment has been criticized, the long-term benefit of being able to resist short-term temptation for deferred gratification has been verified many times.

While the flow experience in an entangled group is a source of happiness, fulfilling and its own reward, this does not mean that the members of the group are constantly happy. Rather, the steps on the way towards happiness might occasionally be full of pain. Any sports trainer knows that triggering anger among her athletes is a sure way to create additional energy. This can be done by swearing at them and insulting them; however, there are better ways to inject small amounts of pain in a respectful way to create energy and positive stress. That anger is a bad driver of energy has been impressively demonstrated by researching racial harassment in the Italian top soccer league.[11] It is unfortunately widely accepted behavior that unruly soccer fans during games start insulting the opposing team. The top league in Italy has many players from Africa who particularly suffer from racial harassment during a game, being verbally abused and sometimes even having bananas thrown at them.

In a natural experiment, researchers compared the period under the Covid-19 lockdown from June to August 2020, when the players played in empty stadiums – without harassment – with their performance afterwards and before, with the harassing audience present. They found that the African players played significantly better in the empty stadiums, while the other players showed no performance difference. This means that the anger generated by the tormented African players did not give them more energy leading to better playing, but rather led to a reduction in their performance by 3 percent. Generalizing from this research, the goal therefore is not to create anger and fear, but to create energy and positive stress to give the individual a highly pleasurable experience of thrill and elation. The question is: how can we introduce the highest amount of gain with the least amount of pain?

2.4   SUCCESS IS THE CAPABILITY TO SUFFER

> Life is beautiful, but it's also a daily struggle. (Simon Gronowski, Holocaust survivor)[12]

Any successful entrepreneur has gone through a lot of suffering and agony while stubbornly pursuing her or his goals to ultimately succeed. Steve Jobs experienced a lot of pain in his childhood, when he was put up for adoption because his biological parents did not feel up to the task of raising their own child. Similarly, Elon Musk was severely bullied as a child at school and was once thrown down the stairs by a group of boys and had to be hospitalized. However, these early painful experiences created tremendous resilience and capability to suffer in pursuit of a long-term goal for Steve Jobs and Elon Musk. The most successful people show a huge resilience to suffering. Both Elon Musk and Steve Jobs had to overcome obstacles early in life to end up at the top later on, along the way redefining their respective industries. The same is true for everybody who wants to reach the top of their profession, for instance, musicians, even if superbly talented, will need to spend decades of ten-hour days practicing to become master performers.

We confirmed this insight in our own research. Having small pain along the way can produce more gain in the end. In an experiment using the Happimeter smartwatch described in Chapter 9, we asked people to do a creative exercise, answering questions like "list as many unusual uses of your pencil as possible" while measuring their happiness with the Happimeter.[13] We found that the people showing the least happiness during the creativity exercise came up with the most creative solutions – in other words, the more pain they experienced while doing the creative work the better was the output of their creativity work. Only when we feel pain, when we have lost something, do we really know how much we value it. We get our happiest moments when something which we have been struggling to achieve, and which seemed almost out of reach, suddenly falls into place. The participants in our creativity experiment who struggled the hardest to deliver a superior result in the end scored the highest producing the best creativity output.

2.5   GROUPFLOW NEEDS BOTH SIMILARITY AND DIVERSITY

Eustress – being positively stressed – is the key prerequisite of getting into groupflow. Only when resilience to stress has been established through loving nurturing in childhood will the grown-up be capable of tolerating the initial pain to get into groupflow. Whether it was rebuilding the caved-in highway bridge in Genova in less than two years, working on the ten-day Covid-19 hospital building construction project in Wuhan or delivering a new software release under an ambitious schedule, delivering superior performance asks for a lot of resilience to stress from the workers. For instance, the construction workers in Genova and Wuhan worked frequently around the clock, bone-tired, and having to make sure they were not injured by the heavy equipment putting the elements into place, causing a lot of pain. But after the bridge or the hospital was up, the workers were deservedly proud to have been part of this bold undertaking. So, working under a lot of external stress, but in a highly motivated group, gives a lot of pain along the way but leads to immense satisfaction at the end.

How can we build eustress to create groupflow? "Be with people you like and do what you like!" That's the advice for workplace satisfaction that my colleague Joao gave me. This is in line with Sigmund Freud's advice when asked for his recipe for happiness: "love and work." I think we all agree with what Sigmund Freud and Joao say. It sounds awfully simple and is awfully hard to do. The sequence of their advice also matters: is it more important to be with people we like, or more important to do what we like? If we have the choice between being with people we like but having a shitty job, or doing what we like but being together with jerks, the former is a better recipe towards happiness than the later. Most of us would probably agree that it is better to clean out the manure in a stable together with a best friend than eating ice cream together with a pathological narcissist sociopath. Ideally of course we want to combine doing what we like with people we like, which brings me back to the main issue: how do I find the people I like? And how do I know what I like to do?

There are countless dating agencies and matchmaking services matching lonely singles on the Internet, and in the brick-and-mortar world doing it the old-fashioned face-to-face way. Similarly, there are zillions of job placement agencies, headhunters and recruiters promising the best fit between job seekers and companies both online on websites such as LinkedIn or Careerbuilder and in the physical offices of companies like Adecco and Randstad. While each vendor is touting its own unique approach, all these companies are matching job and love candidates based on mostly obvious self-declared attributes. While these attributes are helpful in identifying the criteria we are actively searching for in others, we are not very good at knowing what we really want. Steve Jobs said:

> Some people say, "Give the customers what they want." But that's not my approach. Our job is to figure out what they're going to want before they do. I think Henry Ford once said, "If I'd asked customers what they wanted, they would have told me, 'A faster horse!'" *People don't know what they want until you show it to them.* That's why I never rely on market research. Our task is to read things that are not yet on the page.[14]

Applying Steve Jobs' insight to workplace culture, people do not know with whom they want to spend their time until they are spending happy hours with them, and they do not know what they want to do until they actually love what they do. How many times have you planned your dream vacation with huge expectations, only to be disappointed during the vacation because the travel organizer overpromised or because you came with inflated expectations? The goal is to create an environment where the right people are thrown together to thrive while collaborating doing what they love – in other words, creating an environment for groupflow!

To create a team that has a chance to get into groupflow requires a group of people having the right skill and personality mix. The key for a successful team in groupflow is finding the right balance between homogeneity and diversity. On the one hand we are attracted to people similar to us, requiring homogeneous team members, on the other hand "opposites attract" and diversity brings in a broader skill and personality set. In sociology, attraction between people based on their similarity is called "homophily." The concept of "homophily" describes the tendency of people to look for the company of others that are similar to them. The main criteria for how we choose the people we want to spend time with, who we like best, is ourselves. In other words, I want to have people around me that are as similar as possible to myself. Research in homophily has found that these similarities can be superficial, like sharing a name, or they can be more nuanced, like age, gender, ethnicity, social class, income and education level, body fat, size, even eye and hair color. Having a similar first name is a valid selection criterion. For instance, on Reddit, somebody said:

> My maternal grandma is named Gerry (Geraldine) and my grandpa is named Jerry (Jerome). They have a son named Gerald, who goes by Jerry, and named his son

Jerome, who also goes by Jerry. My grandparents have another son named Jerome, who goes by, you guessed it, Jerry. And, completely unrelated, my paternal grand-father is also named Jerry.[15]

More general, the "name-letter effect"[16] has been known since 1985. It says that people are attracted to others that share the same initial or first letters.[17] For instance, Robert will show a tendency to date "Roberta," or at least "Rachel," while Anna will prefer to date Aaron or Andrew over Jacob. The same is also true for last names, where there is a higher percentage of couples sharing their last names than randomness would suggest.[18]

Homophily is in contradiction to the principle that "opposites attract." This principle posits that we like to complement our own weaknesses by teaming up with others bringing complementary experiences and skills that we are missing. Research into personality characteristics has shown that we are mostly attracted to people with similar personality characteristics, however, there are some criteria where opposites attract,[19] for instance an introvert likes to date an extrovert.[20] On the other hand, couples showing similar levels of neuroticism and agreeability have a better chance of staying together over extended periods of time. It does not matter if they are both highly agreeable or quick to get angry, as long as both are at the same end of the agreeability or neuroticism spectrum.[21] Different insights have been found with regards to dominance where a less dominant person preferred to collaborate with a com-plementary highly dominant one.[22]

In order to create an environment of groupflow to innovate and progress, we need to engage in a yin and yang feedback loop alternating between similarity – experiencing happiness through homophily – and diversity – associated with stress and pain (Figure 2.3).

Figure 2.3   *Yin and yang of groupflow*

On the one hand, when engaging with "others like me," applying the "homophily principle," I will be happy, as I know what to expect and will be able to read the mind of the people I am interacting with. However, I will not be exposed to fresh ideas. Interacting with "opposites" will create misunderstandings, friction and stress, but it will expose me to fresh and unknown ideas, triggering me to chart into unknown territory and try out new and unproven things. This will lead to some spectacular failures, creating pain and stress along the way, but will lead to breakthrough solutions. Engaging in a cycle alternating between similarity and diversity is the best way towards innovation and progress.

I have been experiencing the creative influence of this cycle in my own life, where since 2002 I have been traveling back and forth every month between the United States (US) and Europe, between MIT and my native Switzerland. Cambridge is full of creative, inspirational, occasionally weird, unconventional people, while in Switzerland I am embedded in the secure social environment of my extended family and the safety net of my Swiss upbringing. Working at MIT, and teaching courses to students at other universities in places like China, Germany, Chile, Finland, Italy, South Korea, Switzerland and many others, exposes me to numerous novel ideas, greatly nourishing my creativity. But "no pain no gain," I pay a price, experiencing headaches after a red-eyed flight through the night to Beijing or Bangkok, and sleepless first few nights every time I arrive jet-lagged in Boston or Switzerland. I also vividly remember how in the midst of giving a lecture at a university in China I had to run to the bathroom to throw up after a dinner with an ingredient my digestive system did not tolerate. The same happened in Chile while teaching a class, where I had to throw up in the middle of the lecture because I had drunk tap water in the morning which was chlorinated too much for my Swiss stomach. But for nothing in the world would I have wanted to miss the first-hand interaction with foreign cultures and researchers. This way I am learning about new methods and processes in other countries which I would have never discovered by staying put in Switzerland. For instance, I learned from my friend and collaborator Xing Wang, Professor at the Beijing Institute of Technology, about the Chinese concept of Wu Wei mentioned in Chapter 1. Recall that Wu Wei (无为) means "effortless action," "non-action," and "going with the flow," the notion of flow developed as part of Chinese philosophy a long time before Mihaly Csikszentmihalyi defined the flow concept as we know it today.

How can I choose people similar to me? The key problem is "to know thyself." Chances are you were not aware of subconsciously applying the "name-letter effect" and only learned about it by reading it here. While it might sound straightforward to have a liking for people with the same or similar names, people were not aware of this simple preference until psychologist Joszef Nuttin discovered it in 1985. We do not really know ourselves. The same is true of many other preferences you might show. They will only become obvious to you by being made obvious to you by others. Therefore, to learn about yourself, observe yourself in situations together with others, and observe how others respond to you. Our personality is defined by the emotional reactions we show in response to external events. The later parts of this book will introduce the "virtual mirror" that tracks how others respond to you based on your own communication behavior – controlled by your emotions – which will tell you how others see you.

How do I know what I really care about? The key is to observe my emotional response when interacting with others. Whether this response is positive or negative is defined through my moral values which depend on my personality, social background and upbringing.

NOTES

1. Wei, W. (1999). *I Ching Wisdom: More Guidance from the Book of Changes*. Power Press.
2. Csikszentmihalyi, M. (1975). Play and intrinsic rewards. *Journal of Humanistic Psychology*, 15, 41–63.
3. Hosťovecký, M., & Babušiak, B. (2017). Brain activity: Beta wave analysis of 2D and 3D serious games using EEG. *Journal of Applied Mathematics, Statistics and Informatics*, 13(2), 39–53.
4. Brom, C., Buchtová, M., Šisler, V., Děchtěrenko, F., Palme, R., & Glenk, L. M. (2014). Flow, social interaction anxiety and salivary cortisol responses in serious games: A quasi-experimental study. *Computers and Education*, 79, 69–100.
5. Keeler, J. R., Roth, E. A., Neuser, B. L., Spitsbergen, J. M., Waters, D. J. M., & Vianney, J. M. (2015). The neurochemistry and social flow of singing: Bonding and oxytocin. *Frontiers in Human Neuroscience*, 9, 518.
6. Kreutz, G. (2014). Does singing facilitate social bonding? *Music and Medicine*, 6, 51–60.
7. de Manzano, Ö., Cervenka, S., Jucaite, A., Hellenäs, O., Farde, L., & Ullén, F. (2013). Individual differences in the proneness to have flow experiences are linked to dopamine D2-receptor availability in the dorsal striatum. *Neuroimage*, 67, 1–6.
8. Heyman, E., Gamelin, F. X., Goekint, M., Piscitelli, F., Roelands, B., Leclair, E., … & Meeusen, R. (2012). Intense exercise increases circulating endocannabinoid and BDNF levels in humans: Possible implications for reward and depression. *Psychoneuroendocrinology*, 37(6), 844–851.
9. Boecker, H., Sprenger, T., Spilker, M. E., Henriksen, G., Koppenhoefer, M., Wagner, K. J., … & Tolle, T. R. (2008). The runner's high: Opioidergic mechanisms in the human brain. *Cerebral Cortex*, 18(11), 2523–2531.
10. www.dailymail.co.uk/news/article-8517169/Man-51-hadnt-dentist-nearly-30 -years-needs-jaw-removed.html.
11. Caselli, M., Falco, P., & Mattera, G. (2021). When the mob goes silent: Uncovering the effects of racial harassment through a natural experiment. Dipartimento di Economia e Management, Universita degli Studi di Trento working papers.

12. www.nytimes.com/2020/11/20/world/europe/holocaust-piano-brussels-coronavirus.html.

13. Sun, L., Gloor, P. A., Stein, M., Eirich, J., & Wen, Q. (2019, October). "No pain no gain": Predicting creativity through body signals. *Collaborative Innovation Networks Conference of Digital Transformation of Collaboration* (pp. 3–15). Springer.

14. www.goodreads.com/quotes/988332-some-people-say-give-the-customers-what-they-want-but. This is further discussed at www.inc.com/jason-aten/this-was-steve-jobs-most-controversial-legacy-it-was-also-his-most-brilliant.html.

15. www.reddit.com/r/AskReddit/comments/7d3q0l/people_who_are_married_to_someone_with_the_same/.

16. www.psychologistworld.com/emotion/name-letter-effect-attraction.

17. Nuttin, J. M. (1987). Affective consequences of mere ownership: The name letter effect in twelve European languages. *European Journal of Social Psychology*, 17(4), 381–402.

18. Jones, J. T., Pelham, B. W., Carvallo, M., & Mirenberg, M. C. (2004). How do I love thee? Let me count the Js: Implicit egotism and interpersonal attraction. *Journal of Personality and Social Psychology*, 87(5), 665–683.

19. Kristof-Brown, A., Barrick, M. R., & Kay Stevens, C. (2005). When opposites attract: A multi-sample demonstration of complementary person-team fit on extraversion. *Journal of Personality*, 73(4), 935–958.

20. www.personalitypage.com/html/relationships.html.

21. www.psychologytoday.com/us/blog/head-games/201412/do-opposites-really-attract-its-complicated.

22. Dryer, D. C., & Horowitz, L. M. (1997). When do opposites attract? Interpersonal complementarity versus similarity. *Journal of Personality and Social Psychology*, 72(3), 592.

3.   The influence of morality on emotions

While we think we are rational creatures, we are really driven by emotions, and masters in retroactively constructing rational explanations for our emotionally driven reactions. Researchers have defined emotions as strong feelings deriving from a person's circumstances, mood or relationships with other people, contrasting emotions as intuitive feelings with reasoning and knowledge. Emotions are perceived as mental states for the coordination of subsequent movement. Already in 1872, Charles Darwin in his seminal work *The Expression of Emotions in Man and Animal* recognized their importance as evolutionary adaptations for communication and survival. Darwin's key insight was that emotions are universal, which means that when looking at faces of people around the world, emotions such as fear or joy are recognized by all humans independent of race and ethnicity.

Darwin also accepted that emotions are not restricted to humans, but are similarly shown by animals such as dogs, cats, horses, rats and even bees. This view was ignored for most of the last century; the most respected behavioral scientists of the twentieth century such as famed psychologist B. F. Skinner considered animals furry robots who reacted to an external stimulus with an identical response, while humans were seen as infinitely more complex. Today this perspective has been thoroughly revised, and in my own research, studying emotional responses of humans, dogs and horses, we found that emotional behavior of humans is similarly predictable to the behavior of other animals (see Section 20.1). The same machine-learning algorithms make emotional responses to an external stimulus as foreseeable for dogs and horses as for humans.

Researchers still disagree what precisely emotions are and how they function. According to Richard Lazarus,[1] an emotion is executed in three steps. First, an individual conducts a cognitive appraisal with the individual assessing the event cognitively, which cues the emotion and decides on the response: is it anger, fear or disgust? Second, physiological changes happen in the body of the individual and the cognitive reaction initiates biological alterations such as increased heart rate or pituitary adrenal response. Third, an action is executed by the individual feeling the emotion and choosing how to react. However, the bodily response to an emotion, for example anger, can look different from one person to another. There will be a change in heart rate when an individual gets angry, however, the heart rate might go up hugely for one angry individual, while only going up just a bit for another angry individual, depending on their bodily makeup and peace of mind. Just being aware of my anger will reduce my anger.[2] When an emotion is triggered, most of the time not much rational cognition is involved. When reacting to an external event, as described in *Thinking Fast and Slow* by Nobel Prize laureate Daniel Kahneman, the brain has two ways of responding. Kahneman calls them "system 1" – thinking fast – and "system 2" – thinking slow. System 2 is rational and takes time and conscious effort to come up with a solution. System 1 is intuitive and responds in fractions of a second. Computing the distance to the sun takes system 2. Jumping aside when a snake is crossing the path, or catching a ball, is clearly controlled by system 1. Deciding with what emotion to respond to an external event is a system 1 task, it happens intuitively and automatically. However, the brain can be trained to a task which is initially executed rationally by system 2, but over time and after much practice it becomes automatic and is done intuitively by system 1. For instance, multiplying five by five is drilled at elementary school until it becomes intuitive. This means that while an emotional response is a system 1 task, with what emotion to respond for instance to a newspaper article about abortion can be relearned through extended conscious deliberation and exposure to new external influences. For instance, 30 years ago the public may have responded with anger when seeing two men kissing; today many people will just respond with surprise.

While psychologists in the last century assumed that personality characteristics were basically inherited properties of individuals constant over the life of the individual just like genes, more recently a more dynamic view of personality characteristics has evolved. The current scientific consensus is that which emotion is triggered in response to a particular stimulus is dependent on personality characteristics and cultural factors. Personality traits and attitudes towards cultural factors can be relearned and unlearned over the lifetime of an individual. These personality characteristics will then decide what emotion will be triggered by system 1.

Psychologists use different categorizations of standardized emotions. Three of the most popular frameworks are the Ekman framework, named after psychologist Paul Ekman, the Plutchik framework, named after its inventor Robert Plutchik, and the circumplex model. Ekman defined six basic emotions – fear, anger, joy, sadness, disgust and surprise, recognizable through different facial expressions. The Plutchik wheel of emotions includes eight basic emotions – anger, fear, sadness, disgust, surprise, anticipation, trust and joy, separated into three levels of arousal, leading to a total of 24 emotions. Plutchik groups these 24 emotions into subcategories, based on eight stimulus events: threat, obstacle, potential mate, loss of valued person, group member, gruesome object, new territory and sudden novel object. The third emotion framework, the "circumplex model," has two dimensions, valence and arousal. Valence goes from unpleasant to pleasant, arousal goes from low activation (sleepy, bored) to high activation (tense, alert). All three frameworks are useful, but appear somewhat random, indicating that the final word in categorizing emotions has not yet been spoken. In our research using AI to determine the emotion of a person or animal based on body signals, we have experimented with both the circumplex model and the Ekman framework, mostly using the latter, as its comparatively low number of distinctive categories is well suited for machine learning.

Darwin posited that emotions are universal, that is they are experienced by all cultures around the world the same way. This also means that the same facial expressions, independent of ethnicity, of being Asian, Caucasian, African or from other cultures, reflect the same emotions. Today this view is challenged by psychologists, for instance Lisa Feldmann Barrett[3] argues that everyone, based on personal context and experience, will feel and name emotions differently. There are no universal body changes consistent with the experience of an emotional state. In her book Barret lists studies demonstrating that none of the three commonly assumed predictors of emotion – facial expression, physical change such as heart rate and blood pressure, and brain circuity – can be perceived with greater than 35 percent accuracy. For instance, both smiles and scowls can easily be misinterpreted. Famous musician Prince called the ecstatic facial expressions his band members were showing when playing in flow "ugly faces," while smiles might be symptoms of social anxiety as well as of a joyful mood. Culture defines how somebody experiences an emotion, and culture is also strongly influenced by language. For example, people in different cultures will experience anger in a different way, depending on the individual and her or his culture. For instance, the English word "anger" can be translated to German as either *Wut*, *Zorn*, *Verdruss* or *Ärger*, each of which has very different connotations, while in English all are conflated as "anger." While *Wut* is directly translated as anger, it also includes aspects of fury or rage. *Zorn* contains facets of wrath and ire, while *Verdruss* has elements of displeasure and chagrin. *Ärger*, finally, conveys additional feelings of worry and irritation.

Using machine learning can assist in teasing out what the key emotions are across different cultures, aggregating huge numbers of facial emotion pictures for each culture. In a study published in *Nature* in 2020, millions of facial expressions were analyzed[4] using AI from 6 million videos from around the world, from different cultures, races and ethnicities. To link facial expression and associated emotion, the researchers took the emotion labels from the textual description and the context of the movies, extracting the associated facial emotion expressions. They ended up with 16 emotions: amusement, anger, awe, concentration, confusion, contempt, contentment, desire, disappointment, doubt, elation, interest, pain, sadness, surprise and triumph. Through this process, they were also able to assign links between a context and associated emotions, for example "weight training" was positively associated with pain, and "team sports" with triumph. Some connections were also highly culture specific, for instance "wedding" showed positive correlation with surprise and disappointment only in Southeast Asia, while "soldier" only correlated with doubt in Africa. The conclusion from this analysis is that while simple frameworks like the Ekman, Plutchik and circumplex models are useful for analysis, the emotional reality is much more complex, and dependent on an individual's context, background and experiences. However, big data can assist in finding emotions typical of ethnicities and cultures.

3.1   HOW CAN WE REDUCE STRESS?

Emotions are a much richer source of information than the unidimensional concept of stress. Negative emotions such as anger, anxiety, guilt, shame, sadness, envy, jealousy and disgust all create stress.[5] Positive emotions, such as joy, admiration, gratitude and contentment, on the other hand, reduce stress and lead to more prosocial behavior, to better cognitive activity regarding memory and judgment and to better quality of performance.[6] However, for certain tasks, negative emotions can increase cognitive performance. In a project comparing performance of individuals on verbal and visual tasks, it was found that having pleasant emotions improved performance on verbal tasks, while triggering unpleasant emotions increased performance on visual tasks.[7] Further evidence that stress can in fact be positive for certain tasks!

In general, being afraid of stress will create more stress – and shorten your life. In a meta-analysis of the US National Health Survey,[8] the researchers found that there was no correlation between reporting a lot of stress and reduced life expectancy. However, the people answering "Yes" to the additional question "Stress negatively impacts my health" had a 43 percent increased risk of premature death. This means that stress only has negative consequences if I view it negatively by feeling "stressed" and worried about my health. When in flow, I will experience stress too, although this will be positive stress which will not "stress" me, but rather increase my happiness. And as we saw above, it might make me perform better for visual tasks.

The capability to correctly read emotions is key for success. In his bestselling book *Emotional Intelligence*, Daniel Goleman showed that emotional intelligence (or emotional quotient (EQ)) is much more important than rational intelligence (IQ). Emotionally intelligent people read other people's emotions from their facial expressions, from their voice and from their body gestures. EQ is normally associated with empathy and compassion, although a sociopath with high EQ will abuse his or her emotion-reading capabilities for individual personal gain without any regard for the other person.

How can we adjust our emotional responses to reduce stress and increase flow? The goal is to become aware of one's own emotions and adjust them accordingly to obtain the most positive energy and happiness – and the least stress. Emotional responses are shown through "honest signals," reflecting personal values through body language, words and online social networking behavior.

3.2   EMOTIONS CAN REDUCE STRESS

Your ethical values will define with which emotions you will respond to an external trigger. They will define if you respond with anger, fear, disgust or shame to a event. However, according to Buddhist philosophy as for example voiced by philosopher Martha Nussbaum, we should try to ban these emotions in most circumstances from our lives, as they are responsible for creating a lot of stress. We should try to get in a state of mind where joy and sadness are the main emotions controlling our life. The goal should be to resolve our problems with joy and sadness, and try to abstain as much as possible from disgust, shame, fear and anger. In our evolutionary past these emotions were necessary for survival, mobilizing our forces to fight the saber-toothed tigers and refraining from eating spoiled food. However, the more civilization progresses, and the more our basic needs are covered, the less disgust, shame, fear and anger we need. In particular, we should restrict our emotions in response to social transgressions.

Table 3.1 illustrates what happens if somebody commits a "social crime," deviating from established norms of society, for instance if two people of the same gender show mutual affection in public in a homophobic society – committing a social transgression. Based on their personalities, the two people might experience shame, and maybe also fear of being exposed, while the people observing their affectionate behavior might experience disgust and anger. Many people in more open societies in North America and Western Europe might agree that these emotional responses are unnecessary and only result in painful experiences for everybody involved.

Table 3.1   *Response to negative emotions*

	Example	Committer	Observer
Social transgression	Same-sex affectionate behavior in public	Experiences shame and fear	Experiences *maybe* disgust and anger
Ethical transgression	Stealing money	Experiences shame and fear	Experiences disgust and anger

Committing an ethical transgression, such as stealing money or cheating on taxes, will lead to a similar emotional response, with the thief or tax cheater showing embarrassment and shame when being caught and fear of punishment, while public observers will be disgusted and angry at the thief for his unethical behavior. Most people would agree that this similar sequence of emotions is justified as a deterrent against such unethical conduct.

3.2.1   Shame and Disgust

According to moral philosopher Martha Nussbaum – laid out in her seminal work *Hiding from Humanity*[9] – disgust and shame result in discrimination of minorities such as Jews and homosexuals by the majority. As Nussbaum says in another of her books, *The Fragility of Goodness*, human goodness does not fully protect against peril and injustice, in particular, if somebody experiences "moral luck," which means getting blamed or praised for something that the individual did not have control over. To reduce moral luck, we should reduce our morally based condemnation of "deviant" social behavior. Both disgust and shame are hierarchical, meaning that the strata of society in power use it to cement their power. They lead to restrictions of non-harmful activities, which means that whoever cherishes justice, fairness and equality should try to avoid these two emotions when dealing with socially deviant behavior. The way to eschew them for an individual is to self-monitor what triggers disgust and shame and try to adjust one's moral value system accordingly.

However, disgust and shame are essential as a punishment system for people violating ethical norms, for instance stealing and hurting others. In other words, recognizing shame and disgust in response to "deviant" ethical behavior will flag people who are appalled by it, and thus who are more likely to themselves behave ethically.

3.2.2   Fear and Anger

The people who have the most fear are the angriest. This was the insight of my son and his girlfriend, both young doctors in the Covid-19 wards in regional hospitals during the pandemic. Among their patients, most of them well above retirement age, there were calm people who took every day as it came. But there were others who were constantly angry, complaining and impossible to satisfy. But those were also the ones who were the most fearful, fearful to catch additional infections, fearful to be intubated, fearful of discovering additional ailments such as cancer, high blood pressure and diabetes. This means it is hard to separate fear and anger. While in times of external crisis fear and anger can be strong motivators to build up unexpected energy essential for survival, nowadays in our more placid times of abundance, fear creating anger leads to unnecessary stress.

People are particularly fearful of losing the things they value most, according to Maslow's pyramid of needs these would be:

- safety – fear of losing their job;
- power – fear of losing their position of power and influence;
- glory – fear of losing their reputation; and
- love – fear of losing their loved ones.

This means that the more somebody values safety, power, glory and love, the more fearful they will be of losing them, and the angrier they will respond when these possessions are threatened. When archbishop Desmond Tutu during Apartheid in South Africa was asked why he could stay so calm in the view of police brutality, he answered that the only thing the police could take away from him was his life, and he was not afraid of death. Creating an environment without fear will lead to much less anger and stress. By recognizing the restrictions inherent in daily life, and by accepting that these are all perishable goods, that are easily gained and easily lost, we will get into a stage of mindful enlightenment where the main emotions governing our life are joy and sadness.

3.3   ETHICS ARE ~~BAD~~ GOOD FOR BUSINESS

Spinoza, a prominent Dutch philosopher of the early Enlightenment, posits that there is nothing intrinsically good or intrinsically bad, rather they are both relative to the position of the viewer. Things that have classically been seen as good or bad are just good or bad for humans, or a subgroup of humans.[10] Spinoza distinguishes between three kinds of knowledge: opinion, reason and intuition. Opinion or sensory perception, according to Spinoza, is entirely inaccurate, as it merely reflects how our bodies work. Knowledge of the second kind, or reason, encompasses knowledge of the principles of physics and geometry. Knowledge of the third kind is intuitive knowledge, which is controlled by our emotions. Emotions, according to Spinoza, are our means for survival, because each living being, including humans, is trying to survive as long as possible. Additionally, passions or affects are there to direct us to seek what gives us pleasure, and to shun what gives us pain. In particular, Spinoza thinks that living by ungoverned passions will make it impossible for us to live in harmony with each other. Only with the aid of reason can humans distinguish the passions that support virtue from those which are ultimately harmful to oneself and to others.

If we concur with Aristotle that the pursuit of happiness is the ultimate goal of humans, Spinoza gives us the answer that virtue – replacing passion with reason and being good to others – is the path to happiness. Established societal norms posit that ethical behavior is good for business. If employees are too concerned with getting ahead at any price, they will engage in unethical behavior such as bribery, discrimination, ignoring social responsibility and violating corporate governance guidelines. If a company is perceived to behave ethically, it will lead to increased employee performance, job satisfaction, organizational commitment, more trust both by employees and customers and good organizational citizenship.

However, in practice you can be as unethical as you want, as long as you are not caught. Verbal declarations of ethical behavior do not make a company more ethical, however, as long as the declaration is accepted as fact, it makes a company more successful. Enron's code of ethics[11] begins with a letter from disgraced former chief executive officer (CEO) Kenneth Lay, assuring employees that he will conduct business "in accordance with all applicable laws and in a moral and honest manner." He goes on to say "We know Enron enjoys a reputation for fairness and honesty that is respected. Enron's reputation finally depends on its people, you and me. Let's keep that reputation high."

Formerly most admired healthcare technology company Theranos is another example of how riding the ethical high ground on bogus claims will lead to a deep fall. Faked demonstrations, falsified validation reports, misleading claims about contracts and overstated financials – those were some of the transgressions of which Elizabeth Holmes, disgraced founder and CEO of Theranos, was convicted by a jury in the courthouse of San Jose on January 3, 2022. The jury found her guilty not just of behaving unethically, but of breaking the law.

Enron and Theranos are two examples of companies that claimed the ethical high ground, pretending to make the world a better place while actually doing the opposite. Both got rankings as most admired companies and both climbed dizzying valuations before crashing down when their pyramid schemes tumbled. While they were caught, there are numerous examples of similar behavior, just better hidden or executed more smoothly, with the transgressors being lauded as philanthropists.

In capitalist economies it has been accepted wisdom for centuries that Adam Smith's "invisible hand" will transform selfish desire for money, power and glory into collective goods, leading to the best economic outcome such as providing the cheapest bread or aggregating knowledge to be accessible for all. While socialist capitalism prominent in Northern Europe is commonly seen as ethical and morally sound, this is mostly because of established societal norms and trust in society, or in other words by making the invisible hand visible.

That the "invisible hand" of capitalism really will result in ethical behavior of capitalists has been challenged ever since Adam Smith introduced the concept in his seminal work *The Theory of Moral Sentiments*. Adam Smith himself was asking for ethical behavior of the capitalist entrepreneur, but the opposite has been demonstrated many times, with Jeffrey Skilling at Enron and Elizabeth Holmes at Theranos being just two recent examples among many of entrepreneurs who give in to the temptation of behaving unethically for the sake of profit. When the investors of Theranos asked Elizabeth Holmes for details of Theranos' miraculous blood-testing machine, Ms. Holmes always hid behind trade secrets. In other words, the invisibility cloak of the invisible hand was used to hide the non-existing clothes of the emperor, while claiming the ethical high ground.

Ethics defines what is right or wrong – based on the perspective of the viewer. From Jeffrey Skilling's and Elizabeth Holmes' perspective, defining ethics in their own terms, they might have acted perfectly ethically. However, most people would agree that they were driven by personal greed, by their passion for money, power and glory.

So how can we apply reason to overcome our passion for more money, power and glory and behave more ethically? Spain is one of the few countries in the world that offers rehab to white-collar criminals.[12] Corrupt officials, lawyers who were caught taking bribes and accountants embezzling money from their customers can participate in a rehabilitation program while they are serving their sentence in jail. When studying the psychological profiles of these white-collar criminals, the psychologists found that they are no different from ordinary people. They have the same system of values; however, they mentally construct exceptions for themselves. They exhibit "moral disengagement," constructing in their own mind elaborate schemes as to why their misdeeds benefit others and not themselves. They also show egocentrism, thinking only of themselves without concern for the desires and needs of others, and are unable to understand the viewpoints of other people. Their second characteristic is narcissism, an obsession with themselves, by forming an idealized and embellished self-image and an excessive need for admiration. On the other hand, they also show a lack of empathy for the needs and suffering of others, and an exaggerated expectation of entitlement and lack of humility. The Spanish white-collar criminal rehabilitation program thus works with participants on reducing their egocentrism and narcissism, and increasing their humility and empathy. It does so by encouraging the criminals to reflect on their own personality characteristics and raising their awareness of the negative consequences of their misdeeds for their victims. Are there ways to leverage AI to support this process?

3.4 MEASURING PERSONALITY, MORALS AND ATTITUDES TO RISK

Members of the same digital virtual tribe share the same ethics and morals, expressed through similar honest signals of collaboration (see Chapter 12 for a description of the data collection process). Frequently we take our own moral values as a given, without questioning them or understanding that others might live happily with very different morals. In interaction with others, to comprehend their values and behavior, understanding my own behavior, creating awareness of my moral and ethical values and how they differ from others' is key. We have therefore created a system that measures ethical and moral values by interpreting the honest signals of collaboration using AI and machine learning. We are using two different survey-based value self-assessments, the Schwartz value system,[13] and the Haidt moral foundations[14] assessment to collect ethical and moral values. These self-assessments have been used to develop and cross-check our machine learning-based morals and personality prediction systems.

Sociologist Schwartz has identified ten ethical values grouped into five categories:

- *Openness to change*: these people show *self-direction* and independence in thought and action, and search for *stimulation*, novelty and challenges in life. Researchers like Charles Darwin, Albert Einstein and Richard Feynman, and entrepreneurs like Steve Jobs or Elon Musk, would clearly fall into this category.
- *Self-enhancement*: self-enhancing people search for *power*, *hedonism* and *achievement*. For instance, Donald Trump is definitely self-enhancing, doing everything to maintain his chance for a second term as US president, paying 100,000 dollars to Stormy Daniels for a night of sex and branding people who are not as ambitious as he is as losers.
- *Conservation*: these people search for *security*, stability and harmony and they also show *conformity* and restraint in actions that might harm others or violate social expectations or norms. They cherish *tradition* and appreciate the predictability that adherence to established cultural and religious norms provides. Members of the armed forces and of religious orders have been shown to fall into this category.
- *Self-transcendence*: according to Schwartz, these people show *benevolence* in their interactions with others in their ingroup. Some might even demonstrate *universalism*, respect and tolerance for the welfare of all people and of nature, respecting the dignity of humans, animals and plants. Exemplars might be Desmond Tutu and Nelson Mandela.

A second framework assessing ethical values has been defined by psychologist Jonathan Haidt and his collaborators. It distinguishes among five moral foundations: *care* puts strong emphasis on protecting others; *fairness* prioritizes rendering justice based on agreed-on rules; *loyalty* emphasizes standing with one's own group or family; *authority* prefers submitting to tradition and legitimate authority; and *sanctity* is an abhorrence of disgusting food, things and actions.

In experiments it has been shown that doing good deeds indeed carries intrinsic rewards. In a research project, people who voluntarily participated in an act of kindness and morality showed more strength after that act.[15] The researchers stopped random people at a subway station in Boston and asked them to carry a 5-pound weight with stretched out arms for as long as possible in return for a candy bar. Participants then got some money, which they either could keep, or donate to a charity. Afterwards they were asked to repeat the weightlifting exercise. The ones who had donated the money to charity could hold the weight 15 percent longer than the control group. Therefore, for individuals knowing where they stand with regards to these ethical and moral dimensions will not just help them to lift heavier weights, but also increase their capability to tolerate stress in pursuit of goals for the common good.

In our research we have shown that not only do the words you use in your everyday language indicate your ethics and moral values, but even the way you move your body tracked through the sensors of a smartwatch will give away your moral value system and ethical beliefs. Even more, we found that the same indicators – the words you use and your body language – show how willing you are to take risks. Combining all the answers of 140 people who had taken the DOSPERT risk-taking survey, it was found that people who are willing to take social risks, such as defying conventional social norms, are less willing to take ethical risks, such as cheating. People who are members of the "YOLO" (you only live once) tribe, based on their words, are less willing to take ethical and health risks.

In a research project we predicted the moral values of individuals through their body movements measured with the sensors of a smartwatch.[16] The personal moral values were assessed using the Schwartz Value Theory. Data for all variables were gathered through the Happimeter smartwatch-based body-sensing system described in Figure 9.3. Our results show that sensor and mood factors predict a person's values. For instance, we find that more self-centered individuals have lower heart-rate variability. In a second project we calculated the honest signals for each person in a mailbox based on the email behavior of the person.[17] We again found that the words a person used in their email predicted the ethical and moral values of the person. For instance, the more positive and less emotional they were in their language, the more they cared about others.

We also utilized different methods to investigate the relationship between the Five Factor Inventory (FFI) of personality traits of a person and their body movements and online communication patterns. The FFI is also known under the acronym OCEAN – openness, conscientiousness, extraversion, agreeableness and neuroticism. Results are normally collected by having an individual fill out answers to a list of questions through a survey. In our projects we showed that there is no need to fill out the survey, just tracking body movements with a smartwatch or analyzing word usage and online communication patterns will give away the personality of a person.

Figure 3.1 illustrates the results of the surveys for Schwartz values, Haidt morals, the DOSPERT risk-taking survey and the FFI OCEAN personality traits. These surveys are available at www.happimeter.org, so everybody can check how they stand in comparison to hundreds of other people who have answered these surveys.

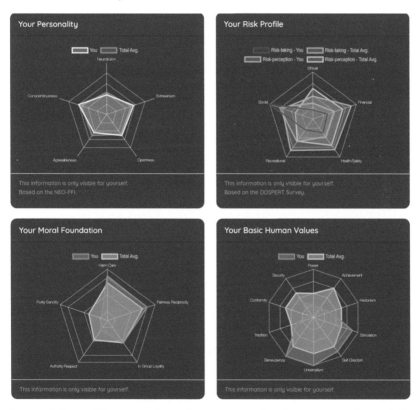

Figure 3.1   My personality values compared to the average values of all participants

Our research illustrates that recent technological advances in AI and machine learning can be employed to analyze a person's values and personality characteristics, combining body sensors and mood states to investigate individual behavior and team cooperation based on an individual's body language and word usage.

NOTES

1. Lazarus, R. S., & Lazarus, B. N. (1994). *Passion and Reason: Making Sense of Our Emotions*. Oxford University Press.
2. www.ahchealthenews.com/2014/01/30/how-anger-impacts-your-heart/.
3. Barrett, L. F. (2017). *How Emotions Are Made: The Secret Life of the Brain*. Houghton Mifflin Harcourt.
4. Cowen, A. S., Keltner, D., Schroff, F., Jou, B., Adam, H., & Prasad, G. (2020). Sixteen facial expressions occur in similar contexts worldwide. *Nature*, 1–7.
5. Lazarus, R. S. (1993). Coping theory and research: Past, present, and future. *Psychosomatic Medicine*, 55(3), 234–247.
6. Lazarus, R. S., & Lazarus, B. N. (1994). *Passion and Reason: Making Sense of Our Emotions*. Oxford University Press.
7. Gray, J. R., Braver, T. S., & Raichle, M. E. (2002). Integration of emotion and cognition in the lateral prefrontal cortex. *Proceedings of the National Academy of Sciences*, 99(6), 4115–4120.
8. Keller, A., Litzelman, K., Wisk, L. E., Maddox, T., Cheng, E. R., Creswell, P. D., & Witt, W. P. (2012). Does the perception that stress affects health matter? The association with health and mortality. *Health Psychology*, 31(5), 677–684.
9. Nussbaum, Martha C. (2004). *Hiding from Humanity: Disgust, Shame, and the Law*. Princeton University Press.
10. Spinoza, B. D., & Eisenberg, P. D. (1977). Treatise on the improvement of the understanding. *Philosophy Research Archives*, 3, 553–679.
11. www.bizjournals.com/columbus/stories/2002/04/01/editorial3.html.
12. www.nytimes.com/2021/05/17/world/europe/spain-corruption-rehab.html?
13. Schwartz, S. H. (2012). An overview of the Schwartz Theory of Basic Values. *Online Readings in Psychology and Culture*, 2(1).
14. Haidt, J. (2012). *The Righteous Mind: Why Good People Are Divided by Politics and Religion*. Pantheon Books.
15. Gray, K. (2019). Moral transformation: Good and evil turn the weak into the mighty. *Social Psychological and Personality Science*, 1(3), 253–258.
16. Sun, L., & Gloor, P. A. (2019, October). Measuring moral values with smartwatch-based body sensors. *Collaborative Innovation Networks Conference of Digital Transformation of Collaboration*. (pp. 51–66). Springer.
17. Gloor, P. A., & Colladon, A. F. (2019, October). Heart beats brain: Measuring moral beliefs through email analysis. *Collaborative Innovation Networks Conference of Digital Transformation of Collaboration*. (pp. 85–93). Springer.

4.   Building blocks of happiness

I don't care about happiness; I care about making money.

That's what a US CEO said to me in 2017, when I was trying to recruit spon-
sors for our Happimeter research project, aiming to develop an AI-driven
smartwatch tool to measure employee happiness. He was fully in line with
the majority of the US population, whose goal does not seem to be happy, but
to make as much money as possible. At least that is what is demonstrated in
Google Trends, where in the US searching for "money" is significantly more
popular than searching for "happiness." This is different from the rest of the
world, where people search more for happiness than for money (Figure 4.1).
I had the same experience, as I was finally able to recruit a European company
as a sponsor for our happiness research.

*Figure 4.1   Google search trends for "happy" and "money" in the
United States (top) and worldwide (bottom)*

The American CEO who was not interested in happy employees, but in having
the most productive and profitable company, was very wrong. As we and
others have shown, there is indeed a strong link between business success and

happiness (see Section 4.1). Happy employees will lead to happy customers, who will be loyal long-time customers.

> I say let the world go to hell, but I should always have my tea. (Fyodor Dostoevsky, *Notes from Underground*)

The link between happiness, ethical values and business success is not straight-forward. As illustrated by the quote of Dostoevsky, people frequently despair about the unfairness of the world and might justify their unethical behavior as necessary to reach their goals. While conventional business literature promotes ethical leaders, more often than not the unethical leader trumps over the ethical one. In his book *Humble Leadership*,[1] organizational development researcher Ed Schein calls for leadership based on trust, humility, integrity and honest conversation. Honesty, integrity and fairness are frequently rated by supervisors as key indicators of a leader's effectiveness.[2] However, it is far from clear that being ethical is actually good for the ethical leaders themselves. Religion tells us to treat others as we want to be treated, with fairness, humility and modesty. However, the founders of ethical religions and philosophies have often paid a high price for introducing these ideas. Socrates was forced to drink poison, Pythagoras was killed by the citizens of Croton, Jesus was crucified, Mani, the founder of Manichaeism, was thrown into jail where he died after a month and many European reformers such as Jan Hus, Girolamo Savonarola, Thomas Cranmer and Jacob Hutter were tortured, beheaded or burned at the stake by their rulers. While everybody would like to be dealt with fairly and prefers interacting with others who are modest and humble, it is not obvious that such conduct is beneficial for the individual showing this ethical behavior. More often than not, selfish behavior carries one much further. The average CEO has not achieved his position because of ethical behavior, but because of ruthless shrewdness. Many CEOs show similarities with sociopaths, combining high EQ with few scruples to apply their EQ to their personal advantage.[3] In a sample of 203 executives chosen by their leaders for a management development program, researchers found that psychopathy correlated positively with creativity, strategic thinking and communication skills, and negatively with being a responsible team player. In other words, the high potentials chosen to be the future CEOs were more likely to be psychopaths, but also more creative, strategic thinkers and excellent communicators, but less likely to be ethical team players. This already begins in business schools, where students majoring in business are more likely to engage in deceptive practices,[4] while condemning others for their deceptive behavior. However, as we will be showing, there is hope for the humble and modest leader in reaping both material and spiritual rewards. Tales abound of initially successful leaders, who combined shrewd tactical behavior with ruthless manipulation of their underlings, only to be murdered by them when the opportunity arose, just like Brutus organizing the senatorial group murder of Julius Cesar, driving his knife deep into Cesar's heart together with his colleagues on that fateful day on the Ides of March in the senate of Rome. Much better to accumulate social capital with your friends, so they will stand with you in times of need, at the risk of not ending up as emperor. More will be said about this when discussing whether it is better to fit in or to stand out (see Section 5.2).

Research has shown that ethical leaders will lead to more ethical organizations. However, this research is problematic, because it is based on self-assessment of the leaders of their ethical behavior[5] – just look at Enron or Theranos for examples of how deceptive these self-declarations are. While there will be some overlap between self-reported ethical values and "ground truth" true behavior, the alignment is spurious and weak at best. Known corporate cheater Enron had one of the best ethical codes, only to be caught in blatantly unethical accounting, which was legal, or rather not explicitly illegal, but totally immoral. Self-declared ethical behavior is thus a weak indicator of true ethical values, as companies and people alike want to be seen as ethical, independent of their true ideals. We can still expect a correlation between true ethical behavior and self-reported values as people are afraid of being caught in the act, and thus will try to live up to their self-reported ethical values. However, if lucrative unethical opportunities arise, more often than not managers will give in to the temptation, independent of the quality and contents of their corporate code of ethics.

The public might actually be smarter than management researchers and business executives, as "ordinary people on the street" think that being ethical is bad for business. In a study asking respondents about the value to society of 40 Fortune 500 firms,[6] people associated high corporate profitability with low societal value. People think that unethical behavior like lowering the quality of service, using deceptive marketing practices, lowering employee pay and adopting worse environmental practices will all lead to higher profits. While there are different company rankings for corporate social performance, the correlation between them is quite low,[7] raising serious questions about their accuracy and validity. All of these rankings have been made by filling out surveys, either by a group of scholars and experts in the field or by employees of the companies answering the questions of the researchers.[8] To the best of our knowledge, other than through surveys, until now there exists no automatic process to automatically calculate ethical behavior and moral values of companies and individuals.

In our own research, we have calculated moral values based on the honest signals extracted from communication archives – described in Chapter 16 – and from language and words that people utilize, using our tribefinder system – described in Chapter 18, using both AI and machine learning to identify ethical and unethical behavior. This means that based on the words people use they can be assigned to different ethical categories or tribes, which we call the bee, ant or leech tribe – see Section 6.2. At the same time, we can measure their emotions and their degree of arrogance or modesty, and fairness or unfairness based on their language. Ants are arrogant and leeches are arrogant and unfair, while bees are modest and fair. As will be shown in Section 19.1, bees are the happiest, while leeches are the angriest and ants have the most fear (Figure 19.10).

We are now coming back to the statement of the CEO at the beginning of this section, who does not care about happiness but is only concerned about making money. As we will see in the next section, there is indeed a strong link between happiness and success.

4.1   HAPPINESS AND SUCCESS

We need to distinguish the emotion of joy from the lasting concept of happiness and satisfaction. Happiness and satisfaction will be reached through the rollercoaster ride of mixing positive and negative emotions, as long as the overall emotional balance is positive. In classical Western philosophy, happiness is frequently seen as the ultimate goal in life. It has been found that happy people are healthier, lead longer lives, have more friends and in general are more successful in everything they do. But what is happiness? The goal of lovers, philosophers and everybody else, happiness is a vague concept that is extremely hard to pin down. Obsessively chasing happiness as the final goal is a recipe for unhappiness. Only if "the way is the goal," if we live by the right values and find deep meaning in what we do, will we also find true long-lasting happiness.

A second key point is that it is futile to expect everlasting happiness. Along the way on the journey through even the happiest life, there will always be moments of sadness, sorrow, anger, fear and disgust. Only if there is some pain along the way on the quest for happiness do we really know what happiness means. A life of constant hedonistic happiness becomes dull and boring. Wild drug-fueled sexual escapades only bring short bursts of fleeting happiness, but not lasting satisfaction with life. Success too early and too effortlessly can easily lead to unhappiness. For instance, musicians who become famous early in their lives have a high risk of dying young. Amy Winehouse died at 27, as did Janis Joplin, Jimmy Hendrix and Kurt Cobain; Avicii died at 28, Elvis Presley died at 42 and Michael Jackson at 50, which does not make the prospects of today's young stars of reaching old age too promising. While we expect material wealth, professional success and fame to bring happiness, the biggest source of happiness is to be with people we love and respect. Thus, the safest and most lasting way to happiness comes through giving and receiving unquestioning love to and from other people in the philosophical sense of Aristotle, who calls it "*philia*." *Philia* is the deep and trusting friendship between two people who are giving to the other without asking for anything in return, which according to other philosophers refers "primarily to relationships among close blood kin."[9] In other words, we should treat others like "kin," with kindness.

People reaching a biblical age are happy people. Reaching old age is an ultimate success metric of having led a happy life. In different studies it has been found that happy old people life longer.[10, 11] In her book *Growing Young*, Marta Zaraska identifies three key properties of people reaching a high age:

- having good *friends*;
- being an *optimist*; and
- being *kind*.

These three criteria for reaching old age are thus also three key prerequisites of happiness. To measure happiness, and the factors causing it, happiness researchers usually collect information about the happiness of their study subjects in surveys of subjective life satisfaction. These surveys assess an individual's overall subjective well-being. Researchers ask questions such as "Taken overall, how satisfied are you with the life you lead on a scale from 0 (totally dissatisfied) to 10 (totally satisfied)?" The resulting scores are then used to correlate happy and less happy people with other factors that might influence their happiness, such as income or health. In fact, it has been found that there is indeed positive correlation between income and happiness – up to a point: once a person earns slightly more than the average income of their peer group, there is no noticeable increase in happiness anymore. Named after the researcher who first discovered it, this is known as the "Easterlin Paradox."[12] In general, there are other criteria besides money that are more reliable predictors of happiness, such as institutional and social trust. This is one of the main reasons why citizens of the Nordic countries Finland, Denmark, Norway and Sweden occupy the top positions in the United Nations World Happiness report[13] as they trust their government, institutions and fellow citizens more than anybody else in the world. Another criterion for happiness is having the feeling of being in control of one's own destiny. This includes being self-employed[14] and thus deciding when and how much to work, but also not being stuck in traffic in a lengthy commute. In fact, researchers found that the duration of the daily commute was a reliable predictor of unhappiness,[15] as was the decision with whom to spend time. This means that being confined to lengthy business meetings – not having self-control – made people unhappy, while being with good friends – as everybody can choose their own friends – leads to some of the happiest moments for a person.[16]

There are some simple recipes for more happiness:

- *Create* something – researchers have found that creating something new will release the same happiness hormone oxytocin as when we have sex or eat delicious food. What you create depends on your personal skills and preferences. During the Covid-19 lockdown many people started baking bread or cookies leading to shortages of yeast and flour in stores. If you are artistically talented you might want to start painting, as did former US president George W. Bush and former United Kingdom prime minister Winston Churchill.
- *Connect* with others – being with people we like is the most reliable source of happiness. So, if you are down, reach out to a friend you have not connected for some time. If you are more adventurous, plan an event that brings you in contact with groups of friends.
- *Crave* nature – nature and trees are never-ending sources of inspiration and happiness. Patients in hospital recover faster and need fewer painkillers if their window faces a park than if it faces an empty wall. A walk in the park – but not a walk on a busy street – will make students more productive and creative. So, get up and take a walk in the park and enjoy the trees!

Happy employees are better employees, leading to more loyal and satisfied customers, rapid growth and more profit. Happiness does not mean hedonistic, sex and drug-fueled parties and exorbitant salaries, but employees working together intrinsically motivated in a job that gives them meaning and fulfill-ment, in a culture of mutual respect, humility and openness. Happiness is not just good for the individual; it is also good for the organization. Happy organ-izations are made up of happy individuals. Positively entangled organizations are happy organizations. Organizational entanglement means creating an organizational culture that deeply cares about all aspects of employee satisfac-tion. Happy employees are more productive[17] and lead to happier customers and suppliers. Happy customers buy more products and will be more loyal in times of adversity, thus increasing the profit and resilience of a company. In a study based on surveys of millions of employees of hundreds of multinational companies by Gallup, the researchers found convincing evidence of a strong correlation between employee satisfaction, productivity and company perfor-mance.[18] Employee satisfaction reduced employee turnover significantly and increased company profitability, employee productivity and customer loyalty. For the financial industry, the correlation was strongest between employee sat-isfaction and customer loyalty and employee productivity. In manufacturing, employee satisfaction was most significant for company profitability.

In their comprehensive meta-study,[19] Sonja Lyubomirsky, Laura King and Ed Diener analyzed 225 research papers about happiness, showing a clear link between happiness and success in all aspects of life. This means that it is not just that your success makes you happy, but that having a predisposition towards happiness will make you more successful. Happy people are more successful in all aspects of private and professional lives such as marriage, friendships, income, work performance and health. Happy people are also more social, active and energetic. They engage in more, more diverse and more active pursuits. Among others, Lyubomirsky, King and Diener list the following consequences of happiness. Happy people:

- are more successful professionally, both having higher income and obtaining faster promotion;
- are more popular;
- are more extrovert;
- live longer;
- are healthier, for instance they show increased immunity against viral diseases such as influenza;[20]
- are more prosocial, more charitable and willing to help;
- are more creative;
- are more active and energetic; and
- have more friends.

This last point, about happy people having more friends, is crucial. Not only do happy people have more friends to start with, but the rich getting richer, more people want to become their friends, so they will get even more friends. Being with people we like is one of the key prerequisites for happiness. Even better, if the people we like, like us back.

4.2   WHAT CAN WE DO TO BE LIKED?

To be a happy team member in flow means being together with others like me, even more, with others who like me. These two points are closely related. I like people that are similar to me, which means that others that are more like me will also like me more. We like people better if we trust them more.[21] For instance, we trust people from our ingroup more, that is people of the same race and ethnicity, social background, age, gender, etc. According to trust researchers, we trust people who are more agreeable, predictable and reliable. In fact, we make decisions about whom we trust based on facial features of others,[22] with features that express less dominance and more happiness rated as being more trustworthy. When looking at a face, our brain makes a split-second decision whether we trust the other person or think he or she is a psychopath and narcissist.[23] The conclusion is thus that there is a four-way relationship between being liked and liking others and trusting others and being trusted by others.

To get our team into groupflow, we need to create a trusting team where team members like each other. The good news is that there are different things we can do to be liked and trusted.

What can you do to be liked?[24]

- Mirror the behavior of the other person – if I copy the body language, gestures and facial expressions, nodding back at my opposite in the same rhythm as she is nodding at me, if we move our hands in similar gestures and walk in lockstep, that will make my opposite more positive towards me.
- Spend time with the other person, even lightly touch them – the more time I spend with somebody, the more the other person starts liking me.
- Make yourself vulnerable – making myself vulnerable by disclosing some of my weaknesses will make the other person like me more, however, disclosing too many weaknesses might undermine my trustworthiness.
- Show positive emotions, smile – if we smile more, our opposites will see us in a more positive light and remember us for a longer period of time.
- Let them talk about themselves – talking about themselves can be inherently rewarding like food or sex, activating the same reward circuits in the brain, and thus letting them see you in a more positive light.
- In extension, this means that you like people most, who
  - mirror your behavior;
  - with whom you voluntarily spend a lot of time;
  - who make themselves vulnerable to you;
  - who show you positive emotions, and smile at you; and
  - who let you talk about yourself.

There are some types of people who are universally liked, similarly there are people that nobody really likes. The key point to be liked is to be not just nice, but to be kind.

4.3   RESPECT AND COMPASSION

Kind individuals show both respect and compassion to others. While compassion and respect are properties of individuals, they also define national culture. For instance, China is known as being more respectful than compassionate, while the US is known as being more compassionate than respectful. And citizens of both countries are not particularly happy, at least compared to small European countries like Denmark, Finland, Iceland or Switzerland, whose national cultures prize both characteristics. For example, Finland makes sure that workers in less qualified professions still get a decent wage sufficient to lead a dignified life. Switzerland is compassionate even with lobsters; it is the only country in the world with a law that forbids boiling them to death. Unfortunately, the US and China, the two most powerful countries on Earth, both vying for global leadership, still have the challenge of building societies that are both strongly respectful and compassionate.

Americans are empathetic to their weak but show little respect to their unqualified workers. Living in the US nearly half the time over the last 20 years, I observed that people with low professional qualifications, like janitors, waiters and cleaners, get little respect. People on the higher rungs of society try to pay them as little as possible, so much so that it is impossible for members of these poorly paid professions – essential for the functioning of cities like Boston, New York or San Francisco – to actually live there. Rather, they have to either sleep in shifts in one-room apartments in windowless basements or spend many hours per day in grueling commutes from poorer towns far away to get to their jobs. Children from such backgrounds, often mistreated by their peers from kindergarten, then take their frustrations out by robbing high-end stores as flash mobs, or at the extreme end in school shootings. On the positive side in the US, there are numerous charities and individuals that engage in countless acts of kindness, compassion and benevolence, assisting the homeless, mistreated animals and others hit by misfortune through no fault of their own.

China is the opposite. In general, the Chinese treat each other with consideration independent of where in the social ladder somebody resides, but they do not have so much compassion for people who are seen as outsiders or animals. In my frequent stays there over the last eight years, I observed that my hosts, usually well-paid academics, company executives and bureaucrats, treated others of lower social status with more respect than their US peers. Unfortunately, I saw little of this compassion for outsiders or animals. In a monastery I saw vendors offering caged birds whose freedom could be bought by tourists as a good deed, for the vendors to go out and catch the birds again for the next tourist. Similarly, I was shocked that in a restaurant I could choose from pigeons sitting in a cage, which would then immediately be grabbed by the cook to be slaughtered and brought back to my table plucked and grilled 20 minutes later. In one extreme example, workers disinfecting an apartment vacated by a Covid-quarantined dog owner bludgeoned the dog to death with iron bars, with the horrified quarantined owner forced to watch the scene on a remote camera.[25] In other cases of over-the-top enforcement of Covid-19 restrictions, at a hospital in Xi'an a woman untested for the virus suffered a miscarriage in the parking lot, and a man with chest pain had to wait for six hours before being admitted to hospital, resulting in his death. Chinese are also not so forthcoming when it comes to giving money to beggars. This has been confirmed by the World Giving Index, which ranks the US as the most generous country, while China has been among the ten least generous countries in the world for ten years in a row.[26]

Therefore, respectful China shows little compassion, while compassionate America shows little respect. In the end, it is in society's best interest to show respect and compassion to all. Treating others with respect is the best antidote against a violent society where those who have live in constant fear of being robbed by the have-nots. At the same time, treating others with compassion ensures that if misfortune hits, others will return the care that one has previously shown, leading to safer and happier lives for all.

The world would be a better place if more people would show compassion for lobsters!

4.4   KINDNESS IS MORE THAN BEING NICE

Showing respect means showing kindness. While it is nice to be nice, it is better to be kind. Being kind to another person is more than being nice, it includes saying things to the other person that might not be nice but are kind. For instance, telling another person that he has bad breath does not sound nice, but it is "kind," as it is in the interest of the other person to become aware of her or his bad breath and take corrective action, for instance brushing their teeth more frequently. It also takes courage to tell somebody that they have bad breath, a willingness to accept pain to give the other person short-term pain but long-term gain – "no pain, no gain."

The word "kindness" includes "being of the same kind" as a synonym for "being related to." Kindness means treating other people as if they were members of one's own family, not just being nice in the moment, but showing lasting kindness that builds trust and relationships over generations.

Figure 4.2 shows what it takes to be kind to other people. It means showing respect to others by being responsive and upfront and honest. It also means empowering others, delegating them responsibility and letting them step up when it is their turn. At the same time, being kind means being fair, caring and inclusive of all members of the team.

Showing respect to people outside one's own ingroup is the key to peaceful relationships. The BlackLivesMatter campaign in the US in response to the 2020 killings of George Floyd, Breonna Taylor and Ahmaud Arbery and the earlier killings of Trayvon Martin in 2012 and Michael Brown and Eric Garner in 2014 illustrates the importance of showing respect. Compare the police response on May 30, 2020 to aggressive behavior of protesters in Brooklyn and in Oklahoma City. In Brooklyn the police officers responded to threatening behavior of the crowd by first slowly driving their cruisers into the crowd and then speeding up, sending protesters scattering. In a similar situation, the Oklahoma City police diffused the tension by "taking the knee," thus showing their respect for the killed victims and solidarity with the crowd, leading to getting applause from the protesters.

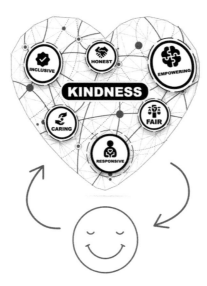

Figure 4.2   Aspects of kindness

In a very different story about kindness, a famous professor at a business school once told me that he was surprised how kind the Nobel Memorial Prize winners in economics were compared to other economists. Economists normally are more known for having huge egos, not for being kind. A few years later, when I had the opportunity to visit the Nobel Prize Museum in Stockholm, I asked the tour guide about her interaction with the winners. She told me that her job included interviewing all the Nobel Prize winners and asking them for some artefacts to be displayed in the museum. She also told me how much she enjoyed the interaction with the winners, and how kind they all had been to her. She explained that nominations for the Nobel Prize have to come from the peers of a scientist. This makes all the difference regarding kindness of the Nobel Prize winners, as their peers are only willing to nominate somebody who is nice and has been kind to others in the past. This means that super-smart jerks have a small chance of winning the Nobel Prize. It pays to be kind, even to potential competitors.

4.5   PERSONALITY CHARACTERISTICS THAT INCREASE HAPPINESS AND LONGEVITY

It turns out there is a direct link between personality characteristics and health and longevity. Having certain personality characteristics is good for your health, while others will reduce your life expectancy and well-being. The most popular personality classification used for psychological research is FFI, which measures the five personality characteristics labelled OCEAN. Openness to experience looks at whether you are stuck in your old ways, or open to new ideas and innovations. Conscientiousness measures your orderliness and tidiness, and how predictable your behavior is and if you do what you say. Extroversion tracks your social behavior: are you an introvert who is happiest alone at home reading a book, or do you prefer to be constantly surrounded by other people and be the heart and soul of a party? Agreeability looks at how easy you are to get along with: are you willing to overlook small offenses and slights, or do you blow up at the smallest offense, imagined or real? Neuroticism measures how much you worry – how moody, easily depressed and anxious you are. In a large-scale statistical analysis with 6904 participants in the US, it was found that all five OCEAN characteristics influence your propensity to have certain diseases.[27] Your likelihood of having high blood pressure, diabetes, cancer, lung disease, a heart condition, a stroke or arthritis are all related to your personality. High conscientiousness, extroversion, openness, agreeability and low neuroticism are all associated with better health. In particular, high conscientiousness and low neuroticism reduce the chance of developing a stroke and lung disease, as does high openness. The causal link between extroversion and agreeability and good health is less prominent. Conscientiousness, doing what you say, showing consistent behavior, cleaning up and being orderly have a direct positive influence on your well-being, as does being open to new ideas, being willing to try out new things, worrying less and adopting an optimistic attitude.

Men who are more conscientious and more open, and women who are less neurotic and more agreeable, live the longest. In a longitudinal study, researchers followed 600 couples living in 1935 in the state of Connecticut over the period from 1935[28] to 2013.[29] Different from many other studies comparing personality with well-being and longevity, the people in the study cohort did not self-answer the FFI survey questions, rather the personalities were assessed by three to five friends of each participant. The researchers found that men with one positive standard deviation increase in conscientiousness had a 29 percent decrease in mortality risk; a similar increase in openness was associated with a 15 percent decrease in mortality risk. Similarly, emotionally more stable and more agreeable women had a 15 percent decrease in mortality risk.

The interesting point is that the personality ratings done by their peers were a better predictor of mortality risk than the self-ratings. For men the effects of the self-ratings were directionally similar to the peer-rated personality characteristics, but smaller with a 13 percent mortality risk decrease for both higher conscientiousness and higher openness. For women, the self-rated personality characteristics were not correlated with any effect on longevity at all. This suggests that frequently we are not honest to ourselves, in particular when assessing ourselves in personality surveys. It also seems that women are even less honest to themselves than men, where at least the effect still remained, although at a reduced size. In a further analysis, the researchers found that friends of a male were particularly good at identifying people with low conscientiousness, and thus with a higher risk of earlier death.

The good news is that personalities change over time. While psychologists in the better part of the twentieth century assumed that once somebody was grown up their personality was cast in stone, it has now been shown that this is not the case. Using the same cohort of 600 couples, when retesting the 600 individuals after one year, the correlation between their original personality values and the answers after one year was about 70 percent; when repeating the test after 20 years, the correlation dropped to 50 percent, indicating large changes in the self-answered personality scores. We are the product of our past experiences, which greatly influence how we act today. For instance, in the same project, the attitude towards marriage of the 600 participants correlated less than 7 percent with the original answers given 20 years before. Conscientiousness correlated at about 38 percent with the ratings given 20 years before. This means that people experienced a huge change in this personality characteristic essential for well-being and a long life. There were also changes of 52 percent in the moral values of the participants over the 20-year period.

Changing your personality is an actionable way to increase happiness and live to an old age in better health. Listen to your friends and try to be more conscientious, more open for new ideas and to worry less. Measure it and be told when to deviate from the good ways. The conclusion therefore is that it is better to ask your friends to assess your personality characteristics than answering the survey questions yourself. Or even better, use an AI system that uses the aggregated wisdom of the swarm to measure your personality based on your honest signals of collaboration, as shown in Part II.

NOTES

1.   Schein, E. H., & Schein, P. A. (2018). *Humble Leadership: The Power of Relationships, Openness, and Trust*. Berrett-Koehler Publishers.

2. Mayer, D. M., Aquino, K., Greenbaum, R. L., & Kuenzi, M. (2012). Who displays ethical leadership, and why does it matter? An examination of antecedents and consequences of ethical leadership. *Academy of Management Journal*, 55(1), 151–171.
3. Babiak, P., Neumann, C. S., & Hare, R. D. (2010). Corporate psychopathy: Talking the walk. *Behavioral Sciences and the Law*, 28(2), 174–193.
4. Shank, C. A. (2018). Deconstructing the corporate psychopath: An examination of deceptive behavior. *Review of Behavioral Finance*, 10(2), 163–182.
5. Mayer, D. M., Aquino, K., Greenbaum, R. L., & Kuenzi, M. (2012). Who displays ethical leadership, and why does it matter? An examination of antecedents and consequences of ethical leadership. *Academy of Management Journal*, 55(1), 151–171.
6. Bhattacharjee, A., & Dana, J. (2017). People think companies can't do good and make money: Can companies prove them wrong? *Harvard Business Review*, https://hbr.org/2017/11/people-think-companies-cant-do-good-and-make-money-can-companies-prove-them-wrong.
7. Sharfman, M. (1996). The construct validity of the Kinder, Lydenberg & Domini social performance ratings data. *Journal of Business Ethics*, 15(3), 287–296.
8. Mattingly, J. E. (2017). Corporate social performance: A review of empirical research examining the corporation–society relationship using Kinder, Lydenberg, Domini social ratings data. *Business and Society*, 56(6), 796–839.
9. Konstan, D. (2008). Aristotle on love and friendship. *ΣΧΟΛΗ. Философское антиковедение и классическая* традиция, 2(2), 207–212.
10. Chei, C.-L., Lee, J. M.-L., Ma, S., & Malhotra, R. (2018). Happy older people live longer. *Age and Ageing*, 47(6), 860–866.
11. Vaillant, G. E. (2008). *Aging Well: Surprising Guideposts to a Happier Life from the Landmark Study of Adult Development*. Hachette UK.
12. Easterlin, R. A., McVey, L. A., Switek, M., Sawangfa, O., & Zweig, J. S. (2010). The happiness–income paradox revisited. *Proceedings of the National Academy of Sciences*, 107(52), 22463–22468.
13. https://worldhappiness.report/ed/2020/.
14. Benz, M., & Frey, B. S. (2008). Being independent is a great thing: Subjective evaluations of self-employment and hierarchy. *Economica*, 75(298), 362–383.
15. Stutzer, A., & Frey, B. S. (2008). Stress that doesn't pay: The commuting paradox. *Scandinavian Journal of Economics*, 110(2), 339–366.
16. Frey, B. S. (2010). *Happiness: A Revolution in Economics*. MIT Press.
17. Oswald, A. J., Proto, E., & Sgroi, D. (2015). Happiness and productivity. *Journal of Labor Economics*, 33(4), 789–822.
18. www.weforum.org/agenda/2019/07/happy-employees-and-their-impact-on-firm-performance/.
19. Lyubomirsky, S., King, L., & Diener, E. (2005). The benefits of frequent positive affect: Does happiness lead to success? *Psychological Bulletin*, 131(6), 803.
20. Cohen, S., Alper, C. M., Doyle, W. J., Treanor, J. J., & Turner, R. B. (2006). Positive emotional style predicts resistance to illness after experimental exposure to rhinovirus or influenza A virus. *Psychosomatic Medicine*, 68(6), 809–815.
21. Rotter, J. B. (1980). Interpersonal trust, trustworthiness, and gullibility. *American Psychologist*, 35(1), 1.
22. Todorov, A., Said, C. P., Engell, A. D., & Oosterhof, N. N. (2008). Understanding evaluation of faces on social dimensions. *Trends in Cognitive Sciences*, 12(12), 455–460.

23. Gordon, D. S., & Platek, S. M. (2009). Trustworthy? The brain knows: Implicit neural responses to faces that vary in dark triad personality characteristics and trustworthiness. *Journal of Social, Evolutionary, and Cultural Psychology*, 3(3), 182.

24. www.independent.co.uk/life-style/sixteen-psychological-tricks-people-you-a7967861.html.

25. www.scmp.com/news/people-culture/social-welfare/article/3156097/china-coronavirus-apology-after-government.

26. www.usnews.com/news/best-countries/articles/2019-12-20/the-worlds-most-generous-countries.

27. Weston, S. J., Hill, P. L., & Jackson, J. J. (2015). Personality traits predict the onset of disease. *Social Psychological and Personality Science*, 6(3), 309–317.

28. Kelly, E. L. (1955). Consistency of the adult personality. *American Psychologist*, 10(11), 659.

29. Jackson, J. J., Connolly, J. J., Garrison, S. M., Leveille, M. M., & Connolly, S. L. (2015). Your friends know how long you will live: A 75-year study of peer-rated personality traits. *Psychological Science*, 26(3), 335–340.

5. Virtual tribes

If wild beasts can be broken to the yoke, it must not be despaired of correcting the man who has strayed. (Michel Foucault, Madness and Civilization, p 78)

Going back to the Stone Age, humans have always split into different tribes, warring at times, collaborating peacefully at others. However, within a tribe or a nation, ingroup loyalty and homogeneity was required and enforced. Only recently has it been accepted that also citizens of Western democracies are split into many virtual tribes.

In his classic work about the history of madness, Michel Foucault describes how deviants from the majority have been (mis)treated over the last centuries. In the age of the Enlightenment, in the eighteenth and nineteenth centuries in Europe, houses of confinement (prisons) were used to lock away criminals, the mad and the jobless. The above quote is taken from the gate to a prison in Hamburg. The prison's goal was to enforce social order, through an authoritarian model which was seen as "adequate to virtue." Through these houses of confinement, the goal was to break outliers to the yoke, pursuing a "one size fits all" approach. The age of Enlightenment led to European national states, successors of the feudal medieval states. Instead of allegiance to a monarch or ruler, national states are based on allegiance to a nation, identified through racial characteristics and shared cultural values. Through allegiance to a figure of authority, be it the French king or emperor, the Austrian or German emperor or the British king, one was made a proud French, Austrian, German or Brit, being a member of the French, Austrian, German or British nation, speaking the same language and having a similar shared "look and feel." People who behaved differently, who did not share the same "look and feel," were locked away in these houses of confinement, be it the gypsies in the Austrian empire or poets and scientists like Oscar Wilde and Alan Turing who were locked away for not hiding their homosexuality. People committing less severe transgressions, such as being poor, were put into confinement to convert them from their obscenely deviating ways to re-educate them to become adjusted members of the nation. If that failed, they were locked away permanently, to avoid diluting the purity of the tribe. Alternatively, they might have been shipped to America or Australia.

Global migration and the internet have been a huge equalizer over the last hundred years. However ultranationalists, or "fatherlanders," are still going strong, for instance #MakeAmericaGreatAgain or as members of the QAnon group, spreading wild conspiracy theories against the enemies of Donald Trump's tribe. Fatherlanders, the members of the ultranationalist tribe, are frequently fundamentally religious; they abhor change and admire authority and tradition.[1] As has been shown in research projects, people with these personality characteristics tend to be prevalent in professions such as the police or the army.[2] While one of their key characteristics is loyalty towards members of their own tribe, they have little tolerance for members of other tribes, as has been shown in research. Also, they are not very open to innovation; they don't like change, they value tradition and they want to conserve things the way they always have been.

5.1   EMOTIONAL REACTIONS INDICATE YOUR TRIBE

According to anthropologists, a tribe is defined as a social group unified by a common culture. A tribe is thus unified by a shared value system, customs, manners and practices. Sometimes we are members of a tribe without being aware of belonging to the same brotherhood. The question is what gets people to self-identify as a member of a tribe, and self-organize and aggregate in a community?

Sociologist Randall Collins introduced the concept of "interaction ritual chains," with interaction rituals acting as key symbols of group membership for keeping people together. Interaction rituals appear if three requirements are met: first, human bodies have to be together close enough to read each others' body language through voice, gestures and facial expressions; second, the humans involved need to focus on the same thing, for instance smoking together or watching the same soccer game; and third, they must feel the same shared emotion, for instance the small pleasure of smoking together or screaming after a goal is scored. If these three conditions occur together, the subsequent interaction ritual will reinforce the emotions and the mutual focus of the participants, creating the feeling of what Emile Durkheim calls "collective effervescence." "Collective effervescence" or "collective enthusiasm" happens when a community gets together, engaging in the same thought and action, thus acting in "collective awareness" or "collective consciousness." A successful interaction ritual has three consequences: first, it triggers a feeling of belonging and solidarity within the group. Second, it generates membership symbols such as flags, but also rituals such as gestures, words or particular persons. Third, it creates emotional energy that gives group members confidence and enthusiasm. This emotional energy can be triggered both by shared delight, for instance if the home soccer team scores a goal, or shared anger, if the opposing team scores.

This means that members of a tribe share the same emotion in response to an external event. Figure 5.1 illustrates what happens if an indigenous inhabitant of Papua New Guinea finds some maggots. He will show joy and be delighted about this nutritious snack. On the contrary, if a New York office worker finds a maggot in her food, she will be disgusted and repulsed.

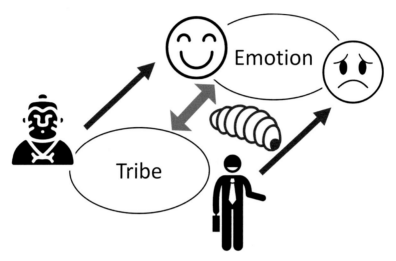

*Figure 5.1   Example of an emotional response to an external stimulus
               dependent on a different tribe*

The same emotional response, as measured through the level of stress hormones in human saliva, will happen if a heterosexual male with strong beliefs about traditional partnerships sees a picture of two men kissing.[3] For a gay man, the same picture will most likely trigger the release of oxytocin, also known as the "love hormone." This means that what emotion a tribe member experiences in response to an external stimulus is dependent on the ethical rules and morals of the tribe.

The fatherlander tribe (shown by the tank in Figure 5.2) will value law and order highly, and unquestioning obeisance of religious authority. In a conservative Islamic society, adultery of a woman might thus lead to anger and disgust, resulting in the stoning of the woman. In a Northern European "treehugger and nerd" society, adultery of a woman might lead to an amicable divorce, and to new love for both former members of the couple.

Figure 5.2 illustrates how the construction of the wall of President Trump on the southern border of the US to keep immigrants and asylum seekers out of the US triggered very different emotional responses among US citizens based on their different moral value systems. Fatherlanders experienced joy and delight, while most treehuggers experienced anger and sadness.

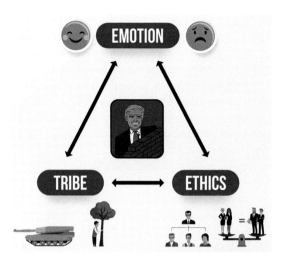

Figure 5.2   *Different emotions triggered by fatherlanders and treehuggers in response to Donald Trump's wall*

In other words, the shared emotional response to an external event will be a key part of Randall Collins' interaction ritual, incentivizing people experiencing the same emotions to external stimuli to join the same tribes. However, in digital virtual tribes the third element of interaction ritual chains, the co-located presence of human bodies, is missing. This is where social media comes in. On Twitter, Reddit, Facebook, Telegram and Signal, people will show their immediate emotional reactions to each other, leading to echo chambers where the same real or fake news is retweeted, reposted and liked at a frenetic pace among the members of the same tribe. If possible, tribe members still try to also be physically close to each other and aggregate at the same location, as this releases neurochemicals such as the bonding and love hormone oxytocin and the feel-good hormone serotonin. This was vividly demonstrated on January 6, 2021, when a tribe of fervent Trump henchmen got together in Washington, DC and stormed the US capitol.

5.2   POWER OR LOVE? IS IT BETTER TO FIT IN, OR TO STAND OUT?

Once you have chosen your tribe, is it better to fit in or stand out? Andre Roussimoff, better known as Andre the Giant, stood out. He towered over everybody, radiating brutal, unfettered force and power. Standing at 2 meters and 24 centimeters, and weighing 236 kilograms, he was one of the most successful show wrestlers of all time. But still, he once told a friend "You know, people think that I have a great life … that I can travel all over and everything … but I see them when they point at me … little kids laugh and say, what kind of a man is he?"[4] With all his success towering over everybody else, he was a lonely man because he stood out and was stared at wherever he went.

Standing out is painful, fitting in is joyful. Being a fully integrated and accepted member of a team, or of a tribe, gives a feeling of belonging and security. Whether it is singing in a choir, playing soccer in a sports club or storming the Capitol on January 6, 2021, being part of a group in flow is instantaneously immensely powerful and rewarding.

Andre the Giant drove a Rolls Royce, owned a ranch in Virginia, flew first class and dined and lodged at the most expensive hotels his entire adult life. Standing out, if done decisively and skillfully, is materially rewarding. Andre the Giant stood out, as did Steve Jobs, or as does Elon Musk. Fitting in is spiritually rewarding, as anybody joining an orchestra, jazz band or soccer team will experience. Standing out makes lonely, fitting in makes happy. While everybody wants to be happy, people follow very different trajectories to reach that goal. Competitive people strive for money, power and glory, while collaborative people prioritize love and compassion over power. Highly competitive people want to stand out, collaborative people strive to fit in. Standing out can also make people happy, but because of other causes. Standing out successfully will give money, power and glory. If you stand out as a leader, towering over your peers, everybody wants to be your friend. However, most likely such friends will also easily leave you once you don't stand out anymore. Or according to social network theory, when standing out you will have many weak ties. Weak ties are links to casual acquaintances and superficial friends. Weak ties are great to get ahead, as they give access to the diverse information and knowledge needed for professional success. However, "weak tie" friends will not go to great lengths to offer assistance in times of need.

Fitting in will give you love. If you fit in, you will have strong ties to the members of your community. Strong ties are links to friends on whom you can rely on in times of need. But maintaining strong ties takes time, as your friends will also expect you to come to their aid when they need help; this means less time to get ahead and stand out.

Regardless of whether we prefer to stand out or fit in, we would all like to have at least some money, power and glory. To succeed, we need to navigate in a carefully balanced equilibrium, deciding at each step if it is time to stand out or if we had better fit in. Standing out means standing up for our opinion, taking risks and sticking our neck out, with the possibility of having it symbolically chopped off. Fitting in means making myself smaller and subordinating my personal wishes and desires to the values of my chosen tribe. It means less glory and power, but the warm feeling of being part of a caring community. One key point is that we can decide to fit in in one tribe and stand out in another one. I discovered this in the first sociometric badge experiment (see Section 14.1) in a bank 15 years ago, where we noticed that a secretary was behaving as a clear introvert, communicating very little, positioned in the periphery of the social network. By chance I spoke with somebody who knew her in her carnival guild, who told me that this could not be, as she was the heart and soul of the guild, acting as a huge extrovert. This means that this secretary decided to invest all her social energy in the carnival guild, making it the center of her life, while the job at the bank was clearly relegated to simply bringing in the money to support her activity for where she got her life's meaning in the guild. In other words, she chose to stand out in the carnival guild and to fit in in her professional life.

In today's globally hyperconnected world we can choose our tribes and whether to fit in or stand out wherever and on the micro level we want, but it turns out that the Indian Varna caste system, which goes back at least 3000 years to the Rig Veda, already came up with assigning each human to one of four castes, which map very well to today's alternative realities.

5.3   FROM VARNA CASTES TO ALTERNATIVE REALITIES

I call the four tribes of the "spiritualists," "nerds," "fatherlanders" and "treehuggers" "alternative realities," as they portray characteristics of four categories of personality-wise orthogonal individuals. They will thus assist people in deciding in which of these alternative realities they belong. While this oversimplification should not be used to pigeonhole an individual, these categories are useful for understanding the general characteristics of a person. Spiritualists provide spiritual guidance, be it as priests and pastors or as meditation coaches and yoga teachers. Nerds are the engineers and scientists, applying and further developing technology, from building houses and roads to computers and rockets. Fatherlanders defend their fatherland, as politicians, managers, soldiers and policemen. Treehuggers protest to the (over)use of technology, wanting to protect nature to create a more sustainable style of living.

Going 3000 years back, these four alternative realities have a direct correspondence to the four castes of the Indian Varna caste system (Figure 5.3). The Varna castes include the brahmins – priests, teachers and scholars; the ksathriya – warriors, administrators and rulers; the vaishyas – farmers, artisans and merchants; and the shudras – laborers and servants. These four castes directly correspond to the four alternative realities. Spiritualists, who strive for higher moral values and ethical behavior, correspond to brahmin intellectuals, priests and teachers, who aim to preserve sacred knowledge over generations. Fatherlanders have an obvious correspondence to ksathriyas, who try to build empires by applying power, in the old days and even today by leading wars, and also by more subtle means as CEOs going on acquisition sprees. Nerds, who believe in the supremacy of science and technology, correspond to the vaishyas, farmers, merchants and artists, who nurture and feed the others. The correspondence between treehuggers and shudras might not be immediately obvious, but treehuggers and shudras are linked by their powerlessness. In Hinduism, shudras are seen as the laboring class, providing services to others. Shudras are the servants of others; they are expected to follow orders of the other three castes without objecting. Fanatic treehuggers, frustrated by the thoughtlessness, unfairness and even cruelty, with whom particularly father-landers and nerds heat the globe, pollute the environment, slaughter whales and cut down trees, struggle with their disentitlement, screaming out their weakness and impotence.

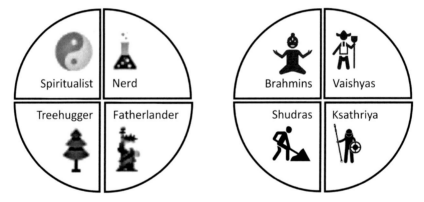

Figure 5.3   The Indian caste system illustrates the professional focus of the four alternative realities

As with everything in life, there are two sides to the coin. Each category, be it in today's alternative realities or in the Indian Varna system going back thousands of years, can be used for good or bad. There are exemplary spiritual leaders like Desmond Tutu, leading through strength grounded in humility, nerds like Steve Jobs changing the way people communicate, treehuggers like Greta Thunberg, carrying the torch of global warming as environmental activ-ists, and fatherlanders who are nation builders like Nelson Mandela.

But there are also spiritual leaders whose contributions to humanity are less clear, although they would all beg to differ (Figure 5.4). Tribal leaders such as

Warren Buffett, spiritual guru of the investment fanatics tribe, or master nerd Vitalik Buterin, creator of cryptocurrency Ethereum, or North Korean dictator and fatherlander Kim Jong-un, or the #extinctionrebellion treehuggers, protesting global warming with mostly non-violent means, are all prominent within their castes. However, none of these later four would probably pass the ethics test raised by Baruch Spinoza, questioning their value to society.

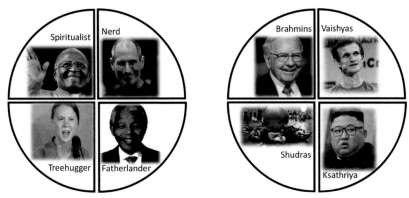

Note: The photos are from www.wikipedia.org.

Figure 5.4   Positive and negative examples of representatives of alternative realities

As has been shown in the earlier discussion about ethics and happiness, one key prerequisite for happiness is the capability to be in control of one's own destiny. This raises the question as to why we need brahmins and kshatriyas. Why are people delegating decisions to their leaders, be it spiritual or worldly? The answer is again based on whether somebody wants to stand out or fit in. If we prefer to fit in with our tribe, we need a leader who is willing to stand out and make decisions. This is the role the brahmins and ksathriyas volunteer for. In other words, decision making and responsibility is voluntarily delegated to spiritual and worldly leaders. Somebody who likes authority and hierarchy will gladly submit to the orders of a brahmin or ksathriya. Many people do not want to take decisions in their private and professional lives, but would rather delegate it to a priest or a manager.

   The key question for people wanting to assume a leadership role as a brahmin or ksathriya is what they can do to stand out as leaders and be accepted by the others as chiefs of their tribe. The answer is that team members want leaders who they can trust. How can one be trusted? By giving trust to others, and by being trustworthy themselves. This means demonstrating consistent behavior, saying what they do and doing what they say. Great leaders have always had the trust of their collaborators. George Washington would not have led the US to independence, overcoming a series of crushing early defeats in 1776 and 1777, if he had not had the full trust of his soldiers.

What does it take to be a trusted leader of a tribe? The leader needs to be entangled with the tribe, sharing the same culture and value system and creating an environment of collective consciousness.

5.4   THE EMERGENCE OF COLLECTIVE CONSCIOUSNESS

We all like to be with people like us, with our tribe – and the same is true of members of other species. Just look at how birds, sheep or fish strive to be with their flock, not to speak of social insects such as bees or ants. One of the main reasons we want to be with similar people is that it is much easier to communicate if we share language, values and context. Sociologist Emile Durkheim called this shared understanding of social norms "collective consciousness." The more similar other people are to me, the more I like them. If I stay together with somebody I like, spending a lot of time together, we tend to get more and more similar and will get more and more aligned in the words we use, our values and moral norms. In prehistoric times millions to hundreds of thousands of years ago this "getting more similar" happened through shared genes. Our ancestor Homo sapiens incorporated the genes of Neanderthals by interbreeding, thus also inheriting some of their personality characteristics, which according to research, include more aggressive traits quite different from the friendlier, self-domesticated personalities of Homo sapiens.[5] Once human language was invented, people had a powerful tool to develop collective consciousness faster by talking about it and gossiping about other people. With the invention of writing which appeared first in 3400 BC in Mesopotamia and shortly thereafter in Egypt, people got more persistent and transportable ways of sharing their values and culture. The invention of printing, which in 200 AD emerged as woodblock printing in China, gave larger and larger groups of people the opportunity to develop collective consciousness by disseminating their ideas even more widely. The invention of the telegraph and the phone made instantaneous sharing of new memes and cultural development on a global scale possible, enabling large groups of people anywhere on Earth to rapidly develop collective consciousness. Today, the internet and smartphone allow us to instantaneously connect on an intimate level with anybody anywhere in the world, sharing ideas and emotions through video chat, Twitter and WhatsApp or WeChat messages. We can reach a single person or a carefully selected subgroup sharing our interests and likes with the click of a button.

A group of people that has developed collective consciousness is able to communicate much more effectively, sometimes even without words. More frequently, code words like "Maga," short for #MakeAmericaGreatAgain, and "sacred" signs and gestures will convey meaning and tell the group what to do and how to act to reach their shared goals. Once the group operates on this level of collective consciousness, it is "entangled." There is also a second key ingredient besides consciousness which is necessary for the successful entanglement of a team, namely shared emotional energy.

5.5 EMOTIONAL ENERGY

What you must understand is that my voice comes from the energy of the audience. The better they are, the better I get. (Freddie Mercury)

In physics, energy is defined as the ability to do work, exerting a force that leads to the movement of an object. For people, interaction with other people, either direct or indirect, will create an emotional response which will lead to the release of energy. Obtaining money, power, glory or love will create an emotional response, giving the person obtaining it energy. For instance, winning a competition or performing for an audience will create emotional energy for the performer. Similarly, in Chinese Taoist philosophy, "Qi" means energy, but can also be understood as the force inherent in all living beings. We all want to be energetic, forceful and full of "Qi." The simplest description of energy as a term in physics is the capability to do work. Applied to humans, the more energy a person has, the more work they can do. An individual can radiate positive energy, being an energy source with whom everybody wants to spend time. A person who is a positive energy source will get others to collaborate with them. Spreading positive energy happens through words, language and body gestures. This goes back to the Greek philosophers, where in classical Greek rhetorical tradition the ability of language to create a "stir to the mind" is called "energia." "Energia" is quantified by the capability of verbal, visual and aural traces to organize and produce collective physical and mental experiences. Energia is associated with the potential to create emotions such as joy, fear, anger, disgust, laughter, tension, pain and relief. A person who is a positive energy source will communicate with others by being heard, seen and read, and thus produce energy by stoking emotions. A group of people will become a collective energy source by sharing positive energy.

Being with your tribe can be a huge source of energy. For instance, a wedding among ultra-Orthodox Jews on November 8, 2020 drew 7,000 guests during the Covid-19 lockdown in New York City. The organizers succeeded in keeping the event secret from the authorities to circumvent the strict Covid-19 lockdown regulations. The organizers described the wedding as "an experience for which words do not suffice" and "a celebration the likes of which we have rarely had the good fortune to experience,"[6] well worth the US$15,000 fine for violating the city's lockdown and isolation rules. Obviously, participants were drawing a huge amount of energy from celebrating with thousands of likeminded people.

Only if the members of a team share their force, their "Qi," through shared goals, motivation and passion will they be entangled. A group of people randomly thrown together without shared goals and motivation will not develop shared energy, and thus will not be entangled. If people communicate through language, body signals and visual cues to build collective energy and collective consciousness they will become entangled. This is what happened at the ultra-Orthodox wedding in New York City, where 7000 people were singing and dancing together in close physical contact at the height of the Covid-19 lockdown.

How does positive entanglement happen? Imagine Bill at the office, who is always smiling, greeting everybody in the morning, asking Mary about her children and questioning Sophia about the health of her old mother. During lunchtime Bill will invite Jeremy to eat lunch together in the office kitchen, discussing the latest sports and political news, while he makes sure that Jeremy gets enough speaking time to express his opinions. In meetings Bill will let others speak first; if he disagrees with something that's said in the meeting, he will deliver his arguments on a factual basis, and make sure not to offend others on a personal level. Compare this to John who comes grumpily in the office in the morning, keeps to himself and if he talks at all he will complain about the weather, the sad state of politics and his poor health. Bill radiates positive energy, his little acts of friendly communication will produce small bursts of energy among Bill's conversation partners, while John spreads negative energy.

Energy for all living beings comes through emotions (Figure 5.5). A lion chasing after a gazelle will trigger huge bursts of fear in the gazelle, leading to the release of large amounts of fear hormones such as adrenaline and cortisone, thus enabling the gazelle to mobilize all her energy to escape the lion as fast as she can. The same is true for humans. Bill spreading positive energy will create positive emotions of surprise, joy and self-esteem among his conversation and meeting partners, while John's negative energy will lead to frustration, disgust and anger among the people with whom he interacts. Bill's conversation partners will be more entangled, while John's negative energy leading to negative emotions will destroy entanglement.

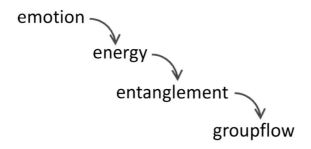

Figure 5.5   Emotions create energy

In the management science literature[7] energy has been defined as "a type of positive affective arousal, which people can experience as emotion." For instance, interaction rituals as defined by Randall Collins, symbols of belonging to a group such as national flags and anthems or the jersey of a soccer club create emotional energy (see Section 5.1) among the members of the group. Their emotions will give them energy and drive them to action. The physical properties of energy indicate how to activate collective human energy for creative and productive use.

According to the First Law of Thermodynamics, the total amount of energy and matter is constant in the Universe. It cannot be destroyed or created, only converted from one form into another. Energy comes in many forms and can be transferred from one object to another, for instance as heat, light or motion. What does this mean for human energy? As energy is the capacity to do work and is transferred from one object to another when a reaction takes place, humans will transfer energy from one person to another by connecting through words, gestures and even direct touch. The collective energy of a group does not appear out of nowhere but is the sum of the energies of the individual group members. If we want to energize a group, we have to contribute our own energy in the form of passion, enthusiasm and dedication, infecting the other group members with our own enthusiasm. This also means that sometimes we must invest energy to overcome pain in order to achieve our goals. This can be as simple as going to the gym in the morning, which is painful and requires considerable energy to overcome the initial inertia, but after the successful workout will lead to starting the day fully charged and energized.

How do emotions transmit energy? Emotions are associated with the "mirror neuron" hypothesis, which conjectures that when we see joy or sadness in somebody else's eyes, this triggers the same emotions in our brain. In their book *Survival of the Friendliest*, Brian Hare and Vanessa Woods write about the "cooperative eye hypothesis." Different from the eyes of our closest relatives, chimpanzees and bonobos, whose eyes appear a solid brown, the outline of human eyes and the iris are clearly visible among the white in the eye. Researchers have found that apes follow the gaze of the experimenter by tracking how the head moves, while humans look at the white in the eyes to follow the gaze. This enables humans to interact with each other much better, looking for the white in the opposite's eyes and "reading the mind in the eye." This means that humans can get energy by seeing the white in their opposite's eye to read their emotional responses. Anything that creates positive emotions will create energy. Bill spreads joy through his optimistic attitude, his humility and his focus on others, thus creating positive energy. Being with people we love will create energy. Showing trust to others will create energy for myself and others to whom I have shown trust. Giving others the opportunity to contribute will create energy for them. Standing with integrity and doing what I say will create energy for me. Listening to others attentively will create energy for others, and for me. Being happy will create energy. Standing out in a positive way will create energy, as will fitting in.

Emotions do not only create energy, but they can also destroy energy. For instance, if in a meeting I am constantly cutting others short, dominating the discussion and forcing my opinion on others, it will drain their energy, as will showing contempt and disrespect. John's negative attitude and focus on his own problems will drain energy from others and destroy entanglement among the teammates of John. Whatever triggers collective emotions also triggers the release of collective energy, be it positive or negative, for instance art, a concert or a soccer match. While energy is released collectively, the emotions triggering the energy release can differ depending on the values of the individual. For instance, when watching a soccer match, the fans of the winning team will show overarching joy, while the fans of the losing team will show anger and frustration. Or in politics, the outcome of the 2020 US presidential election sparked collective anger among the Trump fans, activated collective joy among the Biden fans and generated collective relief in most countries in Europe. This also illustrates that fatherlanders, with their strong "us against them" mentality, will create negative energy in their dealings with "them," their outgroup, the ones who are different from them.

In each team we have members with widely distinctive profiles, some acting as energy sources and others as energy sinks. To metaphorically describe these different behaviors, Chapter 6 introduces member categories inspired by social insects such as bees and ants, and not so social animals such as leeches. Coming back to Bill and John introduced above, Bill, creating energy for himself and others, is a bee, while John, destroying energy wherever he goes, is a leech.

NOTES

1. Barnea, M. F., & Schwartz, S. H. (1998). Values and voting. *Political Psychology*, 19(1), 17–40.
2. Graham, J., Haidt, J., Koleva, S., Motyl, M., Iyer, R., Wojcik, S. P., & Ditto, P. H. (2013). Moral foundations theory: The pragmatic validity of moral pluralism. In Davine, P., & Plant, A. (Eds), *Advances in Experimental Social Psychology* (Vol. 47, pp. 55–130). Academic Press.
3. O'Handley, B. M., Blair, K. L., & Hoskin, R. A. (2017). What do two men kissing and a bucket of maggots have in common? Heterosexual men's indistinguishable salivary α-amylase responses to photos of two men kissing and disgusting images. *Psychology and Sexuality*, 8(3), 173–188.
4. https://prowrestlingstories.com/pro-wrestling-stories/andre-the-giant/.
5. Hare, B. (2017). Survival of the friendliest: Homo sapiens evolved via selection for prosociality. *Annual Review of Psychology*, 68, 155–186.
6. www.nytimes.com/2020/11/24/nyregion/williamsburg-jewish-wedding -coronavirus-covid-masks.html.
7. Quinn, R. W., & Dutton, J. E. (2005). Coordination as energy-in-conversation. *Academy of Management Review*, 30(1), 36–57.

6.   Beeflow, antflow and leechflow

6.1   TRANSFORMING HUMAN RESOURCES INTO CREATIVE SWARMS

We are not resources
We are not capital
We are not talent
We are not labor
We are not manpower.

We are bees
We are all members of the same swarm.

In preindustrial times people were like bees, creating what they needed, growing their grain, baking their bread, sewing and stitching their clothes and building their furniture and houses. Nine thousand years ago, in Çatalhöyük in central Turkey in the Konya Plain, one of the oldest large towns known to historians,[1] up to 8000 people were living in small individual cells. Just like bees in a honeycomb, each family had its own one-room house of similar size, with a fire pit and a bed frame. The one-room houses were all joined together, and people were entering the room from above, leading to a huge, oversized beehive with each family inhabiting one cell. The society seemed to be egalitarian, and there were no palaces, no fortresses and no churches.

With the onset of industrialization, division of labor arose and managers started to manage their resources – one of which happened to be their human resources. But humans don't particularly like to be resources – being a resource implies being a passive asset, being moved around like a pawn in a game of chess without agency and own will. Synonyms like "human capital," "talent," "labor," or "manpower" are not much better. "Human capital" is even worse, as it conveys the connotation of foreign ownership: according to its definition, capital is an asset *owned* by an individual or organization available for a purpose such as running a company or investing. I don't think people want to be owned by their manager or company. "Talent" is somewhat better, as a synonym for natural aptitude or skill; however, the word's origin is similar to "capital" and also has monetary roots as the "talent" was a currency unit of the Greeks and Romans. Again, I don't want to be a piece of money owned by my manager or company for my skill. "Labor" implies hard work and great effort with little interest in creativity and imagination. "Manpower" is no improvement; it stands for the amorphous and anonymous number of people available for work and service, without value of individual ingenuity and originality.

Happiness research has clearly shown that we humans highly value what psychologists call "agency" and "experience": *agency* means the capacity to make independent decisions and being in control of one's own destiny. For instance, happiness researcher Bruno S. Frey found that in already quite happy Switzerland, those Swiss cantons whose citizens have the most to say, that is, they get to vote the most, are the happiest. He also found that being stuck in a traffic jam, when we totally lose control of being able to move when we want to, is assured to reduce happiness and make us miserable. The second psychological property is *experience*, the capability to enjoy and to suffer and to experience compassion and empathy for others.

As "human resources" we are denied both agency and experience. Applied to the corporate environment, agency and experience are well described by the four management principles of W. L. Gore & Associates, a highly successful inventor and manufacturer of the water-resistant fabric Gore-Tex. Established by its founder Bill Gore, W. L. Gore & Associates operates by the four principles freedom, fairness, commitment and waterline. Since its inception, Gore has consistently been ranked as one of the best companies to work for. Gore's associates, as their employees are called, have the freedom to make their own decisions, are expected to treat each other fairly, are empowered to make their own commitments and stick to them and, for wide-ranging decisions affecting the "waterline" of the company, they are counted on to consult with other associates. In other words, they are members of a self-organizing swarm, operating in agency and experience. They are happy bees, and highly successful in that!

The time has come to take back agency and experience from human resources, and create an environment for self-organizing swarms of happy bees. In this book, I propose a social compass to assist us all to become bees, by combining AI and social network analysis to map the social landscape of each individual for more agency and experience. Bees bring creative energy to the team, invigorating and revitalizing team members, increasing the happiness of others interacting with them, in short creating an environment conducive to groupflow. However, there are two other types of insect-inspired behavior that are detrimental to groupflow: the ants, and even worse, the leeches. Instead of energizing a team, they will drain it of energy, leaving everybody interacting with them exhausted, tired and depressed.

You have met these types many times in your corporate lives, the overambitious careerists, who will do everything to be promoted. They will enthusiastically embrace, praise and compliment any idea of the boss, no matter how bad it is. They are the yeasayers, the apple-polishers, the ones who bow in front of their hierarchical superiors while kicking the ones they consider lower in the hierarchy. Welcome to the archetypical members of the ant tribe. While ants might be annoying, you can cope with them as long as you don't cross them. Ants pale in comparison to leeches. Leeches see others only as a means to their own ends. They will try to claim credit for your work and ideas, as they will try to use you to further their own goals. Just like real leeches sucking your blood, they suck your energy and your vitality, leaving you stressed out, exhausted and burnt out.

There are two ways of coping with ants and leeches: either try to get out of their way, evade them and get away from them as far as you can, or work with other bees. Even better though is to try to get ants and leeches to change their behavior, and help them to become creative and productive team players, and behave like bees.

6.2   BEES BRING THE HONEY

Flow experience can be reached in many areas, from sports, art and music, to professional teamwork. Mihaly Csikszentmihalyi even describes criminals enjoying their burglaries, and the extreme example of the Marquis de Sade enjoying his sadistic behavior. Perfectly legal flow activities will cause pain to some of the involved parties, for instance dog and cock fights in some parts of the world, bull fighting in Spain or boxing matches in the US and elsewhere. It is therefore worthwhile to divide flow experiences into three different categories sorted by positivity for the involved parties: first, the enjoyable experience of creating something radically new that has never been there before; second, the gratification derived from competing against others or oneself in sports ranging from mountain climbing to computer games; and third, the pleasure one gets from ripping off others, leading to pain for the losers and delight for the winners. I call these three categories beeflow, antflow and leechflow (Table 6.1).

Table 6.1   Beeflow, antflow and leechflow

	Goal	Benefits	Example
Beeflow	create	to self + to others	Create painting, play jazz in a band, design new product
Antflow	win	to self	Play online game, play soccer match
Leechflow	exploit	to self (from others)	Devise pyramid scheme, engage in mobbing

Bee hives are entangled organizations with bees being the masters of entanglement. Bees communicate through waggle dances, touching each other's bodies rhythmically, similarly to jazz musicians swinging their bodies to the tune of their music. Bees are also good for everyone. Not only do they produce honey which is widely loved and was the main sweetener for millennia, honey also has valuable medical properties. But most importantly, bees are absolutely essential as pollinators, pollinating up to 80 percent of all cultivated crop plants. Without bees there would be no apples, no cherries, no peaches, no nuts and no herbs. Without bees, life as we know it would be impossible.

Ant hives are similarly entangled organizations capable of amazing feats, self-organizing to solve complex tasks, for instance creating pheromone trails to food sources and herding larvae of other insects to drink their fluid. However, if two ants from two different ant hives meet, a fight to death will arise. Ants are immensely competitive. While they collaborate inside their hive, they conduct epic battles between different hives. For instance, the invasive Argentine ant forms super-colonies with up to 1 trillion individuals in Southern Europe and the US. At the border between the super-colonies there is constant warfare, for example that of two super-colonies in Southern California in which researchers estimate that up to 30 million ants per year die in monumental battles.

Leeches are unentangled, each fighting for their blood meal on their own. Leeches are parasites, that attach their suckers to their prey animal and feed on the blood of their host. In the front of their mouth they have three teeth, which they slice through the skin of the host. Once attached, they use a combination of mucus and suction to stay attached to the skin of their host, while consuming their blood meal. Leeches also excrete a weak anesthetic to soothe their prey while inserting their teeth into them, until it is too late. While leeches have been used for medical bloodletting for at least for 2500 years, they carry parasites in their digestive system, and bacteria, viruses and other parasites from previous blood meals can survive within a leech for months and infect the next host. Although leeches have limited medical use, life without leeches, without having to worry about a leech bite in leech-infested water, would be a better life. If bloodletting really is necessary – most of the time it is not, more people have been killed through excessive bloodletting than have been saved – this can also easily be done by the doctor in other ways.

There are also human bees, ants and leeches that offer valuable lessons about flow and entanglement. Human bees are people who derive their joy and meaning in life from creating new things. It seems there is a subgroup of the overall population that draws particular pleasure from creating new things and gaining new insights. Researchers have found that for some people, creative insights and the "eureka moment" trigger the same neural reward as when we eat food we like, have an orgasm or consume addictive substances.[2] In other words, some people experience creative insights as intrinsically rewarding. This explains the puzzle solvers, starving artists, underpaid researchers and innovators tinkering with new ideas in their garages. Human bees are creators. Creating new things creates joy for the creator. While the creation process might include painful moments along the way, the joy at the end of the process, when the final product is there, more than pays for it. One of the main reasons for experiencing the joy of creation is the flow experience. For instance, flow is prominent when making music. This starts with little children who experience flow in music learning and making.[3] Flow is experienced when composing music, and the flow experience is the main motivation[4] for musicians playing together in bands and orchestras. Other typical human bees might be inventors, authors, painters, sculptors, researchers and engineers. They pollinate society with new ideas, ensuring innovation and progress. Bees create positive entanglement among themselves by creating human creative swarms.

However, not everybody draws intrinsic satisfaction from gaining creative insights. There is a large(r) part of the population that does not like change, but likes to follow the example of others, and would like to keep everything as safe and solid as it "always was in the good old times." Those are the ants. Ants are (most of the time) not hurting anybody, but they are not creating anything new. Ants are followers. Their happiness comes from being in company with others like them. Human ants like to aggregate in large crowds and occasionally demonstrate the madness of crowds. A prominent example of human ants following each other in a flow experience were the nearly 500,000 participants of the Sturgis Harvey Davidson motorcycle festival in August 2020, flouting Covid-19 distancing rules and leading according to one study[5] to an additional 260,000 Covid-19 infections, 19 percent of the US total of that month, resulting in US$12.2 billion of additional public health expenditure. People investing in Bitcoin, non-fungible tokens and other pyramid schemes for speculative purposes are today's successors of the Dutch investors creating the black tulip craze in the seventeenth century in Holland, where prizes of black tulip bulbs spiked to astronomical heights before crashing and losing any value. When buying a highly prized unique black tulip bulb, the Dutch investor probably reached the flow state. Ants can also reach the flow state just being on their own. For instance, playing computer games provides a pleasurable flow experience. Researchers investigating flow of computer gamers found[6] that indeed the feeling of flow was a key reason for online gaming addiction.

Human leeches are different from bees and ants by being obsessed about getting as much money and power as possible and doing whatever it takes to grab it. Leeches are bloodsuckers. Their happiness comes from winning and getting everything for themselves. Human leeches are the people that are trying to profit from others by bending the rules to their own advantage. Their goal in life is to amass as much wealth and money as they possibly can. They consume the honey of the bees, profit from their pollination and also milk the ants. Class action and malpractice lawyers, hedge fund managers, merger and acquisition bankers and "activist investors" would be archetypical professions preferred by human leeches, for instance, the investors of drug price-gouging companies Valeant and Turing Pharmaceuticals.[7] While a leech might get into flow, leeches destroy the entanglement of others. Leeches might reach group-flow for example by becoming the head of a mafia family.

Table 6.2 illustrates the moral values and personality characteristics of archetypical groupflow tribe members, using the Haidt and Schwartz moral value frameworks and the FFI personality characteristics introduced in Section 3.4.

Table 6.2   Personality and motivation of groupflow tribes

	Bee	Ant	Leech
Values	Self-transcendence Self-direction/benevolence	Tradition/authority Conformity/security	Achievement/power
Personality	Openness	Conscientiousness	(Neuroticism)
Morals	Fairness/care		Unfairness
Risk taking	Social risks	Financial/health risks	Ethical risks

These three categories are orthogonal to another framework describing what we value most, intelligence (IQ), empathy (EQ) or creativity (CQ). A believer in IQ will value measurable achievements, such as a position of power and glory, while somebody who values EQ will look for emotional closeness with groups of others. A believer in CQ draws satisfaction from creating new things, be it paintings, software or pastry. As human energy is limited, there is only a finite amount of time and other resources that an individual can invest in either intelligent, empathic or creative endeavors. This means that when calibrating the total energy an individual can spend as "1," the sum of IQ, EQ and CQ will be one, or written as a mathematical equation, $IQ+EQ+CQ=1$. The individual will distribute her energies among these three different groups of activities according to her priorities. Mapping IQ, EQ and CQ to bees, ants and leeches, bees will obviously be motivated mostly by CQ, and leeches will value IQ above everything while (ab)using their IQ for selfish manipulation of others to advance their own goals. Ants will be in the middle, combining IQ and EQ.

Obviously, the world is neither black nor white, and we all possess attributes of all categories. We are sometimes bees, frequently ants and, if we get the opportunity, we might even behave like leeches. In every society there are taking leeches and giving bees. An entangled organization would like its members to be givers, not takers. A single selfish leech has the potential to destroy the entanglement of a swarm of bees. The goal is to make sure that in the end there are only bees and ants in the group, and prospective leeches are turned into bees by making their parasitic behavior obvious to them. While it is up to each individual to decide on their behavior, choosing to be a bee, an ant or a leech, their honest signals and virtual tribe memberships (see Chapter 5) will give them away.

Mihaly Csikszentmihalyi does not distinguish between flow being reached as an individual, for instance as a lonely rock climber, or as a group, for instance being a member of a jazz band. This book focuses on groupflow and what organizations and individuals can do to reach it. More precisely we focus on beeflow, and what we can do to create groupflow in organizations to operate as creative swarms of bees. For instance, a great exemplar of group beeflow has been described by Dietmar Sachser in his book on theater flow.[8] A theater ensemble reaches groupflow through many rehearsals, developing collective awareness and feeling as one unified whole. As German actor Fritzi Haberlandt says, "It's a form of intoxication that makes you happy." However, if there are too many ants and leeches in a team, it will never reach groupflow, or even if it reaches groupflow, it will soon be destroyed.

6.3 BEEFLOW STARTS IN CHILDHOOD

Being a bee also means being persistent, suffering through the birthing pains of a new idea when others still don't understand it and fighting through obstacles and resistance to get the idea off the ground. To be resilient to pain and external pressure requires somebody to rely on who gives unconditional love. Besides having suffered a lot in their youth, both Elon Musk and Steve Jobs also had loving mothers who were key to their future success. After Steve Jobs was put up for adoption by his biological mother, he was adopted by Clara and Paul Jobs, and in his words, "was blessed to have the two of them as parents." Elon Musk's mother gave him extraordinary freedom, but also taught him that "you have to work hard to make your own luck"[9] while as a divorced mother with three children the family lived hand to mouth. Early on the members of the family had a reciprocal relationship: Maye Musk, the mother, was the care-taker of the family, but the children also took turns taking care of her. While Maye was in Toronto to set up her PhD program at the University of Toronto in 1989,[10] her 15-year-old daughter Tosca decided that the whole family should move to Canada and sold the family house and car on her own. When Maye came back, the only thing left for her to do was sign the sales contract.

In his book *Aging Well*, George Vaillant stresses the importance of having stable relationships to build resilience against adversity.[11] Vaillant describes the results of three longitudinal studies, where researchers followed hundreds of people from birth to death from different strata of society. Besides not smoking, not drinking excessively, not being overweight and exercising, the most important criterion is to be in a warm and loving relationship – in other words being well entangled. Vaillant compares the success of a man who was born in poor circumstances in Boston's South End, with no money and regularly beaten by his father. However, this man reported having an older brother who acted as his protector and supported him through his struggles while growing up. He lived to an old age, achieving considerable financial success owning his own business. Vaillant compares him to a group of men studying at Harvard, not lacking financial support in their youth, however, being emotionally neglected by their parents who were busy participating in the social life of Boston's high society. They all died unhappy and lonely, comparatively young in their 60s, their wealth gone, some of them also becoming alcoholics.

A similar research project conducted in the 1960s by Betty Hart and Todd Risley[12] further supports the importance of having positively nurturing support in the first few years of a child's life. The "30-million-word gap" study followed the lives of 42 American families with small children over two and a half years. In the age before digital audio analysis the researchers painstakingly recorded and counted the number of words the parents in these families exchanged with their children. They grouped the families into three categories: low status, frequently on welfare; blue-collar working class with functioning but relatively low-income non-academic parents; and high-status professional families with mostly academically educated parents. They found that the welfare families, often led by single mothers, exchanged 15 million words, while the high-status families spoke 45 million words with their children. Even more, they found that in high-status professional families, the ratio of encouragement of the parents towards the children compared to discouragement was about six to one, corresponding to a professional parent giving 166,000 encouragements and 26,000 discouragements to the child. This was radically different in welfare families, where the ratio was one encouragement to three discouragements, corresponding to totally 26,000 encouragements compared to 57,000 discouragements. When checking the academic performance five to seven years later, the researchers found that the number of words children were exposed to in years one to three significantly predicted their academic performance six years later.

Indian educator Sugata Mitra created another experiment that illustrates the importance of loving, supportive relationships for children in their initial years. In the slums of Kalkaji in Delhi he pioneered the concept of minimally invasive education through his "hole in the wall" experiment. By providing protected computers to children in slums – the "holes in the wall" were computers in an ATM-like case – Sugata Mitra found that the children were teaching themselves computer skills, English and math just by being able to access the computers and the internet. He made sure that only children could use the computers, by having plastic covers on the keyboards where only small arms would fit and iron seats in front of the computers that were too narrow for the bodies of adults. He compared the educational performance of the self-taught slum children with the performance of children attending some of the best schools in India, where he found that his slum children performed almost as well as the children from the good schools. By adding a support network – the granny cloud[13] – the slum children improved their performance to the level of the children from the good schools. The grannies were from the United Kingdom and initially they were just chatting with the slum children, but soon they started sharing stories, songs, puzzles and games to reach out to the children. Some of the grannies even traveled to India to visit "their" children. As this example illustrates, besides having access to the internet through the hole-in-the-wall computers and sharing insights in small children groups clustered around the computers, it was the loving positive feedback provided by the grannies that made all the difference.

So, what does this mean for aspiring bees? It is key how the "wet nurse" bees treat their young. They need a supportive, trusting environment, the "granny club" that helps them get through the pain while coming up with new ideas and taking these new ideas through the difficult gestation period. In the corporate world, this nurturing environment corresponds to a culture where people are not afraid to "speak up," where they dare to object to their superiors if necessary and where it is OK to make mistakes. "Speaking up" to superiors should be part of positively reinforcing communication, using six positive sentences for one negative, similar to the loving and nurturing parents in the "30-million-word gap" project. This is a culture where there are no stupid ideas and people are respected as individuals, independent of where they are in the corporate hierarchy. A straightforward way to show this respect is to be on time for meetings. The saying "punctuality is the politeness of kings" has been attributed to Louis XVIII of France in the early nineteenth century, as this is the only way for an absolute monarch to show respect. Similarly, superiors don't have to be punctual, but by being punctual they demonstrate that they respect their subordinates. Thus, having a culture where meetings start on time is an "honest signal" of a bee culture.

6.4   "BEE IN FLOW"

> The men of experiment are like the ant, they only collect and use; the reasoners resemble spiders, who make cobwebs out of their own substance. But the bee takes the middle course: it gathers its material from the flowers of the garden and field, but transforms and digests it by a power of its own. (Francis Bacon, *The New Organon*)

What's the difference between a lawyer and a leech? Answer: After you die, a leech stops sucking your blood.

Since historical times, some professions have been associated with bees, ants and leeches. Bees create, ants toil and leeches destroy. In jokes and proverbs, some occupations are exemplars of bees, ants and leeches. Although these generalizations are a huge oversimplification, there is more than a grain of truth to these analogies. Researchers have found that personality is aligned with profession.[14] If somebody's personality fits well they are more successful, measured by a higher salary.[15] People choose a particular profession because of their personality, for instance it has been shown that economists choose their career because they value money more than ethical behavior.[16] According to the annual Gallup ethics survey, nurses and doctors are seen as the most ethical professions, while bankers, lawyers, managers, car salespeople and politicians are seen as the least honest and ethical.[17] In another survey among 652 Israeli professionals,[18] bankers and managers were craving for power, doctors and social workers valued benevolence and universalism, accountants strove for security and tradition, while artists and scientists searched for self-direction. So, there are indeed archetypical bees, ants and leeches among the different professions.

Bees *create* honey and they pollinate flowers; according to some estimates a third of all food we eat is dependent on bee pollination. Human bees create products as bakers, chefs, tailors, painters, sculptors, engineers, builders, authors, composers and inventors. They are primarily motivated by the joy of creating, by trying to solve a problem or creating a better product. They genuinely want to help and make the world a better place.

Ants *toil* by running around and collecting food for their hive, fighting and killing ants from competing ant hives. Just like the real ants, human ants scurry around, working hard, competing and sometimes fighting obsessively as competitive athletes, vendors, lawyers, accountants, managers and surgeons. They are predominantly motivated by the wish to win and acquire fame.

Leeches *destroy* by lurking hidden at the bottom of ponds and lakes waiting to attack their prey, to suck vertebrate and invertebrate blood. Human leeches, motivated by power and money, show an unstoppable appetite for wealth as hedge fund managers, venture capitalists, class action and malpractice lawyers and beauty surgeons.

But the behavioral boundaries between the three virtual tribes are fluid and permeable. Bees, behaving like leeches, are not beyond attacking and robbing honey from a weaker beehive. Ants can grow wings, as the queen and the male ants do for their wedding nights. Ants can also switch from competing with other hives to collaborating, as some wood ants (*Formica paralugubris*) in the Swiss Jura do, which instead of fighting, collaborate across thousands of colonies,[19] with resounding evolutionary success.

The boundaries are similarly fluid between human bees, ants and leeches. There are artists who create counterfeit copies of famous paintings, and malicious hackers who use their coding skills to break into IT systems to extract a Bitcoin ransom. On the other hand, there are venture capitalists acting as innovative entrepreneurs, lawyers who are fighting for human rights and surgeons reconstructing shattered limbs of victims of accidents and wars.

The key point is that we all should try to be more like proverbial bees, independently of what we work as. There are professions such as competitive athletes, factory workers, lawyers, venture capitalists and hedge fund managers, where the nature of the profession is geared towards ant- and leech-like activity, but everybody can be a bee in flow, whatever their profession is.

NOTES

1. www.scientificamerican.com/article/an-ancient-proto-city-reveals-the-origin-of -home/.
2. Oh, Y., Chesebrough, C., Erickson, B., Zhang, F., & Kounios, J. (2020). An insight-related neural reward signal. *NeuroImage*, 116757.
3. Custodero, L. A. (2012). The call to create: Flow experience in music learning and teaching. In Hargreaves, D., Miell, D., & MacDonald, R. (Eds), *Musical Imaginations: Multidisciplinary Perspectives on Creativity, Performance, and Perception* (pp. 369–384). Oxford University Press.
4. Fritz, B. S., & Avsec, A. (2007). The experience of flow and subjective well-being of music students. *Horizons of Psychology*, 16(2), 5–17.
5. Dave, D. M., Friedson, A. I., McNichols, D., & Sabia, J. J. (2020). The contagion externality of a superspreading event: The Sturgis Motorcycle Rally and Covid-19 (No. 13670). Institute of Labor Economics. http://ftp.iza.org/dp13670 .pdf.
6. Chou, T. J., & Ting, C. C. (2003). The role of flow experience in cyber-game addiction. *CyberPsychology and Behavior*, 6(6), 663–675.
7. www.health.com/mind-body/6-insane-examples-of-prescription-drug-price -increases.
8. Sachser, D. (2009). *Theaterspielflow: über die Freude als Basis schöpferischen Theaterschaffens*. Alexander-Verlag.
9. www.insidehook.com/article/tech/elon-musk-childhood-revealed-maye-musk -memoir?utm_source=direct&utm_medium=inline&utm_campaign=related.
10. www.dailymail.co.uk/news/article-8056455/New-memoir-model-Maye-Musk -sheds-light-billionaire-son-Elons-upbringing.html.
11. Vaillant, G. E. (2008). *Aging Well: Surprising Guideposts to a Happier Life from the Landmark Study of Adult Development*. Hachette UK.
12. Hart, B., & Risley, T. R. (1995). *Meaningful Differences in the Everyday Experience of Young American Children*. P. H. Brookes.
13. http://thegrannycloud.org.
14. King, D. D., Ott-Holland, C. J., Ryan, A. M., Huang, J. L., Wadlington, P. L., & Elizondo, F. (2016). Personality homogeneity in organizations and occupations:

Considering similarity sources. *Journal of Business and Psychology*, 32(6), 641–653.

15. Denissen, J. J., Bleidorn, W., Hennecke, M., Luhmann, M., Orth, U., Specht, J., & Zimmermann, J. (2017). Uncovering the power of personality to shape income. *Psychological Science*, 29(1), 3–13.

16. Frey, B. S., & Meier, S. (2003). Are political economists selfish and indoctrinated? Evidence from a natural experiment. *Economic Inquiry*, 41(3), 448–462.

17. https://news.gallup.com/poll/245597/nurses-again-outpace-professions-honesty-ethics.aspx.

18. Knafo, A., & Sagiv, L. (2004). Values and work environment: Mapping 32 occupations. *European Journal of Psychology of Education*, 19(3), 255–273.

19. Chapuisat, M., Bernasconi, C., Hoehn, S., & Reuter, M. (2005). Nestmate recognition in the unicolonial ant *Formica paralugubris*. *Behavioral Ecology*, 16(1), 15–19.

7.   Entanglement is more than collaboration

For more than 2 billion years, unicellular microbes thrived, until they decided to entangle by fusing their cells. We are only capable of doing complex things, like building a computer, using our hands to type on the keyboard, compose a musical masterpiece, play a piece of Mozart on the piano or pursue a complex line of thinking, because our ancestors, monocellular organisms, decided about 600 million years ago to join forces and merge into the first multicellular organisms. Even to today's unicellular organisms, entanglement gives a huge advantage, for instance the bacterium Pseudomonas fluorescens forms multicellular mats on surfaces to gain better access to oxygen.[1] However, once the mats exist, individuals who do not produce the glue necessary to form the mats will thrive and grow faster than their siblings working for the collective. But in the end, a collective with too many free-riders – individuals unwilling to contribute to the common good – will starve the mat and destroy it. This is already a classic "tragedy of the commons" where a community with too many individuals who are too greedy and not willing to work for the good of the community will destroy it. The multicellular organisms with the most collaborative unicellular organisms where each cell is willing to behave altruistically by putting the common good over its own profits will be the most successful. In other words, the most entangled multicellular organisms will be the most successful. Organizations whose individual members are the most altruistic and most oriented towards the common good of all members will be the most successful.

The concept of "entanglement between two people" and of "entangled swarms" is inspired by quantum physics, where two particles can be entangled over long distances. Entangled particles will share the same properties, which, when changed for one entangled particle, will be changed instantaneously by the other particle too. For instance, if the angle of rotation in space for one quantum particle is changed, its entangled twin anywhere in this world will change its position too. Recently, quantum entanglement has even been shown between one particle circling earth in a satellite, while the other was residing on a base station on earth's surface. The same is true for entangled people. They will know what the entangled others feel and desire almost instantaneously, because they keep them in their mind, and as they know them extremely well, they are able to predict their reaction to events as soon as the event touches the other person.

In the animal world there are numerous examples of entanglement. Social insects such as bees, ants and termites are perfect exemplars. For instance, without central control, termites self-organize in huge mounds with millions of members where they coordinate to create a perfect micro climate to maintain a "garden" of fungi for food. Termites of the genus Macrotermes communicate through pheromones and other as yet unknown ways to build mounds of up to 8 to 9 meters of height, which, through thermoregulation, provide a moderate temperature throughout the day in the most arid and inhospitable climates. If intruders come into the nest, the termites bang their heads against the wall to create vibrations and release pheromones that call the termite soldiers. Similarly, entangled hives of carpenter ants create farms with aphids which they farm like cows, milking a sugary secretion similar to honeydew for food. Beehives coordinate through a "waggle dance," where a "leader" bee communicates the location of a honey source or a promising new location for a swarming beehive by dancing and rhythmically touching the other bees with her body.

How does entanglement among humans work? Multicellular organisms communicate through synchronous oscillation. Just look at our heart that is keeping our body functions synchronized through its rhythmic beat. The same is true for entanglement among different individuals. Similar to bacteria, termites, bees and ants, entangled humans form organizations that subconsciously communicate to reach a common goal. For instance, simply walking through a company's cafeteria will tell you if this is an entangled organization – the atmosphere will be radiating a positive vibe with people sitting together at tables, smiling and greeting when passing each other, and engaging in animated discussions, while in a non-entangled organization, people in the cafeteria will sit morosely by themselves at the tables, devouring their food and not greeting or talking to each other.

If two strangers are locked together in the same room for extended periods of time, they will either start to like each other and become entangled in the process, or they will kill each other. A Quora author describes a beautiful story that perfectly illustrates this process of entanglement:[2] At the end of a class at a university, a male student, Arjun, was finishing some work in the classroom, while Kriya, a female student, was also still idling in the classroom to wrap up classwork. They did not know each other besides having seen each other's faces during class. Kriya was waiting for her brother to pick her up but he was late by at least one hour, so Arjun offered to accompany Kriya to the bus to get home. However, when they wanted to leave the classroom, the door was locked and there was no way to get out, as the classroom was on the third floor and it was impossible to get out other than through the door. Both Arjun and

Kriya tried to call their friends on their cellphones to come and help them get out, but none of them was around and available. Kriya got really afraid and suspicious about being locked in the room with a male stranger. Arjun noticed how upset she was and asked her to watch a short funny movie on his phone about two strangers locked in a room. This took away the fear from Kriya, and in turn she showed Arjun a short movie she particularly liked. They took turns showing each other favorite movies and started sharing some other small secrets. During the whole time Arjun made sure to always keep at least a meter away from Kriya, which further alleviated her fear and assured her that he was trustworthy and would not harm her. When Kriya's brother finally appeared to get them out of their locked classroom, both Kriya and Arjun were truly sorry to leave and step out of the magical atmosphere that had engulfed them. Fast forward three years, Arjun and Kriya were still dating each other and planning to get married.

This story strikingly demonstrates how entanglement among strangers develops, from disgust and distrust to building up trust by mirroring each other and sharing small secrets, leading in the end to mutual love and entanglement. The key for building successful entanglement is getting away from seeing differences to seeing commonalities. This is what Arjun successfully did by creating a common basis of finding short movies that both Arjun and Kriya liked. Mirroring each other, sharing small secrets and the same movies built up entanglement and engagement. Looking at long-time successfully married couples, they share the same habits, preferences, political leanings, even the same little gestures and body language. The same entanglement also happens between humans and their companion animals like dogs or horses.

As the story of Arjun and Kriya illustrates, entanglement is like a successful marriage. A well-entangled couple has no need to talk, each spouse will immediately know what the other wants to say and will be able to communicate without words. Going through a divorce means breaking up an entangled relationship. A disentangled couple has been moving apart, until there is no common ground anymore and the entanglement is broken.

7.1   CHARACTERISTICS OF ENTANGLED ORGANIZATIONS

Individuals in teams that are collaborating well, be it spouses, competitive dancing couples, soccer teams, orchestra members, competitive sailing teams or any other entangled group, are all connected in five ways. Entanglement between any two individuals is characterized by:

1. synchronization in movements (physical and virtual);
2. shared emotions (same response to same stimulus);

3. shared language (using similar words to describe the same event);
4. shared facial expressions (responding with similar facial expressions to the same stimulus); and
5. shared values (tribes, ethics, morals).

In our research over the last 20 years we have investigated these five ways in hundreds of research projects. Their validity has been demonstrated in many different settings in small teams and large organizations, in non-profits and businesses.

7.1.1 Synchronization in Movements

People who are entangled will start mirroring each other's body movements. In interpersonal dialog, they will look each other in the eye and start nodding in synch. Groups of people on the dance floor will start to synchronously move their bodies to the beat of the sound, people in the audience of a circus performance will start clapping in synchronicity and spectators at a soccer game will start singing in a chorus to encourage their team. The same behavior also happens in electronic communication, where entangled people synchronously send and receive email messages or change their social network position in synch with each other.

7.1.2 Shared Emotions

Entangled people will show the same emotional feedback when reacting to an event. For instance, people in the same cultural space will show the same emotion in response to an external stimulus. Indigenous people in the Amazon rainforest might be delighted when discovering crickets or maggots as part of a future delicious meal, while city dwellers from New York might experience disgust when exposed to the same animals. Similarly, people with strong ethics will be disgusted when learning about the drug manipulations of Martin Shkreli, who as CEO of Turing Pharmaceuticals raised the price of a Daraprim pill from US$13 to US$750. The AIDS patients dependent on Daraprim to keep their Toxoplasmosis under control would be in despair when learning about the price hike, while the shareholders of Turing would be delighted about the windfall profits. There are three differently entangled groups – the ethically conscious, the AIDS patients with Toxoplasmosis and the amoral investors – showing different emotional reactions to the same event.

7.1.3   Shared Language

Entangled people will use the same words to describe an event. For instance, the engineering team investigating the Genoa bridge collapse in August 2018 will talk in technical terms about the tendons giving in to external stress, the journalists focusing on the human tragedies resulting from the drivers killed in the disaster will use compassionate and emphatic language to describe the same event, while the relatives of the people killed in the collapse will be in despair. Similarly, in his letter to shareholders, activist investor Bill Ackmann used enthusiastic language to describe the business model of pharmaceutical company Valeant, which similarly to Turing pharmaceutical bought up other companies manufacturing effective medications and then jacked up the price while investing very little in research. When investigating this behavior, the US Securities and Exchange Commission used very different words expressing disgust to describe Valeant's behavior, while the diabetes patients who suddenly experienced an 800 percent price increase for Valeant's recently acquired pill Glumetza used language expressing pain and fear.

7.1.4   Shared Facial Expressions

The emotional response of differently entangled people will be mirrored in their faces. People who are entangled and respond in the same way to an external event, for instance seeing a maggot, will thus show similar facial expressions. Or think back to the soccer World Cup semi-final in 2014 when Brazil lost against Germany 7 to 1. The faces of the Brazilian fans inside the Estadio Mineirao showed growing pain ending in despair, while the faces of the German fans showed utter delight, mixed with growing compassion for the Brazilians as the German goals were piling up. This means that inside the same physical space there can be different groups of differently entangled people occupying alternative realities. Looking at the face of a person sitting beside a Brazilian soccer fan in the Estadio Mineirao would tell the fan if his neighbor was rooting for "us" – the Brazilian team – or "them" – the German team.

7.1.5   Shared Values

Entangled people of the same virtual tribe will respond in the same way to an external stimulus. For instance, different groups will react very differently to refugees crossing their national borders. Ultranationalists will respond with rejection and repulsion, while welcoming people will respond with sympathy and compassion. For instance, research has shown that ultranationalists (which we term "fatherlanders") crave the cultural values of tradition and authority with less emphasis on caring and fairness, while people with a more open personality prioritize caring and fairness over tradition and authority, so when watching a report of Syrian refugees arriving in Germany in 2015, the values of the viewer would have been reflected in facial expressions, words and other emotional responses.

7.2 HOW TO CREATE ENTANGLEMENT BETWEEN INDIVIDUALS

In historical armies, the task of the drummer was to create entanglement among the soldiers. The pulsing beat synchronized the individual soldiers, getting them to advance in lockstep and become one frenzied mass of attacking warriors. This is still shown in the marching columns in the parades for instance of the Chinese, North Korean or Russian armies today, taking place to the rhythmic beat of military bands. But there are many other, more peaceful ways in which groups of people can become entangled. In our research we have studied entanglement ranging from small teams to entire nations, from direct one-to-one exchanges between two individuals to formal interaction by phone, email and online media in large companies and global organizations. The way two people communicate shows how much in synch and thus how "entangled" and in groupflow they are. The goal of our research is to create methods and tools for tracking and supporting "entanglement" between individuals, in particular within the same organization or tribe, wherever they might be on earth, with the aim of creating an environment where groupflow will emerge spontaneously. "Entangled organizations" communicate in shared awareness. If something happens to the organization in one part of the world, it is immediately felt and responded to in other parts of the world. People can be entangled in both positive and negative ways. While in this book we will focus on positive entanglement, people can also be negatively entangled. For instance, a wife might be entangled in an abusive relationship with a man who beats her but she is unable to disengage from him. The victim of a hijacking might be entangled with the hijacker, as famously happened when Patty Hearst, the granddaughter of publicist William Randolph Hearst, was taken hostage by terrorists in 1974 and started identifying with her kidnappers, even joining them on bank robberies.

Positively entangled individuals engage in compassionate and nurturing interaction. Personal relationships, partners in married and otherwise committed couples, are prime examples of entangled teams. But any members of a successful team, in business or recreational activities, are entangled. Nobel

Prize winner Daniel Kahnemann has the following to say about his collaboration with his long-time partner Amos Tversky:

> Amos and I discovered that we enjoyed working together. Amos was always very funny, and in his presence I became funny as well, so we spent hours of solid work in continuous amusement. The pleasure we found in working together made us exceptionally patient; it is much easier to strive for perfection when you are never bored. Perhaps most important, we checked our critical weapons at the door. Both Amos and I were critical and argumentative, he even more than I, but during the years of our collaboration neither of us ever rejected out of hand anything the other said. Indeed, one of the great joys I found in the collaboration was that Amos frequently saw the point of my vague ideas much more clearly than I did. Amos was the more logical thinker, with an orientation to theory and an unfailing sense of direction. I was more intuitive and rooted in the psychology of perception, from which we borrowed many ideas. We were sufficiently similar to understand each other easily, and sufficiently different to surprise each other. We developed a routine in which we spent much of our working days together, often on long walks. For the next fourteen years our collaboration was the focus of our lives, and the work we did together during those years was the best either of us ever did …
>
>   Until geographical separation made it too difficult to go on, Amos and I enjoyed the extraordinary good fortune of a shared mind that was superior to our individual minds and of a relationship that made our work fun as well as productive. Our collaboration on judgement and decision making was the reason for the Nobel Prize that I received in 2002, which Amos would have shared had he not died, aged fifty-nine, in 1996.

As Daniel Kahnemann explains, a culture supportive of entanglement will increase the effectiveness, productivity and happiness of the entangled people, teams and organizations. How can an organization and how can the individuals working at the organization create entangled teams? The secret of creating entangled teams is to find matching team members and connect them in a positive way, just like Daniel Kahnemann "found" Amos Tversky. So, the next question is: "Who are the right team members?" The answer is "People like me," that is, people who share the same values, respond similarly to unexpected events and who have similar societal beliefs. This was certainly the case for Daniel Kahnemann, who invited Tversky as a guest speaker to a seminar at Hebrew University in Jerusalem that Kahnemann was teaching. When they had dinner together after the seminar, they discovered their shared interests and beliefs and started their long-term collaboration.

   In order to find "others like myself," this also means that the first step is to know about myself, what my personality characteristics are, what my ethical values and societal beliefs are and so on. Based on knowing myself, I can then set out to find others like myself. We might think that we know who we are, however, a lot of research has shown the opposite. We might either vastly underestimate or overestimate our fairness, we might assume our belief for

God and fatherland as a given, only to be shaken if others see us in an entirely different light. Creating entanglement between two people means building awareness for the feelings of others, to understand how they see others and how others see them. Only when there is extensive overlap between self-image and the image that others have of the individual are we ready to connect and entangle with similar people who share the same values and beliefs. Spending time in an entangled group is a reliable way to happiness.

Creating a happily entangled swarm requires three steps (Figure 7.1):

1. learn about myself;
2. develop awareness of others about me, and increase my awareness of their needs, strengths and weaknesses; and
3. connect and entangle with the people in my environment who are the most similar to me.

For instance, professional musicians playing together perfectly demonstrate the entanglement process.

Figure 7.1   Steps to happy entanglement

7.3   SWINGING IN FLOW: SYNCHRONIZING LIKE A JAZZ MUSICIAN

Orchestras are great exemplars of entangled organizations. When the Boston Symphony Orchestra plays Beethoven, it demonstrates the perfection of a fully entangled team. The main means of communication of a classical orchestra is synchronization by the conductor, with the musicians picking up and interpreting the body language of the conductor. However, entanglement among professional classical musicians playing together over decades is far more than the musicians reading the body language of the conductor in real time. For instance, at New York's world-famous Orpheus Chamber Orchestra, active since 1972, musicians practice a collaborative leadership style – without a conductor – where the musicians lead themselves democratically. Members of Orpheus are all musicians of the highest caliber, frequently holding teaching positions at the most prominent conservatories and universities in the New York area such as Juilliard or the New England Conservatory. This means that they speak the "musical language" at the highest level, capable of instantaneous communication in rehearsals and concerts without using words.

Jazz musicians take entanglement a step further by communicating without furtive glances and coordinating without words. They do not have to look at each other, they communicate through their ears, as they have internalized the rules of jazz, and thus each of the members of a jamming jazz band knows by listening to the music what their part is, when they have to step back and when to step up and take the lead. Studying videos of jazz musicians improvising, we identified seven principles of how they communicate while jamming together. Comparing two YouTube videos where two ragtime pianists, Tom Brier (www .last.fm/music/Tom+Brier/+wiki) and Adam Swanson (www.adamgswanson .com) are improvising together nicely illustrates the seven principles. Tom Brier and Adam Swanson are well known in the field, having won different prizes and performed at many festivals. Both of them also started as child prodigies, discovering their calling as professional ragtime pianists early on in their lives. Over the years both have performed and competed at different festivals across the US. Two YouTube videos recorded in 2008 and 2010 where Tom and Adam out of the blue began playing the "Chopsticks" rag together illustrate how groupflow between the two musicians emerges. The first time this happened was at the tenth Sutter Creek Ragtime Festival (www .youtube.com/watch?v=H-8bSZa4Fjg) and the second time was at the West Coast Ragtime Festival (www.youtube.com/watch?v=ku2r8HdKong). The first time, in 2008, Adam had been playing the first few bars of "Chopsticks" as a joke, not knowing how Tom would respond to it. Also, at that time, Adam did not know the full "Chopsticks" rag after the first few bars. Tom took up the challenge and started playing, Adam had to pick up the tune and learn it on the fly. The second time, in 2010, Adam was well prepared, and Tom and Adam started grooving for 9 minutes, as recorded in the video. In the 2008 event, Adam turned "Chopsticks" first into the "Tim Baileys" rag and then, both in 2008 and 2010, into the "Tiger Rag." Along the way, Tom and Adam switched keys on each other, thus creating brief periods of dissonance, before getting back into synch. In their mutual interplay, Tom and Adam wonderfully illustrate the key principles of entanglement by rotating leadership:

1. They are seamlessly passing control from one to the other.
2. Whoever has a creative idea takes the lead, and the other follows.
3. They are masters of their profession.
4. The one who knows less learns from the master.
5. They play and synchronize by ear.
6. Competitive collaboration leads to the perfect product.
7. They do it for the fun of it!

7.3.1   They Are Seamlessly Passing Control from One to the Other

In improvisation sessions, the musicians are switching the lead at least half a dozen times. Thanks to this rotation in leadership, creativity is flourishing, with unpredictable but highly enjoyable and stimulating results. Initially Adam plays a few bars of "Chopsticks," which Tom then picks up and continues by making up a trio section on the spot. Leaders easily take turns in the leadership role, leading to an unpredictable but high-quality end product.

7.3.2   Whoever Has a Creative Idea Takes the Lead, and the Other Follows

Initially, Adam challenges Tom to play with him a more complex tune, "Car-Barlick Acid." Tom accepts but when Adam starts playing "Chopsticks" as a joke, Tom takes up this joke and keeps on playing "Chopsticks," improvising and adding new sections along the way, until Adam changes their melody to "Bill Bailey," flexibly picked up by Tom. Adam finally leads over into "Tiger Rag." Leaders are in perfect synch, with the one who knows the tune best taking the lead and the rest of the team following along, until another team member has a better idea, which is then adapted by the rest of the team. This also means that they are willing to give up leadership when somebody else is more qualified. Whoever is most competent steps up to the task.

7.3.3   They Are Masters of Their Profession

Adam and Tom were both child prodigies who started at a young age playing ragtime. Playing rag is rarely played to make a living, but always because the player is passionate about playing it. In the two videos the two artists are participating at a festival, but they still use the opportunity of having a break to play together even more. The two sessions are completely unplanned and unrehearsed, nevertheless they lead to a stunning performance, because the two masters speak the same (musical) language and are able to communicate through their music. They both have huge talent and passion for their art, which allows them to coordinate effortlessly and to easily switch roles. The one who is best qualified for a task becomes the leader until somebody else comes along who is better qualified.

7.3.4   The One Who Knows Less Learns from the Master

In their jamming session, the lead goes from Adam, who challenges Tom with a few bars of "Chopsticks," to Tom, who knows the tune and takes the lead, training Adam on the fly. Adam quickly masters it so well that he can take the lead to successfully introduce "Bill Bailey," bringing Tom along, who then steps up leading the way, until Adam again jumps ahead by switching over to the "Tiger Rag." This means that entangled teams are also learning networks, where more junior members are constantly trained by the master.

7.3.5   They Play and Synchronize by Ear

In their communication and interplay, the "media is the message." Adam and Tom speak the same musical language; even more, they breathe it, and their brains are wired in the same way. Both had been infected by the "ragtime virus" at five years old, and since then each has played for hours every day. They have the basic rhythm and melody in their DNA and can play the classic "Maple Leaf Rag" in their sleep. Cooperation and playing together comes to them as naturally as breathing, they do not need conscious effort to collaborate, rather this happens in their subconsciousness.

7.3.6   Competitive Collaboration Leads to the Perfect Product

If each of the players had jammed and improvised alone, never would an end product of this quality have come out. This session lives from the musical tension and creativity of these two top musicians, who nurture each other's creativity in playful competition, thriving in creativity and trying to beat each other with new ideas, leading to the perfect collaboration. This is competitive collaboration at its best, much more than the sum of its parts!

7.3.7   They Do It for the Fun of It!

Adam and Tom enjoy playing together so much that they utilize the break in their concert to play even more. Grooving and jamming for them is not work but sheer pleasure that energizes them. Entangled team members join their group not for money, but because they are intrinsically motivated to work together towards their shared goal to develop a superior product.

In our research we have studied jazz musicians playing in a concert wearing sociometric badges and smartwatches, and through facial emotion recognition, as described in subsequent sections, where we found them to be perfect exemplars of entangled teams, mirroring each other's expressions and emotions interacting in flow.

7.4 ENTANGLED TEAMS SHARE THE SAME EMOTIONS

> After watching an adoring Indianapolis crowd scream for Mr. Trump — the only thing Mr. Mnuchin could compare it to was when Mick Jagger had taken him to a Rolling Stones concert — Mr. Mnuchin was convinced that Mr. Trump would win.
> (*New York Times*, August 30, 2020)

"Emotions are the great captains of our lives and we obey them without realizing it" – this quote by Vincent Van Gogh makes it clear that while we think that we are rational creatures controlled by reason, the opposite is true. The ecstatic, enthusiastic, adoring, screaming crowds at Donald Trump's rallies shared the same emotions of uncontrolled exuberance and ecstasy, telling Mr. Mnuchin, the future secretary of the treasury of the Trump government, where to place his bets and throw in his lot with Donald Trump.

In many situations we behave highly irrationally, driven by emotion and passion. The key point in these situations is that we are not aware that our emotions have taken over and control what we do, rather we still assume that we behave rationally, driven by clear logic. It is therefore highly desirable to get an early warning system that alerts us when our emotions are overwriting the logic circuit. Even more, knowing what sort of action triggers what sort of emotional response is a clear sign of what one's values are, and to which tribe one belongs.

Imagine you are going to a circus performance. When stepping through the entrance into the circus tent you are full of pleasant expectation. While sitting under the large tent roof and watching a troupe of trapeze artists, you experience a tickling sensation but are mostly relaxed while watching the dazzling spins and jumps of the artists. Occasionally you might hold your breath at a particularly daring jump. Once the artists have finished, you and all other members of the audience start clapping, initially individually and asynchronously, but becoming more and more synchronized, clapping in step for a few minutes, which gives you the pleasant feeling of being part of a large, happily entangled crowd. At the same time the trapeze artists, waiting for their performance, have their hearts racing, triggered by fear and thrill. Once they are on stage, climbing up the rope and swinging on the trapeze, somersaulting and flying through the air, they are fully concentrated and focused on their exercises and on each other, their fear now gone, immersed in the flow of their acrobatics. Once they have finished flying through the air, back on firm ground, they stand on the stage, breathing heavily but smiling happily and relieved, bowing to the audience while soaking up the well-deserved applause.

In this scenario there are two different groups at the same place, under the roof of the circus tent, which are strongly entangled within their own group but only weakly entangled with the other group. The spectators experience a sequence of emotions starting with pleasant expectations, moving on to positive thrill and excitement and ending in happy relaxation. The artists exhibit a very different emotional sequence, starting with fear and worry, leading to the highest concentration and immense positive stress and ending in huge relief and happiness. If we had a way to anonymously measure the emotions of everybody under the roof of the circus tent, we could easily tell who is an artist and who is a spectator without knowing anything else about them. In our research we have done precisely that, not for circus artists but for other similar scenarios such as theater plays and musical concerts and rehearsals using body sensors, facial emotion recognition and AI.

In our studies we equipped professional actors in a theater play and jazz musicians using the smartwatch-based Happimeter system described in Section 9.4 and measured their emotions using machine learning and AI. At the same time, we also captured the emotions of the audience through face emotion recognition with webcams. We noticed different entanglements between the actors and the audience. While the actors were exhibiting shared fear and stress, the audience was entangled in surprise and happiness. We also noticed that when an actor was walking from the stage to the audience, to involve them in the performance, this triggered fear among the audience – most likely people were afraid to be picked by the actor for an experiment. However, once the "thrill of maybe being chosen" was over, the relief of the audience was shown as happiness in the faces of the spectators. This means that the audience first was entangled in collective fear to be selected, which then led to entangled happiness once the danger of being chosen was over. This point illustrates that exposing a team, in this case the audience, to a small pain, is a good way to build entanglement among the team. See also the discussion about "no pain, no gain" in Section 2.3.

We did similar experiments in the office environment, using the same smartwatch-based Happimeter system. We found that clearly knowing your emotions was helpful to better manage your emotions. Using the Happimeter smartwatches, we found that the body of the wearer of the watch predicted emotions such as stress or the degree of understanding in a classroom setting. In a project analyzing a series of meetings in the research lab of a high-tech company, we found that the way they moved their bodies predicted their perceived meeting productivity. The more participants differed in moving their bodies on the chairs during the meeting, the more productive they found the meeting. In other words, taking turns being active during the meeting gave participants the feeling of being more engaged and entangled with the other participants. Alternating between sitting motionless and focused at one time, and animatedly gesticulating at other times during the meeting was an indicator of an engaged and entangled participant.

In another experiment in the classroom, we measured tiredness of the students and quality of the teaching, comparing it with the degree of entanglement of the students with the teacher. This was done by inviting the students in the class to wear the Happimeter watch, and periodically polling them on the watch by vibrating it and asking them to enter their assessment of the quality of the teaching and their tiredness. We found that the body movements of the students indeed predicted their understanding of the materials and their degree of tiredness. The most predictive attributes of the students were their heart rate and body movement. In other words, the way their hearts were beating and the way they were fidgeting on their seats predicted to what extent they were immersed in the presentation of the teacher. Note that there was no general pattern; for some students, a higher heart rate and less fidgeting was an indicator of being entangled with the teacher, while for others it was a lower heart rate or moving around on their chairs more. This confirms our findings from previous projects with the Happimeter smartwatch, where for some people increased heart rate indicated happiness, while for others lower heart rate was a predictor of happiness. The point is that heart rate is an individual characteristic of a person, just like hair color or eye color; machine learning deciphers the differences between individuals and creates a combined model to accurately predict the mood of the wearer of the smartwatch.

7.5   SHARING FACIAL EXPRESSIONS

> The face is the mirror of the mind, and eyes without speaking confess the secrets of the heart. (St. Jerome)

In their 2020 book *Survival of the Friendliest*, Brian Hare and Vanessa Woods compare our Homo sapiens ancestors with the Neanderthals. The Neanderthals had a highly sophisticated culture, burying their dead, caring for their sick and adorning themselves with paint and jewelry. They also were stronger than Homo sapiens, barrel-chested and muscular. Based on comparative experiments with dogs, foxes, chimpanzees and bonobos,[3] Hare and Woods support the self-domestication hypothesis first formulated by Richard Wrangham. The self-domestication hypothesis posits that Homo sapiens from after 80,000 years ago showed marked signs of self-domestication compared to Neanderthals. Neanderthal skulls show signs of a strong influence of testosterone, the "male sex hormone" triggering aggression and competitive behavior, while Homo sapiens skulls and skeletons show influence of serotonin, a hormone regulating mood and emotions. The more testosterone is produced during puberty, the thicker the brow ridge in the face and the longer the face. Hare, Woods and other researchers found that the brow ridge of Homo sapiens' skulls over the last 80,000 years reduced by 40 percent, while faces became 10 percent shorter and 5 percent narrower, indicating lower levels of testosterone compared to Neanderthals. Serotonin on the other hand seems to change skull structure by making it more globular, more like a balloon or a light bulb. Every other skull of early hominins except Homo sapiens had low, flat foreheads while Neanderthals had skulls shaped like footballs. Only we Homo sapiens have the balloon-like globular skull indicative of lower testosterone and higher serotonin levels. Lower testosterone and higher serotonin also reinforce the influence of another hormone, oxytocin, on social bonding. Eye contact between parents and babies creates oxytocin, making both parents and babies more loving and feeling loved. This result ties in with the theory of "facial width to height ratio," which posits that men with higher facial width to height ratio with broader, rounder faces are more aggressive, while men with thinner faces are more trustworthy.[4] For instance, among 743 faces of Finnish soldiers in the winter war against Russia during the Second World War,[5] soldiers with thinner faces had a higher rank, while soldiers with rounder faces had more children. The perception of aggressiveness of wider faces led to better outcomes in a negotiation game among Chinese MBA students,[6] while CEOs are more wide-faced than their comparable peer group.[7] As St. Jerome says above, reading the face of a person will show many facets of personality characteristics and emotions.

In our own research we have studied the facial and voice emotions of people in various settings, such as concerts, theater plays, business meetings and in the classroom. We conducted a series of research projects using facial emotion detection systems using webcams. For instance, we tracked the emotions of 34 students participating in a semester-long virtual seminar. The students worked in eight teams, collaborating mostly over long distance. In a bi-weekly, two-hour online meeting using Zoom video conferencing, they presented their project progress. We tracked the emotion of their faces using face emotion detection and compared it with the quality of their presentations, by collecting a score from each participant asking "How many points would you give this presentation?" at the end of each one. Not surprisingly we found that happy faces correlated with highly scored presentations, while bored, neutral faces correlated with low scoring presentations. But we also found that the wider the spread in positive and negative emotions among the audience, the higher the score of the presenter. In other words, if the audience was riding an emotional rollercoaster, viewers scored the quality of the presentation much higher.

In another project we analyzed the facial emotions of jazz musicians in a rehearsal at the Berklee College of Music, who were rehearsing with a famous musician in preparation for a big concert. When tracking the emotions through the Happimeter and facial expressions, we found the same as with the students in the Zoom video-conferencing analysis: the more their facial expressions reflected fear and anger – most likely anger about themselves because they were not fulfilling their own high expectations – the better their performance was, measured through the Happimeter worn by others. In other words, going through an emotional rollercoaster was a recipe for playing better.

We also measured emotions of participants in meetings using the Happimeter. However, there we found the opposite. While an emotional rollercoaster is good for a performance in theater or music, meeting participants do not really appreciate emotional rollercoasters; rather they prefer meetings in harmony.

7.6   SHARING THE SAME LANGUAGE

Another powerful indicator of being entangled is using the same or at least similar words to portray the same event. Members of the same tribe use the same words to describe what they see and think. In his play "Pygmalion," Bernhard Shaw describes the story of Henry Higgins, a professor of linguistics in highly class-conscious United Kingdom just before the First World War. After a chance encounter with foul-mouthed flower girl Eliza, who he overhears swearing in the worst British underclass dialect, Higgins enters into a wager with Colonel Pickering, another upper-class Briton interested in linguistics. Higgins commits to converting the flower girl Eliza into an upper-class girl, fit to be a duchess, simply by teaching her how to speak like one. After much turmoil Higgins succeeds in this endeavor having her accepted as a full member of the British upper class, just by changing the way she speaks and the words she uses. This illustrates that sharing similar words to describe similar events is enough to identify membership among entangled members of a tribe.

The same is true for spouses, who start using each other's words and expressions while also mimicking each other's gestures and behavior. Children start using the words and expressions of their parents, greatly contributing to setting them up for future success or failure in their adult lives. In a nutshell, the way parents talk to their children, using many loving words or using fewer negative words, is one of the key predictors of how much children learn later in life, and how resilient they are towards failure. This is discussed in depth in Section 6.3.

As we have demonstrated in our research, the propensity to use the same words and expressions extends to consumer tribes and fans of a particular brand. This property of members of the same consumer or political tribe using similar words can be used to discover the personality characteristics of individuals. We have built a system called Tribefinder, the technical details of which are described in Chapter 19, to automatically identify members of a tribe based on word usage.

7.7   NEGATIVE ENTANGLEMENT

While entanglement is an overwhelmingly positive phenomenon, entanglement also has a dark side. The generals and soldiers supporting North Korean leader Kim Jong-un suppressing their own population are as negatively entangled as the members of the Ku Klux Klan, a Sicilian mafia clan or the affiliates of a Mexican drug cartel. Negative entanglement can also be found in the business world. A stark example of negative entanglement was Lehman Bros and how their CEO Richard Fuld infamously created a culture of fear, financial constraints and normalization of mistreatment on the part of employees. He built an organization that was negatively entangled. The regulators and society asked why nobody spoke up. We now know it is not simple to speak up in negatively entangled organizations. It's the same as bystanders asking "Why doesn't she just leave him" when talking about an abused woman. When used negatively, entanglement will stifle speaking up and diversity of thought, which is another key indicator of effective teams. Misalignment in honest signals (see Section 11.1) can be used to pinpoint and identify negative entanglement.

Figure 7.2   Religious fanatics dancing amid graves in a churchyard

There can certainly be too much entanglement, as shown in medieval dancing manias. In the Middle Ages, large groups of people infected each other with the "dance plague," dancing madly until they fainted from exhaustion. For example, in 1518 in Strasbourg, a woman began to madly dance, without music, for the first six days alone and after a month 400 people were dancing together. Historians report that up to 15 people per day dropped dead from exhaustion through dancing (Figure 7.2).

Today's raves are similar to the dancing manias centuries ago. At the annual Love Parade in Berlin, later in Duisburg, close to a million people danced in a state of trance for days, occasionally supported with a little chemical help. But again, this large-scale entanglement is quite risky. At the Love Parade in 2010 in Duisburg, 21 people were crushed in a panic, injuring 500.

Nazi Germany is another prime example of negative entanglement. In a social network study, criteria for the rapid adaptation of Nazism were identified.[8] The researchers found that the more social cohesion there was in a town in the Weimar Republic before the rise of Nazi Germany, measured as membership in sports clubs, pigeon breeders' associations and choirs, the higher the subsequent percentage of Nazi party members. "Interacting as equals while singing or discussing rabbit breeding did not fortify Germans against the lure of an extremist party." Rather, the more entangled the population of a town was as rabbit breeders and choir singers, the more it lubricated the spread of ideas of a murderous regime. Ultranationalists such as the Nazis make a strong distinction between "us" and "them." While ultranationalists give and expect loyalty from the members of their own ingroup or tribe, they deny humanity to their outgroup. The Nazis put members of other tribes such as Jews, gypsies and homosexuals into extermination camps, to create a fully negatively entangled society by annihilating everybody who was "different."

NOTES

1. Libby, E., & Ratcliff, W. C. (2014). Ratcheting the evolution of multicellularity. *Science*, 346(6208), 426–427.
2. www.quora.com/What-will-you-do-if-you-are-locked-in-a-room-with-a-girl.
3. Hare, B. (2017). Survival of the friendliest: Homo sapiens evolved via selection for prosociality. *Annual Review of Psychology*, 68, 155–186.
4. Haselhuhn, M. P., Ormiston, M. E., & Wong, E. M. (2015). Men's facial width-to-height ratio predicts aggression: A meta-analysis. *PLoS One*, 10(4), e0122637.
5. Loehr, J., & O'Hara, R. B. (2013). Facial morphology predicts male fitness and rank but not survival in Second World War Finnish soldiers. *Biology Letters*, 9(4), 20130049.
6. Yang, Y., Tang, C., Qu, X., Wang, C., & Denson, T. F. (2018). Group facial width-to-height ratio predicts intergroup negotiation outcomes. *Frontiers in Psychology*, 9, 214.

7.   Alrajih, S., & Ward, J. (2014). Increased facial width-to-height ratio and per-
      ceived dominance in the faces of the UK's leading business leaders. *British
      Journal of Psychology*, 105(2), 153–161.
8.   Satyanath, S., Voigtländer, N., & Voth, H. J. (2017). Bowling for fascism: Social
      capital and the rise of the Nazi Party. *Journal of Political Economy*, 125(2),
      478–526.

8. Creating entangled collaborative innovation networks

A fully entangled creative team will work together as a COIN. COINs are small teams of intrinsically motivated people who collaborate over the internet to create something radically new. The work atmosphere in a COIN thus corresponds to a team in groupflow. To reach flow, team members must be intrinsically motivated by the goals of the COIN. The COIN creation process is inspired by bees and consists of embedding the COIN core team into a larger ecosystem of collaborative learning networks and collaborative interest networks that carry the innovative ideas and products of the COIN over the tipping point, towards wider societal acceptance. For instance, the development of the mRNA vaccine against Covid-19[1] is the product of a sequence of COINs, starting with the discovery of mRNA 60 years ago. COINs of researchers in the US, Canada and Europe worked together, using the molecule to direct cells to make viruses that would strengthen the immune system, developing ways to transfer these genetic molecules to the human body and leveraging decades of HIV research targeting the "spikes" of the HIV virus. In early 2020 these different fields of research all came together, when the "spike" of the Covid-19 virus was encoded in mRNA molecules and converted into vaccines. Two of the COIN leaders, Anthony Fauci, who would go on to lead the US response to Covid-19, and Barney Graham, a leader in his lab, started their long and until then unsuccessful journey researching HIV vaccines in the 1980s. However, what they learned while tackling HIV was essential for fighting viruses attacking the respiratory system such as the coronavirus. They were soon joined by numerous collaborative learning networks, among them scientists at BioNTech, Pfizer and Moderna, who picked up their latest results from scientific pre-publications and got to work manufacturing effective vaccines, testing them with thousands of volunteers in collaborative interest networks until they could be safely injected into billions of people to protect them against the coronavirus.

COINs are the most productive engines of innovation ever. Any successful startup will be born out of a COIN, while large companies and other large organizations struggle to keep their ecosystems of COINs alive and vibrant.[2] In our research over the last 20 years, we have been studying COINs at hundreds of organizations, ranging from jazz orchestras, teams of surgeons, open-source communities and startups – for instance biotech at MIT-Kendall Square[3] – to Fortune 500 firms with hundreds of thousands of employees. What we found is that to fully unleash the power of COINs, entanglement among team members is key. They need to have a shared context and shared values which allow them to communicate without words, through "honest signals," body language and shared action. In other words, they should be members of the same virtual tribe, sharing the same morals and characteristics. Entangled members of COINs operate in an environment of positive energy; being humble, kind and compassionate gives positive emotional energy, while avoiding overconfident, arrogant and egotistical behavior which drains energy and creates a toxic work environment.

I started studying COINs 20 years ago, initially analyzing open-source communities and Wikipedia editors. In the meantime, I have researched and analyzed hundreds of commercial and non-profit organizations. I was frequently brought in as a COIN midwife, to assist in getting a nascent or struggling COIN off the ground. Figure 8.1 describes the COIN creation process that I have applied in these projects. It is very much inspired by the bees. When a beehive has grown too large, it splits into two halves, with the old queen and half of the bees leaving their old home and following the queen to a new home.

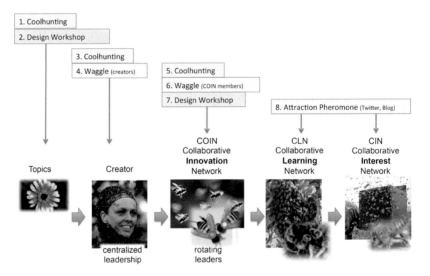

Figure 8.1   Exemplary collaborative innovation network creation process

The process starts with the bees leaving their old home and clustering around the old queen on a branch somewhere near the old hive, while a small number of the most adventurous bees scout for a new home. When one of them thinks she has found a new dream home, she will fly back to the swarming bees to conduct a waggle dance enticing other bees to follow her and check out the potential new home. The more excitedly the successful scout does her waggle dance, the more other scouts will go out and check the new home. If they also like what they see, they will come back to the swarm and join the waggle dance. This goes on until a threshold is reached, where the entire swarm gets excited and starts vibrating and heating up. When the swarm has reached a certain temperature, it will explode in an instant and all bees will start flying, following the guidance of the excited scouts who direct the swarm to the new location. While flying with the swarm, the scouts will spray attraction phero- mones to further motivate and direct the flying swarm to the new home. The new home has also already been marked with attraction pheromones to attract the swarm to settle in and commence building the new home.

The process for human bees works the same. This has been verified both by studying numerous COINs and by employing it when trying to jump start a fledgling COIN.

The key prerequisite for successfully creating a COIN is that the members are there not because they are paid to be there, but because they care about the cause. The first step when creating a COIN is to decide on the initial task that the team wants to tackle. For example, I was involved in creating a COIN for addressing infant mortality in the US, sponsored by the Maternal and Child Health Bureau of the US Health Resources and Services Administration. To get the COIN off the ground, a passionate group got together to hunt for solutions to address the stubborn issue of health disparity in the US. Different from other wealthy Western countries, in the US, health is strongly correlated with income, with infant mortality in the lowest income bracket being similar to a developing country. To develop radical innovations tackling this issue, a COIN creation process was officially kicked off through a workshop. Before the workshop, the organizing group did a "waggle dance" like the bees, which attracted other bees to their honey source or told them the location of a potential new home. The human "bees" did their waggle dance to attract other social workers and public health officials to their cause. In the workshop the team brainstormed, collected and sorted different ideas. It finally decided on developing a framework for creating community action networks, bringing together disadvantaged families with community elders, social workers and government officials. In the next step the team decided on its informal leaders. This happened with volunteers stepping up to assume leadership roles.

Once the COIN was set up and running, group members formed subteams or individually worked on solutions, while getting together on monthly Zoom meetings to update each other on their progress and to collaborate on further developing new products. It was surprising how well this brainstorming process over Zoom worked. There were about a dozen members in the COIN, each of us at a different location, having a Zoom window open and a shared Google document. This shared editing in the Google document was amazingly productive, with each of the COIN members typing their thinking and ideas in the online document in real time, editing and answering each other's comments. It even looked a bit spooky, having 12 people at the same time typing in different parts of the document. Management of the project was via rotating leadership, with members assuming a leadership role based on the skills they brought to the table and the task that needed to be completed.

After the initial products and solutions had been developed, the COIN members started spreading the "attraction pheromone." A COIN will recruit other potential bees in this phase by teaching them the tools and methods that the COIN developed. In the case of the infant mortality COIN, this phase consisted of organizing webinars, building a website and writing documents about community action networks for other social workers across the US. These social workers who learned from the initial COIN further distributed the materials and invited young mothers, fathers and other family members to them. These families with young babies from disadvantaged backgrounds in the community action networks form the collaborative interest network, the end users of the product that the COIN had developed.

COINs have been around for a long time, turbocharged by the emergence of the internet and the web. The creation of the web by Tim Berners-Lee and his colleagues, Wikipedia by Jimmy Wales and Linux by Linus Torvalds are all poster stories of disruptive innovation by COINs. Every successful startup, not just Apple, Google or Facebook, has at its core a COIN. The challenge for large organizations and companies is to maintain an environment encouraging the emergence and growth of COINs. The virtual mirroring process, which uses the social network analysis and AI tools described in Part II to find COINs, measure emotions and identify tribes, is introduced in Chapter 9. It describes the actions individuals and companies can take to turn their organization into a beehive of entangled COINs.

NOTES

1.   www.nytimes.com/2022/01/15/health/mrna-vaccine.html.
2.   Gloor, P. A. (2006). *Swarm Creativity: Competitive Advantage through Collaborative Innovation Networks*. Oxford University Press.
3.   Allen, T. J., Gloor, P., Colladon, A. F., Woerner, S. L., & Raz, O. (2016). The power of reciprocal knowledge sharing relationships for startup success. *Journal of Small Business and Enterprise Development*, 23(3), 636–651.

9. Virtual mirroring

If a man has lost a leg or an eye, he knows he has lost a leg or an eye; but if he has lost a self – himself – he cannot know it, because he is no longer there to know it. (Oliver Sacks)

Just like the human body shivers when it has a fever, an organization frequently has a vague feeling that something is amiss but is unable to pinpoint what is wrong. Similar to a thermometer measuring the health of the body, we propose a novel approach to assessing and improving individual and organizational mental health by calculating a series of communication metrics between individuals in the organization. Offering individuals the opportunity to reflect on their own communication behavior has the potential to change those behaviors and ultimately improve their happiness and the quality of their relationships with others. Just like mirror neurons put the self and the other back together and map the actions of the other into the self, our virtual mirroring process is grounded on the idea that self-awareness requires socialization and continuous dialog about the impact that our words and behaviors have on others.

Showing the impact of your actions can really change your behavior! In a fascinating research project in California,[1] half of 1332 students in an ethics class read and discussed a paper and watched a video about the suffering of animals slaughtered for human consumption. The other half of the students read and discussed a paper about charitable giving. Unbeknownst to the students, after the ethics class, their purchasing behavior at the campus cafeteria was monitored for the duration of a month. The students discussing meat consumption reduced their meat consumption by 7 percent. This effect occurred not just right after the class but remained until the end of the observation period. This experiment shows that showing somebody the consequences of their own behavior clearly impacts their future behavior. In our use of virtual mirroring, we are using the same effect to improve communication behavior, groupflow and happiness. In dozens of projects, we have shown that individuals and teams change their communication behavior, if the way they communicate and the impact of their behavior is shown to them. If people know which communication behavior makes them more collaborative, and thus more successful, they will change their behavior for the better.

9.1   INSIDE – OUTSIDE – ENTANGLE

The combination of social network analysis and AI allows individuals and organizations to radically improve their collaboration by measuring it, to increase it and reach groupflow. Computing a virtual mirror of their and others' communication behavior will give individuals insight to change their interaction for the better. This chapter introduces practical steps of what you and your team can do to reach optimum creativity and productivity through groupflow by creating an entangled organization. It presents the groupflow creation process, consisting of the three components "inside," "outside" and "entanglement." The individuals gain insight from the inside by looking at their individual virtual mirror to understand how they see themselves. They are exposed to the outside view by getting honest feedback from others about their communication behavior to discover their weaknesses and whether they have been truthful to themselves. Applying the principle "no pain, no gain," they learn to accept their shortcomings and turn them into strengths. Finally, in the entanglement phase, they form entanglement through synchronizing with their team members, increasing individual happiness and creating collective awareness and high organizational performance.

The initial inside phase consists of measuring and mirroring the individual communication behavior back to the individual. This basically means creating "selfies" of the communication of oneself with others, and of the individual values, personality characteristics and risk behavior. In particular, it means creating a "my-selfie" to honestly assess how I see myself, and how this differs from my desired self-image. It also includes an "other-selfie" to assess how others see me, and how this differs from my desired self-image. Finally, it includes creating a "group-selfie" to assess my position among my friends and collaborators, how they see me and how this is different from how I would like to be seen by my peers.

Individuals obtain a potentially painful outside view by searching for and accepting their shortcomings. This means accepting the "other-selfie" that will tell me where my self-image differs from the view that others have of myself and where my weaknesses are. Willingness to improve oneself includes readiness to accept pain in the short term for long-term gain. The Romans built their empire "per aspera ad astra," or over the stones to the stars. This means facing reality, even if we don't like it, and being willing to initiate change and follow through on it. In the context of groupflow, team members must be willing to embrace a challenging task without knowing if they will succeed. If they succeed, they will be rewarded not just by the accomplished task, but even more by the positive flow experience of working together and having had a great time together.

The entanglement phase creates an entangled organization by making predictions about how the organization will operate in the future, based on an analysis of the organization's communication archives. It will synchronize interaction among individual team members, just as a drummer synchronizes a column of marching soldiers. In parallel, the inside and outside views will show individuals the consequences of their actions and influence their behavior towards more empathy and humility, key characteristics of an organization with high collective intelligence.[2] An entangled organization will think and act as a single organism, just like the two mice whose brains were synchronized through implanted electrodes by a team of researchers at Northwestern University in Evanston, Illinois. They implanted a device into the cortex of the brains of two mice that allowed researchers to synchronize the brain by sending synchronous rapid pulses to the device that triggered neurons in the cortex of the two mice. The researchers then put the two stranger mice together in a cage.[3] When the light diodes placed in the brains of the two mice were turned on through the electrodes and started flashing in sync, the mice could not get enough of each other, and wanted to stay close together in their cage.[4] Turning on synchronicity triggered the desire for closeness; when the synchronicity was turned off, the mice lost interest in each other.

While we cannot implant electrodes into human brains to start entanglement, there are procedural steps we can take to increase synchronicity among team members. Similar entanglement effects are experienced by humans singing together in a choir, dancing together and screaming their lungs out at a football game. This means that to induce groupflow in a team, members have to start interacting in synchronicity. In order to act synchronized and in a coordinated way in a creative team, personality characteristics like humility and empathy are essential, while narcissism and egocentrism definitively get in the way.

What can we do in our work and private lives to create such nourishing relationships of trust and respect? Everything starts with knowing ourselves. However, while we all think we know who we are, the reality is very different. The image I have of myself is not the image that others have of me. Only when these two images are in alignment will it be possible for me to communicate with others on the same level and understand my opposite. To discover mismatches between self-perception and the perception others have of me, the best way is to look at how I communicate with others, and how others communicate with me. If in my communication with others I am describing myself in very different words from how others see me in their communication with me, if in direct contact I am not capable of looking others in their eyes, if it takes me weeks to answer an email or WhatsApp message or if others never answer my messages, I should know I have a problem. Figure 9.1 describes the steps as to how virtual mirroring is creating entanglement by extending awareness of self to awareness of others.

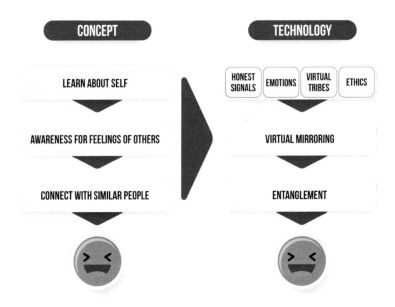

Figure 9.1   How virtual mirroring creates entanglement

A person learns about herself by looking at her "honest signals of collaboration" and other characteristics of individualism and personality gleaned from
her communication records such as email, Skype, Twitter and smartwatch
sensors. Computed from communication logs and body sensors, "honest
signals" measure emotions, attitudes towards social issues through the "virtual
tribes" and ethical and moral values of a person. These values are shown to the
individual in the "virtual mirror" of her communication behavior, helping her
to better know herself. In the virtual mirror she will also learn how others see
her, compared to the image she has about herself. This knowledge will help
her to become entangled with the people around her, leading to fulfilling and
rewarding relationships in her private and professional lives, resulting in better
collaboration and highly productive, happy work teams.

9.2   THE THREE STEPS OF VIRTUAL MIRRORING
TO CREATE ENTANGLEMENT

To get people to behave more socially responsible it takes both the carrot and
the stick. Colorado Mesa University (CMU) got through the Covid-19 pandemic much better than many other universities using virtual mirroring. This
illustrates the power of showing students the simulated consequences of their

behavior to educate them about better social distancing[5] and being more honest in reporting a potential Covid-19 infection. Early in the pandemic, CMU's leadership decided to offer its students an on-campus experience despite the risk of clusters of Covid-19 outbreaks. They collaborated with the MIT and Harvard Broad Institute to implement a sophisticated virtual mirroring system combining insight through self-management with institutional oversight. To manage the unruly students and limit their social activities, CMU employed a three-pronged approach. They provided insight to the students through the Scout smartphone app developed by Pardis Sabeti and her team at the Broad Institute. Each student had to track and enter their health symptoms on the Scout app every day, giving the students an early warning sign that a Covid infection might be on the way. Every time students went to their (socially distanced) classroom teaching, showing a green light on the Scout app permitted entry, and if the light was red they were sent to Covid testing; if the test came back positive, they had to go into quarantine.

This self-monitoring insight component was combined with an oversight component, as the sewage installations of the student dorms at CMU were controlled by a wastewater monitoring system also developed at the Broad Institute. This allowed CMU leadership to recognize outbreaks in dorms early, as the Covid-19 virus can be traced through human feces. Frequently, individual Covid-19 incidence from the Scout app and Covid-19 indication through the wastewater location system did not match, as students wanting to keep their social activities alive were less than honest in entering their symptoms in the Scout app. There was thus more Covid-19 shown in the wastewater monitor than the Scout smartphone app was implying. Subsequently, to discover these infected students, CMU did blanket Covid testing in the dorms where wastewater analysis indicated Covid, despite the Scout app indicators being negative. By wielding this "stick," students who were less than honest when entering their symptoms were discovered and sent to quarantine, and larger outbreaks were thus avoided. To further reduce and ideally eliminate this irresponsible and dishonest behavior, "Operation Outbreak," another smartphone app for increasing socially responsible behavior, was deployed[6] among the student population. It simulated the spread of infectious diseases by randomly jumping by Bluetooth from an "infected" smartphone to the smartphone of another user close enough to "catch the disease." This way it showed the students that socializing and getting too close to others was dangerous and educated them about more responsible socially distanced behavior. Combining these three steps led to a socially aware and responsible student population and very low Covid-19 infection rates at CMU compared to other US colleges.

The process applied at CMU beautifully illustrates how behavior can be made more responsible and collaborative through virtual mirroring:

1. *Insight*: Do a self-assessment, which was done with the Scout app at CMU. When doing the self-assessment, people might not be honest to themselves. More generally, this means tracking individual communication behavior, to understand how the individual communicates with others. The individuals also assess their moral values, personality and attitude to risk. This will tell them more clearly who they are in their own eyes.

2. *Oversight*: Monitor true behavior to identify cheaters, such as with the wastewater monitoring system at CMU. This gives an organization an overview of its communication structure. The goal is to create a social landscape mapping the lay of the land within the organization and in interaction with the outside world. This overview map will assist the organization's leaders to improve productivity, creativity and satisfaction of the organization's members.

3. *Entanglement*: Show individuals the impact of their behavior in a safe environment, such as with the contagion spreading modeling app given to the CMU students. This means comparing their own morals, personality characteristics and communication behavior with others and adjusting their conduct with regards to socially desirable behavior, increasing humility and empathy and reducing egocentrism and narcissism.

These three steps, giving insight into communication behavior, providing oversight of negative behavior and supporting entanglement by making them more empathic, can change people towards more collaborative and socially responsible behavior.

9.3   USING A SOCIAL COMPASS FOR VIRTUAL MIRRORING

The technology to build this virtual mirror is based on the Social Compass introduced in Chapter 20 by analyzing communication activities of individuals embedded in social networks and showing them the consequences of their communication behavior (see Figure 20.1). This analysis starts with taking a survey measuring the moral values (see Figure 3.1). Figure 20.3 illustrates the My-Selfie view of the Social Compass virtual mirror on the smartphone.

The virtual mirror can also be aggregated on the departmental level. This gives organizations a privacy-respecting way to measure and visualize employee satisfaction and communication behavior. Figure 9.2 illustrates the virtual mirror for a fictional organization made up of the three departments IT, marketing and sales.

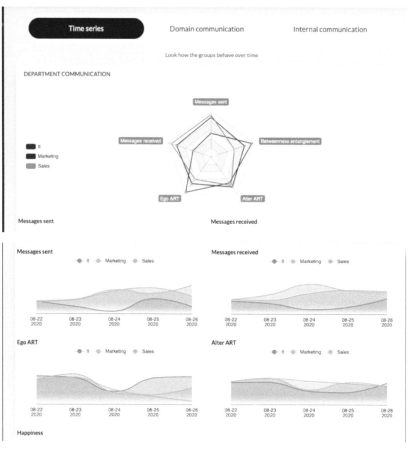

Figure 9.2   *Web-based virtual mirror comparing the honest signals for the three departments IT, marketing and sales*

The virtual mirror uses the AI tools described in Chapters 13–18 to calculate the honest signals of each person based on their communication archive. It also aggregates individual information on the department, project, customer and location level. It gives individual and aggregated feedback on how well a person or department is doing compared to the peer group, and what the person or department can do to change their communication behavior for better outcomes. For instance, once I realize that spending time with a particular person will make me unhappy, I will initiate change, by either helping that person to change her behavior or by avoiding her altogether. Similarly, if in a business setting I know that customers will be more satisfied if they get honest answers in a timely fashion, and I have been slow in my answers and have used overly positive language, I will adjust my behavior to respond honestly in a timelier way. Likewise, if I am told that my communication style comes across as overbearing and dominating and I am suppressing the creativity of my teammates, I will change my behavior to be humbler and more team oriented. Also, if I realize I am not engaged with my team members, I might change my behavior to respond to individuals directly and more rapidly to become more entangled with the team.

Virtual mirroring brings real results in the corporate world. In a project with a global service provider with over 80,000 employees, we collected anonymized email data for 24 of their large customer accounts out of a total of 250 large customers. Each customer account was providing services such as payroll processing or call center services to a large customer such as for example Bank of America or Pfizer with dozens to hundreds of workers. The account leader at the service provider got virtual mirror information similar to the one shown in Figure 9.2. At the same time, the satisfaction of the customers was measured using the Net Promoter Score, a metric that asks customers how likely they are to recommend their service provider to their friends. After eight months of virtual mirroring, the 24 customer accounts exposed to virtual mirroring of their email showed a significant improvement in customer satisfaction, increasing the contentment of their customers by 18 percent compared to the other over 200 non-mirrored accounts.

One key aspect of virtual mirroring is not just measuring the networking behavior, but also the emotions, in particular the happiness of individuals.

9.4   INCREASING HAPPINESS BY VIRTUAL MIRRORING WITH THE HAPPIMETER

> Happiness depends on ourselves. (Aristotle)

As discussed in Section 4.1, happiness has been an overarching goal of mankind at least since Aristotle spoke of Eudaimonia. According to Aristotle, happiness starts with us. Only if we know ourselves can we be happy. Thus, it is essential to know what makes us happy and unhappy. However, measuring happiness has been elusive and until now has almost exclusively been done by asking survey questions about self-perceived happiness. We have created a novel happiness measurement device, tracking happiness and stress through changes in body signals with a smartwatch – the "Happimeter." It predicts individual emotions from sensor data collected by the smartwatch, such as acceleration, heartbeat and activity. Figure 9.3 illustrates the key components of the Happimeter. It consists of a smartwatch, currently either an Apple watch or an Android Wear watch, that measures body signals of the wearer, such as heart rate, movement through an accelerometer and speech energy through the microphone (no content is recorded). The data are then transferred to a smartphone, where it is shown in the Happimeter app. The Happimeter app also includes the meeting balancer which supports turn taking in meetings to encourage more balanced speaking time among meeting participants. The data are sent from the smartphone to a machine learning server in the cloud, which computes the happiness of the wearer of the watch based on the body signals with an accuracy of 75 to 80 percent. Additionally, users can register on a website, to form teams to track their team happiness as well as their individual happiness and other emotions over extended periods of time.

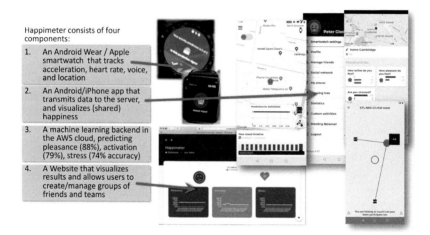

Happimeter consists of four components:

1. An Android Wear / Apple smartwatch that tracks acceleration, heart rate, voice, and location

2. An Android/iPhone app that transmits data to the server, and visualizes (shared) happiness

3. A machine learning backend in the AWS cloud, predicting pleasance (88%), activation (79%), stress (74% accuracy)

4. A Website that visualizes results and allows users to create/manage groups of friends and teams

Figure 9.3   Happimeter overview

The Happimeter was tested in many different settings. For instance, it was given to 22 employees in the innovation lab of a bank for a period of three months to measure their individual happiness, activity and stress. The participants were randomly divided into an experimental and a control group of similar size. In an initial training phase lasting a few weeks, both groups wore the watch and entered their subjective happiness, activity and stress levels several times a day. These user-entered ratings were then used to train a machine learning system using the sensors of the smartwatch to subsequently automatically predict happiness, activity and stress. In a second phase, only the experimental group was told their happiness, together with recommendations of what they could do to increase their happiness if the Happimeter noticed that happiness was low. The experimental group received ongoing feedback about their mood and which activity, sensor signals or interaction with other people made them happier or unhappier. The control group did not get any feedback about their predicted and manually entered emotions.

Figure 9.4 illustrates the individual insights that users of the Happimeter get from the website. They learn what precisely, for instance the weather, changes in location or the time of day, makes them unhappy. They are also told if other people they are interacting with (these also need to wear the Happimeter) will increase or decrease their happiness. Note that the Happimeter can only show correlation, not causation. It could well be that Joao Marcos is an indicator of my unhappiness not because I don't like him, but because I regularly travel with him in the subway, which is always late and thus makes me unhappy.

Figure 9.5 shows the default recommendations that Happimeter gives to users to increase their happiness, when the Happimeter predicts that the wearer of the Happimeter is unhappy, stressed and unactive. These suggestions given in response to a combination of pleasance, activation and stress can be changed by the user.

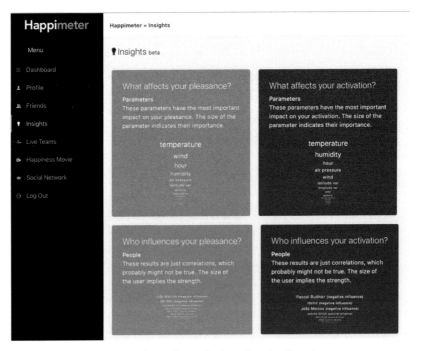

Figure 9.4   Individual insights calculated by the Happimeter

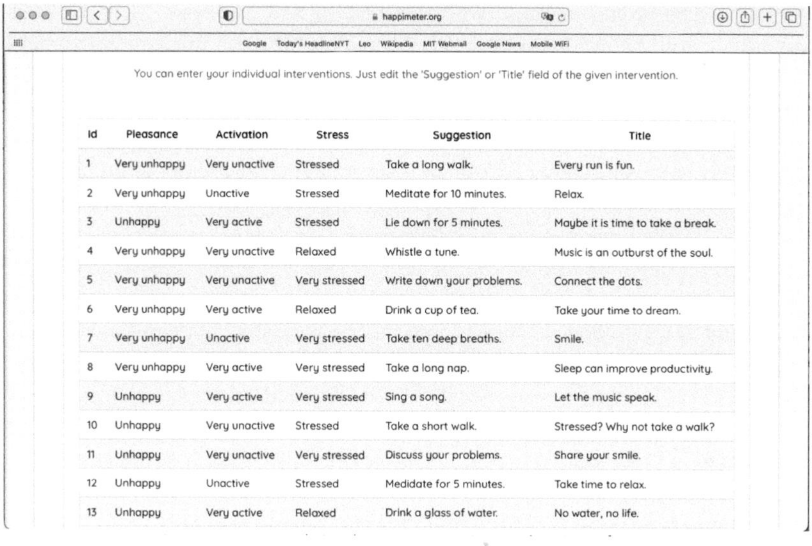

You can enter your individual interventions. Just edit the 'Suggestion' or 'Title' field of the given intervention.

Id	Pleasance	Activation	Stress	Suggestion	Title
1	Very unhappy	Very unactive	Stressed	Take a long walk.	Every run is fun.
2	Very unhappy	Unactive	Stressed	Meditate for 10 minutes.	Relax.
3	Unhappy	Very active	Stressed	Lie down for 5 minutes.	Maybe it is time to take a break.
4	Very unhappy	Very unactive	Relaxed	Whistle a tune.	Music is an outburst of the soul.
5	Very unhappy	Very unactive	Very stressed	Write down your problems.	Connect the dots.
6	Very unhappy	Very active	Relaxed	Drink a cup of tea.	Take your time to dream.
7	Very unhappy	Unactive	Very stressed	Take ten deep breaths.	Smile.
8	Very unhappy	Very active	Very stressed	Take a long nap.	Sleep can improve productivity.
9	Unhappy	Very active	Very stressed	Sing a song.	Let the music speak.
10	Unhappy	Very unactive	Stressed	Take a short walk.	Stressed? Why not take a walk?
11	Unhappy	Very unactive	Very stressed	Discuss your problems.	Share your smile.
12	Unhappy	Unactive	Stressed	Medidate for 5 minutes.	Take time to relax.
13	Unhappy	Very active	Relaxed	Drink a glass of water.	No water, no life.

Figure 9.5   Recommendations by the Happimeter to increase happiness of wearer

As in quantum physics we observed a "Heisenberg Effect" – simply measuring a system changes the behavior of the system. When the participants were made aware of their measurements, they changed their behavior: members of the experimental group that received happiness feedback were 16 percent happier and 26 percent more active at the end of the experiment than the control group which did not get any feedback. No effect was observed for stress in this experiment.

9.5   THE VIRTUAL MIRROR IS NOT ABOUT ME, IT IS ABOUT THE OTHERS

During the Covid-19 lockdown, Zoom and other video-conferencing systems mushroomed, becoming essential tools for conducting business meetings, online teaching and staying in touch with loved ones. However, many users felt stressed about video conferencing and asked to go back to phone and conference calls. Personally, I hate conference calls – in my days as a consultant at PwC and Deloitte 20 years ago I spent 60 percent of my time being trapped in calls, the mobile phone stuck between ear and neck and the muscles in the neck getting stiffer and stiffer as time on the call progressed. While nobody knew who else was listening in, only one person at a time could speak, with everybody else being a mostly bored eavesdropper. By the sound of the voice of the speaker, listeners had to guess who that person was and what their emotion was, which could become quite tricky, particularly if participants were numerous and speakers became agitated. Over the last 20 years, video conferencing partially replaced conference calls, until finally the last two Covid years brought a decisive boost to Zoom and its competitors, definitively relegating conference calls to a niche. Compared to phone calls, video-conferencing calls are a much richer interaction experience, as they allow users to see each other, thus opening up other communication channels to convey emotions among all participants through facial expressions and in the chat window. On the downside, it becomes harder to hide the pajamas that participants might be wearing and the food they are eating during the calls. And as always when something is (too) successful, video-conferencing naysayers and alarmists discover obstacles and impediments. Among a vocal minority, Zoom fatigue and video-conferencing burnout after a year of intensive video calls brought Clubhouse – a voice-only podcast and voice chat app – and a backlash against video conferencing with requests to go back to phone and conference calls.

I very much prefer video conferencing over conference calls. As a traveler around the globe for the last 25 years, I have been a video-conferencing user of the first hour. Since 2005 I have been teaching the distributed COINs course with participants from different universities around the world, using video-conferencing tools, experimenting with Webex, Adobe Connect, Google Hangout, Zoom and many other products. While, particularly in the early days, there were many video-conferencing hiccups and glitches, there is no way I would want to go back to phone calls. In fact, it would have been impossible to teach the COINs course just using a conference call for the students to interact with each other synchronously across multiple time zones and multiple classrooms. But also for applications other than online teaching, virtual video-conferencing meetings offer a much higher interaction quality than voice-only conference calls.

I noticed that video-conferencing refusers seem to be particularly stressed by their own picture on the screen. Instead of focusing on the other participants, we become obsessed with our own appearance in the little window on the screen, fussing over our haircut, shirt, the background and the angle of the camera. Ignoring my own image on the camera, instead trying to look the other participants in their (remote) eyes, takes away this stress, just like we have no chance to constantly check our own appearance when in face-to-face meetings. This is not to say that we are not constantly aware of, if not obsessed with, our own appearance in meetings with others. This was already obvious to Louis XIV, the Sun King, when he created the Hall of Mirrors in his royal palace in Versailles. By getting his nobles to focus on their own appearance in the mirrors, he distracted them from scheming and plotting against his rule.

With virtual mirroring we have the same concern. By creating a virtual mirror of our own communication behavior, and learning about how we are seen by others, we can greatly improve communication quality and business performance. However, the ultimate goal is not for me to shine, but to focus on the emotions of my conversation partners, on the effect my communication has on them, and on making sure that they feel fully respected and happy. Yet, there is a thin line between focusing on the counterpart and focusing on myself by making myself more attractive. There is a reason why people have a "Zoom shirt" ready to pull over their crumpled t-shirts and obsess over haircuts and facial wrinkles.

Research has repeatedly found that attractive people are more successful. *Being more attractive means forgetting about self.* It's hard to look your best on a selfie and it's much easier to look happy and relaxed when a friend is taking your picture, particularly if you are immersed in your activity and not aware that your picture is being taken. In our own research[7] we asked almost 200 university students in a survey about their advice and friendship networks at the beginning and the end of a course, and also had them rate the attractiveness of their classmates. Additionally, we asked them to rate the intelligence and creativity of the other students. While we found that students who were rated more intelligent and creative grew their advice network the fastest, the students seen as the most attractive acquired the most new friends over the course of the semester. In other research,[8] it was found that more attractive people are considered more able by employers and are more confident, which means increased wages, better social skills and they are more likely to get elected to public office and get called back to job interviews more often. Good looking CEOs bring better returns, attractive teachers teach better and attractive students get better grades and have more dating success.

Psychology gives us some straightforward advice on what we can do to be more attractive.[9] For a start, being nice makes you attractive, as does being authentic and open. Being an active listener, paying attention to others and only saying something when you have something to say is another way to increase attractiveness. Showing a positive attitude and looking your counterpart in the eyes with a friendly smile will also make you more popular. On the other hand, complaining is a recipe for chasing others away, as is being overly confident and cocky.

Being in flow means trying to get rid of mind-wandering, with the aim of "living in the moment," even making the self disappear. Self consists of memories. We tend to very selectively remember, trying to banish unpleasant recollections, while positive remembrances will be magnified. The goal is to be at peace with yourself, accepting the good and the bad memories of the past while living in the present. Coming back to Zoom fatigue, this means accepting how we look, not looking at our own picture in the Zoom window but looking at the faces of others. In this regard, Microsoft Teams is ahead of Zoom, in that it shows the picture of the owner of the camera in a small window, while the faces of the other participants are shown in much larger windows, so it is easier to focus on them. Zoom per default shows the speaker at the top in a large window, which unfortunately influences the speaker to focus on her or himself, and not the other participants. In this regard, Zoom still offers a virtual mirror which focuses on the self, not on how the self is interacting with others. In your own virtual mirror, try to focus on the others and forget yourself!

9.6   OUTSIDE: SEEK THE PAIN – CREATE POSITIVE STRESS

In the documentary movie "An Inconvenient Truth", former US vice president Al Gore talks about the dangers of global warming, showing each of us a virtual mirror of how our actions might be causing environmental change and global warming. Similarly, through virtual mirroring of individual communication patterns, everyone might be forced to face personal inconvenient truths. In the virtual mirror others will tell you through the "Other-Selfie" who you really are – even if you don't like it. Just like with global warming, we can either keep our unhealthy old ways until the world blows up in our face or face them head on and initiate corrective action. Virtual mirroring points out individual weaknesses; ideally, an individual seeks out the pain and accepts their deficiencies and converts them into strengths. Frequently the fastest way to reach a goal is also the most inconvenient one. Admitting inconvenient truths gets people out of their comfort zone and will force them to change. Oprah Winfrey showed the same willingness to face inconvenient truths when admitting to experiencing sexual abuse in her childhood on her show. This was at the same time extremely painful and liberating, and built bridges with her audience, as her humility and empathy made her more accessible to her viewers.

As has been mentioned before, frequently we are very bad judges of ourselves. Our friends do a much better job of assessing our personality. For example, as already discussed in Section 4.5, in a longitudinal survey of 600 adults tracking changes in personality over time, the researchers found that our friends are much better judges of our personalities than we are ourselves.[10] The researchers partially explained the higher accuracy of friends' personality assessment through the capability of aggregating assessments of multiple friends for an individual. This wisdom of our friends can be aggregated in even higher numbers through AI to predict for instance individual moral values based on the combined honest signals of large groups of people.

Figure 9.6 illustrates the difference of an employee in his self-rated moral values and the moral values predicted through the language he is using in email, as well as through his body movements with the Happimeter. For instance, we see that he thinks of himself as a fair person and not particularly concerned about purity and sanctity. The machine learning model tells another story, with a very high degree of purity and sanctity and a much lower fairness score than the self-assessment would suggest.

Emotions can also be tracked in video meetings through facial emotion recognition. By showing the aggregated emotions of participants in real time, the productivity of a meeting can be improved.

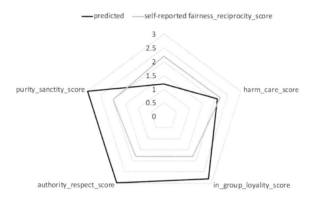

Figure 9.6   *Difference between self-rated moral values and moral values predicted automatically by machine learning*

Figure 9.7 illustrates an emotion-tracking system built by students in the COINs course that tries to encourage an "emotional rollercoaster." Using a similar system, and comparing the emotions shown in the faces during the meeting with perceived meeting outcome, we found that an "emotional roller-coaster" was correlated with more productive meetings.[11] Just showing happy faces was not enough for a productive meeting, it was much better to show a mix of happy, surprised and fearful faces. Having only neutral faces, on the other hand, was a predictor of unproductive meetings.

Besides the "emotional rollercoaster," another predictor of productive meetings is "turn taking," the more turns different people take and the more they alternate in speaking, the more productive the meeting will be. We first noticed that using sociometric badges[12] (see Section 14.1).

Figure 9.8 shows the web version of the meeting balancer, which demonstrates the turns between participants in a video conference. Showing these turns and indicating individuals when they talk too much or too little is highly efficient in democratizing speaking time and thus will increase the experience of meeting participants and the overall creative output of the meeting.

Figure 9.7   Measuring and mirroring emotions in video meetings

According to Mihaly Csikszentmihalyi, working in flow means being in positive stress or eustress. Working in a team in groupflow does not mean unimpeded, unlimited, unending happiness. Rather, as shown in earlier chapters (see Section 2.3), going through iterative phases of external stress and pain will lead to flow and happiness. Overcoming pain and uncertainty might in the end produce huge joy when the definitive product is finally here. Intrinsically motivated people, working in beeflow inspired by their cause, and not by money, power or glory, are more resilient towards adversity while working on their project than teams of ants or leeches, and are thus in a much better position to reach groupflow.

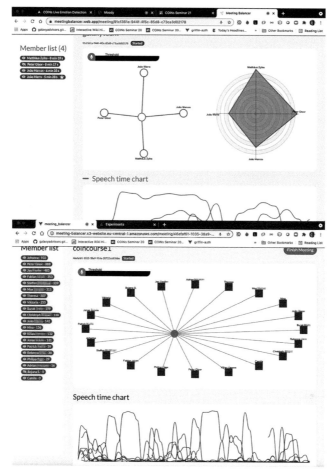

Figure 9.8   Meeting balancer measuring turn taking in video-conference meetings

NOTES

1. Schwitzgebel, E., Cokelet, B., & Singer, P. (2020). Do ethics classes influence student behavior? Case study: Teaching the ethics of eating meat. *Cognition*, 203, 104397.
2. Woolley, A. W., Chabris, C. F., Pentland, A., Hashmi, N., & Malone, T. W. (2010). Evidence for a collective intelligence factor in the performance of human groups. *Science*, 330(6004), 686–688.
3. Yang, Y., Wu, M., Vázquez-Guardado, A., Wegener, A. J., Grajales-Reyes, J. G., Deng, Y., … & Rogers, J. A. (2021). *Wireless Multilateral Devices for*

Optogenetic Studies of Individual and Social Behaviors. Nature Publishing Group, pp. 1–11.

4.   www.nytimes.com/2021/05/25/science/optogenetics-brain-social-behavior .html.

5.   www.nytimes.com/2021/05/17/health/coronavirus-broad-colorado-mesa-sabeti .html.

6.   www.cell.com/cell/fulltext/S0092-8674(20)31084-9.

7.   Colladon, A. F., Grippa, F., Battistoni, E., Gloor, P. A., & Bella, A. L. (2018). What makes you popular: Beauty, personality or intelligence? *International Journal of Entrepreneurship and Small Business*, 35(2), 162–186.

8.   www.businessinsider.com/beautiful-people-make-more-money-2014-11?r=US &IR=T#attractive-people-are-more-sought-after-as-romantic-partners-11.

9.   https://theartofsimple.net/10-ways-to-instantly-become-more-attractive/.

10.   Jackson, J. J., Connolly, J. J., Garrison, S. M., Leveille, M. M., & Connolly, S. L. (2015). Your friends know how long you will live: A 75-year study of peer-rated personality traits. *Psychological Science*, 26(3), 335–340.

11.   Rößler, J., Sun, J., & Gloor, P. (2021). Reducing videoconferencing fatigue through facial emotion recognition. *Future Internet*, 13(5), 126.

12.   Olguın, D. O., Gloor, P. A., & Pentland, A. S. (2009, September). Capturing individual and group behavior with wearable sensors. *Proceedings of the 2009 AAAI Spring Symposium on Human Behavior Modeling*, 9.

10. Steps to entanglement

What are practical and proven steps to create and nurture entanglement among team members? Creating entanglement is hard. In his classic book On Dialogue,[1] David Bohm describes the importance for a team to spend time together in the same room, "just" listening and talking to develop mutual understanding and harmony. Spending hours and hours – Bohm talks of days – together will help develop the shared vocabulary and the implicit contextual meaning of words which are essential for fruitful communication and mutual understanding. Team members will accept everybody's point of view equally and non-judgmentally, leading in the end to a fully entangled team. According to Bohm, the key is the willingness to listen, even if somebody totally disagrees with what the other person says, to just build a shared understanding and "agree to disagree."

When I joined Coopers & Lybrand, a predecessor firm of PwC, a long time ago as a young consultant, I was sent to consultant bootcamp, where I was taught the key consulting principle "Listen – think – consult – act!" This means that when meeting a prospective customer on a first engagement, do not brag to show how smart you are, but start by listening. Once you think you have understood what the customer is trying to say, think it through and compare it with what you already know, to position it in context. Then start consulting others (and Google), asking for advice on how they see the problem and how they would tackle it. Only then, after going through the previous three steps, "listen – think – consult," start speaking and acting. This is very different behavior compared to what I have seen from many super-smart, overconfident, cocky young consultants with freshly minted MBAs from top business schools. Later in my career, rising through the ranks of PwC and Deloitte and making partner at both organizations, this principle served me well. As a partner, the main job is selling engagements to customers. In my sales presentations with prospective customers, I realized that they did not want to hear how smart I was, but they wanted me to listen to their story, to understand what their problem was and then come up with the best solution. As a rule of thumb, I found that if the prospective customer did 80 to 90 percent of the talking, I had a very high chance of subsequently getting the engagement. This means that to get entangled with the customers, let them do the talking and listen to what they have to say. Good leaders always talk last, such that everybody else has a chance to contribute their opinion. It is all about listening and letting others do the talking!

10.1   SIX STEPS TO BECOME AN ENTANGLED TEAM MEMBER

Entanglement and groupflow have profound consequences for building high-performing teams with happy members. They influence team member selection, the teamwork process and interaction among team members. Based on hundreds of projects analyzing and creating COINs over the last 20 years with organizations ranging from Fortune 500 high-tech and financial firms to non-profit foundations, charities and open-source communities, I found six principles for the individual and three principles for the organization to support groupflow.

This section describes the six steps you, as an individual, can take to become a better and happier member of a better team.

10.1.1   Intrinsic Aligned Motivation

Be a bee! You need to find meaning in the teamwork you do. Only if the team members share *the same* vision and goals will they work together well. Ideally, they work in the team not because they are paid to do it, but because they deeply care for the task they are trying to accomplish. However, sharing the same vision, for instance #MakeAmericaGreatAgain, can be reached by very different means. Although they share the same goal, members of the Trump tribe see a totally different way for #MakeAmericaGreatAgain than members of the Bernie Sanders tribe. Thus, team members should all share similar values and morals – be members of the same tribe. For instance, combining somebody who craves power and authority with benevolent universalists will cause pain for both. Better if both either strive for self-enhancement or for self-transcendence. For instance, combining "up or out" McKinsey consultants and "value-generating" Goldman Sachs bankers with social workers passion-ate about reducing infant mortality and Amnesty International coordinators caring about asylum seekers will not work well. Similarly, authority-seeking team members will not collaborate well with others who prioritize fairness and caring over ingroup loyalty and tradition – just look at "red state" America and "blue state" America living side by side in different alternative realities. When creating a new COIN in my own work I make it a point not to mention compen-sation in the beginning, as I never want to recruit team members that are just in it for the money. Rather I found that the best work is done by volunteers, who are passionate about the task and don't care about making as much money as possible. If the work is done well, rewards will come by themselves.

10.1.2   Diversity – Mediated by Homophily

Ours and research by others has shown that team members with diverse backgrounds will lead to better and more creative results, as team members will complement each other's strengths and weaknesses. However, there can also be too much of a good thing, a deeply religious factory worker from the Midwest might not speak the same language as an Ivy League-educated lawyer. The same might be true for the Southern Korean waiter in the same team as a South African rugby player. While some diversity in personality characteristics between team members has been shown to be good, for instance having extroverts and introverts in the same team, it is preferable to mediate diversity with a shared background, for instance having two US Midwest factory workers in the same team, with one having a South African friend and the other having a South Korean friend. The two factory workers will speak the same US Midwest English but will bring diverse experiences from the interaction with their friends from different cultures.

10.1.3   Turn Taking – One Queen Bee Alone Dies

In our research we found that taking turns in leadership is essential for the success of creative teams. A leader who is not able to delegate a task to whoever is best qualified to do it will burn out very quickly. Good leaders are the best in their team, great leaders recruit others to their team who are better than them. Great leaders also empower more junior team members and give them recognition and responsibility. Figure 10.1 shows the meeting balancer app which is part of the Social Compass and Happimeter smartphone app. It illustrates the turn taking among participants in our team meeting, showing the speaking activity of team members in two subsequent meetings. In the first meeting on November 5, 2020, I am dominating the discussion, as shown on the left-hand side by the large square on the right and the red ball near me showing that I hijacked most of the meeting time. This is also clear in my speaking activity, as shown by the soaring red line in the middle-left of the picture. The second meeting on November 12, 2020, on the right-hand side of Figure 10.1, shows the positive effect of virtual mirroring on more efficient turn taking. Now all members take even turns, my speaking activity is very low and the other team members are talking much more. This is also shown in the picture on the very right, showing that my speaking activity is now very low while the others are contributing much more.

Figure 10.1   Turn taking in meetings: mirroring speaking time and turns leads to more even distribution of speaking time

10.1.4   Selective Entanglement

In our research we found that the right type of entanglement is essential for successful teamwork. There can also be too much of a good thing. A huge organization which is too far entangled will be stifling and choke off all creativity. It is better to have smaller, highly entangled teams – COINs – connected by weaker organizational entanglement. In a closely knit team, members do not just collaborate on the task of the team but also care, respect and know about each other as human beings. They become more like an extended family than a team focused solely on the efficient execution of the tasks allocated by management. This means being kind to each other, talking about more than work when being together and knowing the personal likes and dislikes of other team members. For instance, a good friend of mine remembers the preferred pastries of his work colleagues, and whenever he is expecting them for an official meeting he makes sure to pass by the local bakery and buy some to have them ready for the meeting.

10.1.5   Acknowledge the Virtual Mirror

A team member needs to be willing to look in the virtual mirror and accept inconvenient truths. In our research, we found that just the willingness to accept a virtual mirror was a predictor of future success. For example, in a project measuring interaction between employees using sociometric badges (see Section 14.1) there were two group managers who did not believe in our project and asked to be equipped with fake badges which did not give them any results. Wearing the fake badges would not show their colleagues that they were not participating in our project. While of course we did not tell anything to their supervisor, about half a year after our project was finished, both managers were relieved of their management function and released from their jobs to basically await retirement (this was a socially minded enterprise where long-term employees were kept until retirement). "Acknowledging the virtual mirror" means accepting constructive criticism from others. It also means being willing to improve one's own ways of doing things if there is a better way, instead of sticking to the old ways just because of tradition and because "it has always been like that."

10.1.6　Increase Emotional Awareness

Team members should become aware of their own emotions. This is non-trivial; while we think of ourselves as rational creatures, we are driven by emotions. We think we know our emotions; the truth is that we mentally adjust our emotional interpretation through our personal value system. Using facial emotion recognition in Zoom meetings, we have found that becoming aware of one's true emotions will make the meetings more productive for all participants. Willingness to frighten and shock, providing an emotional rollercoaster, will make meeting participants more engaged and improve meeting outcomes. Additionally, we should also be aware that aspiring to a state of constant happiness for all team members is not good for the team; in order to reach the flow state and deliver superior results, it is better to operate in the team by the "no pain, no gain" principle. Therefore, the team and its members need to be prepared to live in the emotional rollercoaster where joy and happiness take turns with fear, anger, sadness, disgust and surprise. There will be times of joy and happiness, but there will also be times of stress. Using a tool such as the Social Compass will show the individual their emotions at any point in time and support them to get in flow. It will alert them of unnecessary negative emotions and stress and help them to become better collaborators.

10.2　THREE STEPS FOR BUILDING ENTANGLED ORGANIZATIONS

Besides guiding the behavior of the individual, creating and nurturing entanglement for groupflow also profoundly impacts the management of organizations. The previous section showed six steps that everyone can take to be a better team member. This section introduces three guidelines essential for leaders and managers to improve teamwork and collaboration in their organization.

10.2.1 Weakly Connected COINs – Strong Ties within Teams, Weak Ties across Teams

Strong ties build trust and happiness, while weak ties help in information sharing and knowing about opportunities and resources. The goal should be to create high-functioning teams – highly connected internally – whose members work in entanglement and groupflow, while interacting on an as-needs basis with members from other teams. The best corporate networks have highly entangled "islands" connected by comparatively weaker ties between the islands. COIN theory supported by Dunbar's number sets an upper limit of about 150 people for each island, although depending on the task they might also be much smaller. Anthropologist Robin Dunbar posits that since ancestral times our brains have developed to keep track of the personal strengths, weaknesses and preferences of at most 150 other people, as illustrated by the average size of native tribes, military companies and church parishes. The aim of larger organizations should be to build an "archipelago" with "islands of trust." Each island is a COIN of close collaborators. The inhabitants of each island draw satisfaction and happiness from interacting with each other. Occasionally they board their canoes to paddle to another island when there is a need for additional information and resources from outside their core team. Figure 10.2 shows the email communication network of the 2020 COINs seminar illustrating the archipelago made up of different islands. Each student is a node; I am represented by the labeled large node in the center of the network. The different teams – forming the islands – are clearly visible, the

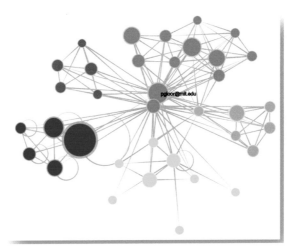

Figure 10.2   Team network of the COINs course

size of a node shows the influence of team members based on how much novel words they inject into the team discussion (see Chapter 17). The purple node right beside me is a teaching assistant helping teach the course; he and I are the connectors in the archipelago of connected teams. However, we are not the most influential team members – this role is held by students in the different teams, as shown for instance by the large blue node on the lower left.

10.2.2   Creating Synchronicity

Entanglement on the organizational level can be measured through synchronicity of interaction. Just like the heart sets the rhythm for the human body, in an entangled organization communication happens synchronously, with informal and formal leaders setting the pulse. This entanglement can for example be measured through the rhythm of email exchanges, or the similarity of changes in network structure dynamics. The left chart in Figure 10.3 shows the email activity of the students participating in the 2020 COINs seminar. It illustrates the rhythm of the COINs course. Synchronization and entanglement come from the initially weekly, later bi-weekly meetings, with a peak of email activity before each meeting. The right side in the chart shows my entanglement with my colleagues in my team based on the email activity of my colleagues in their message exchange with me. Whenever the two lines representing one of my colleagues and I are getting close, we exchange emails more synchronously and at higher frequency (see Chapter 18).

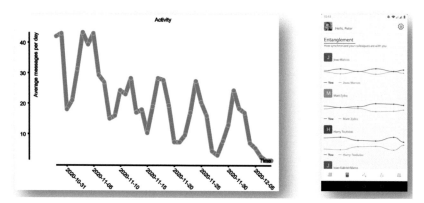

Figure 10.3   Entangled activity pattern of the COINs course (left) and in my research group (right)

10.2.3   Know the Tribes in Your Organization

An organization will only work well if its members share the same value system. In this sense an organization is a tribe, consisting of different clans with each clan having its own sacred symbols and values. Figure 10.4 shows again the email network of the 2020 COINs course participants with the connections drawn by the emails exchanged among students and teachers. The nodes are colored by the tribes computed from the words each student or teacher used in their email. As the chart shows, there are no "fatherlander" participants in the course, and students in the same team share mostly the same values. Most team members are "treehuggers" while the team on the lower left with the nodes shown in green is made up of "nerds." The peripheral blue nodes did not use enough words and can thus not be assigned to a tribe. This picture illustrates that well-working teams are members of the same tribes sharing the same values.

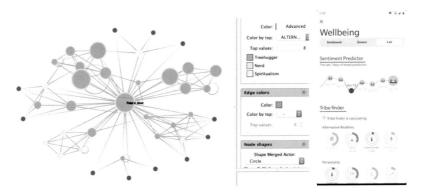

Figure 10.4   Tribal structure of the students in the COINs course (left) and my personal tribes in the Social Compass (right)

The screenshot of the Social Compass on the right of Figure 10.4 shows my personal tribes for the last seven days, for example showing that I am mostly spiritual and nerdish up to April 16, 2021. The Social Compass also displays the tribes of my communication partners, based on the emails that other people send to me. The Social Compass will calculate their tribes for the last seven days based on the words in their emails to me. Knowing the personality characteristics and personal values of my communication partners will greatly assist me in better communicating with them. Note that this calculation of their tribes happens exclusively on my smartphone, using the emails they have sent me.

To resume, an entangled organization consists of an archipelago of COINs, COIN members are connected by strong ties and the different COINs are linked by weaker ties. The COINs and the entire organization interact synchronized with a shared heartbeat. COIN participants are members of the same tribes, sharing personality, moral values and attitudes to risk.

How can these things be measured? Part II of this book introduces an AI-based method implemented as a set of tools, combining social network analysis with emotion recognition through analyzing text and body language. The toolset uses communication archives such as email and Slack, but also facial and voice emotion recognition in direct one-to-one interaction to construct a virtual mirror of the communication behaviors of the involved individuals.

NOTE

1.   Bohm, D., & Nichol, L. (2013). *On Dialogue*. Routledge.

PART II

Measuring groupflow

11. AI makes emotions measurable by aggregating the wisdom of the crowd

Computers and the internet empower us to measure interhuman interaction on a high level of granularity and detail. Sensors combined with AI give us the capability to constantly analyze and interpret communication. In Part II of this book, we will learn how to leverage the most recent technological advances of the internet – wearable technology, cloud computing and AI – to measure happiness, well-being, workplace satisfaction and stress, and mirror back these measurements to the individual. This will lead to more connected, collectively aware, entangled team members, and thus to teams collaborating in groupflow.

The recent progress in AI allows users to successfully accomplish typically human tasks of common-sense pattern recognition that were impossible for humans until now, such as recognizing human faces and writing newspaper articles. While the "wisdom of crowds" has been described and tested many times, AI also combines the limited intelligence of isolated individuals to empower these isolated individuals to accomplish tasks which would be impossible for the individual to achieve in isolation. For instance, there is a test called "reading the mind in the eye"[1] that tests EQ by showing only the eyes of a face and asking the reader to correctly identify the emotions of the person belonging to the face. This is one of the tests to identify autistic people, it has also been shown that men perform much worse in this test than women. When I took the test, I got about 50 percent of the faces wrong. Using facial image recognition, AI can get up to 90 percent accuracy recognizing the emotion of a face. This is done by combining the wisdom of the crowd: a machine-learning system is trained with thousands of face pictures which previously have been labeled by different people with the emotion that the individual person doing the labeling thinks she sees in the face. Thus, even if an individual is as bad as I am at recognizing the correct emotions of others from looking at their eyes, combining the collective EQ of many people allows the AI system to make a 90 percent accurate prediction. It gives the "emotionally challenged" individual a tool for accurately recognizing the mood of the person the individual is talking to. For instance, wearing smartglasses, a user can apply this automated face emotion recognition to look at other people's faces, and have the computer tell the wearer of the smartglasses the emotions of the people the wearer is looking at, thus overcoming a potential deficiency in reading the mind in the eyes.

Figure 11.1 shows the view from the smartphone camera of an app that we built that runs on an Android phone in combination with the Vuzix smartglasses. It captures the face of the person that the wearer of the glasses is looking at – in this case I am looking at myself, while wearing the Vuzix glasses running our software. The picture on the smartphone shows to the wearer the emotions of the person the wearer is looking at. In this example I get confirmation that I am showing a happy face.

Figure 11.1   Emotion recognition with Vuzix smartglasses

On the technical level, we combine social network analysis, online social media tracking, machine learning and AI to build a social map of the self and its environment as the foundation for measuring and improving entanglement in groups and between two individuals. Our approach tells you where you are on the journey of finding yourself, knowing who you really are and how to better navigate your social landscape for a happier future. Our approach includes the calculation of human emotions from facial expression recognition and body language through sensors. The same methods are applied to analyzing global networks such as Twitter or Reddit to find entangled swarms of Trump followers and global warming activists. In organizational networks constructed from communication archives such as email, entanglement in teams, departments, branch offices and divisions of companies and other organizations can be measured. In direct interpersonal interaction among two individuals and in small teams, their degree of entanglement can be tracked. Our approach is based on social network analysis, a statistical method based on graph theory to compute the structural properties of networks and compare them with the business task that the members of the network are working on. In addition, we also use Natural Language Processing to analyze the content of network interactions, such as the content of tweets, emails and Skype, Teams or Slack messages. Using image and sound processing we calculate emotions from facial expressions and from voice as well as from body movement captured by the sensors of a smartwatch. All of these metrics extracted from communication archives are fed into a time series analysis of changes over time. Using these values as inputs for machine learning will predict the future behavior of network nodes – individuals and groups – based on their statistical properties. Analyzing online social media using this method will foresee tomorrow's mood regarding Donald Trump,[2] the spread of Covid-19 through online social media[3] and what will be the most popular news story tomorrow.[4] Creating online virtual tribes shows customer demographics based on their online expressions. Examining corporate email allows a company to create a "weather forecast" of tomorrow's customer and employee and supplier satisfaction. Tracking body signals of individuals through smartwatches and face and voice emotion recognition with cameras and microphones will calculate individual and team happiness and meeting satisfaction.

11.1 MEASURING INTERACTIONS

An individual can only get in groupflow in the company of others. While groupflow most easily is reached in face-to-face interactive collaboration, it can also happen virtually. An example is a virtual performance of 58 children of the One Voice Children's Choir performing together on Zoom the song "Memories" by Maroon 5.[5] This is a perfect showcase of a team reaching the flow state together while being physically apart. The degree of entanglement can be measured as direct synchronous interaction between humans such as between the children in the One Voice Children's Choir, who influence each other instantaneously through voice and body gestures shown on the webcam to get into flow. We can also measure asynchronous interaction between participants such as two teams of TikTok creators responding to each other's challenges by recording similar dance moves to the same song, for example the different videos produced reacting to the "Blinding Lights Dance Challenge."[6]

Besides measuring interactions through body gestures, we can also measure interaction through words. You have probably been entangled many times on WhatsApp, Signal, Telegram or WeChat with your loved ones in a quick dialog exchanging short messages and smileys and other emojis in minutes or seconds. The same, at a slower pace, can also happen by email, where the speed of response and the intensity of turn-taking is an indicator of the degree of entanglement between two people exchanging emails. It also can happen globally, exchanging messages for instance on Twitter or Reddit, be it about #BlackLivesMatter, #MeToo, #MakeAmericaGreatAgain or about GameStop on the WallStreetBets subreddit.

How can this interaction be measured formally and precisely? Measuring human communication dynamics can be done on the individual, the organizational and the global levels. Figure 11.2 illustrates the methods and tools described in this book to measure interaction among humans.

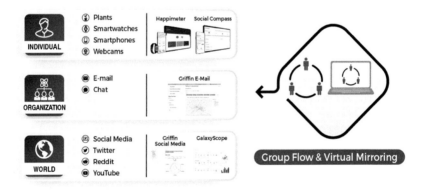

Figure 11.2   Individual, organizational and global ways of measuring social interaction

On the individual level, we can measure interaction through body signals captured by smartwatches, facial expressions captured by webcams and location tracking and interaction measured by smartphones. We also can use plants as biosensors to capture human emotions and interactions (see Section 20.1). On the organizational level we can use email archives and archives of chat interactions such as Slack or Microsoft Teams. On the global level, Twitter is most prominently used to measure interaction, while other online social media tools providing communication data are YouTube comments and Reddit. Unfortunately, Facebook, which would be a great source of social network information, is closed to automatic computer-based analysis thus it cannot be easily analyzed.

The process to building an entangled organization starts with knowing oneself. While we all think we know who we are, in reality there is a huge mismatch between the person I think I am and the person others see in me. I might think I am a fair, considerate, gregarious, popular individual. However, when asking others, if they are honest, they might tell me a very different story, of experiencing me as a biased, egoistic, disliked or isolated individual. However, through our "honest signals" we are telling others who we are without saying it explicitly: how you move your body and your use of words will give you and others deep insights into your personality. The words you use in emails and other online communication tools such as Twitter, WhatsApp, Slack or WeChat will identify your emotions, personality characteristics, ethical values, attitudes towards risk and to what virtual tribes you belong.

The same information can also be found from the way you move your body. This can be measured easily and non-obtrusively in a privacy-respecting way either with the body sensors of a smartwatch or through facial emotion recognition with a webcam, smartphone camera and smartglasses. We have built a set of tools based on AI, using millions of observations of people to train our software. We have collected anonymized data records of people communicating with others over the internet, communicating within large organizations and in face-to-face interaction, analyzing Twitter archives, email logs and the sensors of smartwatches and sociometric sensors. These communication logs have been compared with personality characteristics, ethical values and understanding of fairness assessed with different personality tests such as the FFI, an ethical and personal values survey (the Schwartz value survey) and a fairness survey (the moral foundations test) (see Chapter 5).

There are two types of honest signals:

1. *Actionable*, when I learn about them, I can change my behavior. For instance, how quickly *I* respond to others, and what words I use when communicating with them.
2. *Non-actionable*, simply informing me what others think about me. For instance, how quickly *others* respond to me, and what words they use when communicating with me. I can only influence the behavior of others indirectly by changing my own behavior.

Figure 11.3 shows the three structural ways of measuring human interactions. We can look at the networking structure of how people connect, we can look at the emotions the people are showing and experiencing while interacting and we can look at the content of what they say in their interactions.

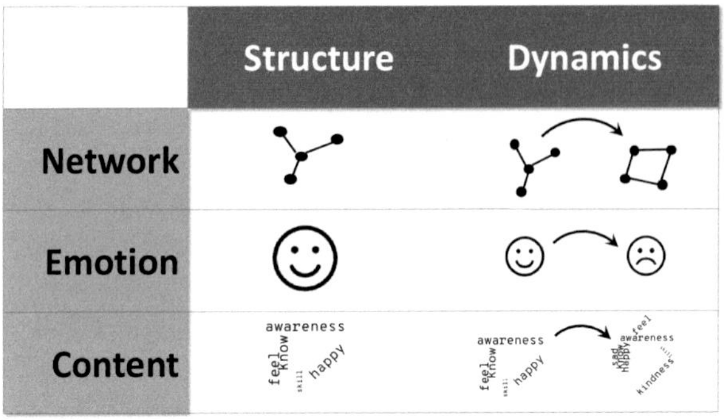

Figure 11.3   Three dimensions of measuring interactions

Measuring *network structure* will calculate the influence of people based on the structure of their personal network, tracked through communication archives such as email, Twitter and face-to-face interaction records from smartphones and other sensors. *Networking dynamics* will measure how the interaction structure changes over time, for instance measuring if somebody becomes less central over time, or the speed with which others respond to an individual.

Measuring *emotions* of an individual in a particular context will give insights about the personality, ethical values and risk attitudes of the individual. These emotions can be tracked through facial expressions, body posture, body signals like heart rate or arm movement and also through the emotions expressed in written language used in communication with others. *Changes in emotion* can be used to measure outcomes of an interaction. For instance, in class presentations, theater performances and music concerts, when analyzing the emotions of the audience, we found that presentations that produced an emotional rollercoaster of surprise, happiness, disgust, fear and anger were rated higher by the audience in the end than a presentation that produced a constantly happy facial expression among the listeners.

Measuring *content* will show the creativity of the people exchanging the content. A group that uses highly specific words deviating from the rest of the organization is more creative. Looking at the *dynamics of how novel words spread* through the group will also pinpoint the most creative and influential group members. The more a new word or concept is being picked up by others, and the faster it spreads, the more creative and influential the creator of the new concept is.

NOTES

1. http://socialintelligence.labinthewild.org/mite/.
2. Guo, T., Jelinewski, T., Mittermeier, G., & Veihelmann, T. (2019). Predicting the emotions and topics of Donald J. Trump based on Twitter data. Seminar Paper in 2019/20 COINs Seminar, www.dropbox.com/s/4olcg8qorwsvjzi/COINs1920 _FinalPaper_Group2_final.pdf?dl=0.
3. Sun, J., & Gloor, P. A. (2021). Assessing the predictive power of online social media to analyze Covid-19 outbreaks in the 50 US states, www.preprints.org/ manuscript/202106.0105/download/final_file.
4. Sun, J., & Gloor, P. (2020). Towards re-inventing psychohistory: Predicting the popularity of tomorrow's news from yesterday's Twitter and news feeds. *Journal of Systems Science and Systems Engineering*, 1–20.
5. www.youtube.com/watch?v=XB6yjGVuzVo.
6. www.buzzfeednews.com/article/laurenstrapagiel/blinding-lights-tiktok-dance -challenge-parents.

12. AI-based interaction analysis between humans (and other living creatures)

The analysis process to predict human behavior from communication logs through machine learning, natural language processing (NLP) and social network analysis follows four steps. These four steps are introduced in this section. We will not discuss general principles of machine learning, NLP and social network analysis, as there are many excellent books about these topics. Rather, this section will outline how to use these techniques for predicting human behavior by analyzing archives of traces of human-to-human and human-to-other living creatures interaction such as email or GPS sensor data. The aim is to find general patterns of human behavior indicative of future actions. Learning about these patterns, and then analyzing past behavior and comparing it with desirable behavior – "the best against the rest" – will change future behavior towards better performance and happiness.

The general process consists of four steps (Figure 12.1):

1. Collecting the data from body sensors and communication archives. This means for example tracking heart-rate values, accelerometer values of a smartwatch or collecting the mailbox of a person.
2. Converting the data into features or variables suitable for machine learning. This means for example converting the $x/y/z$ coordinates of an accelerometer into an energy vector, or calculating network centrality measures of the emails of all people in a mailbox.
3. Determining the "ground truth" of a training sample, for example collecting FFI personality characteristics of a large enough sample of people through surveys, or the human resources performance ratings for employees where high-performing networking behavior should be identified. Or labeling a subset of email messages manually by assigning an emotion rating to each message. A sample suitable for machine learning should consist of at least 100 cases, better many more, and the values should be evenly distributed.
4. Feeding the features which have been calculated in step 2 into a machine-learning system such as Rapidminer, Knime or a Python framework such as scikit-learn, predicting the dependent or target variable from step 3 using the data from step 2 to build a machine-learning model.

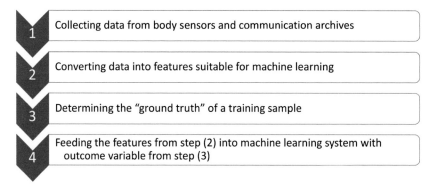

Figure 12.1   Four-step process to predict future behavior from
communication logs

Now the four steps will be discussed in more detail.

12.1   DATA COLLECTION

The first step consists of collecting the interaction data. The body response to direct interpersonal interaction can for example be tracked through brainwaves, heartrate, body movement, voice pattern and facial expression. Brainwaves can be measured with EEG sensors from companies such as Muse, Emotiv and OpenBCI. In our experiments we used the Muse headband to measure Alpha waves in the frequency range of 7.5–12.5 Hz, which occurs during wakeful relaxation with closed eyes, and Beta waves ranging from 12.5 and 30 Hz indicative of normal waking consciousness. However, when comparing Alpha time series of different users of Muse at the same event, we found little correlation among the different users,[1] indicating that the measurements were not very accurate. Also, the Muse software development kit is not supported anymore, therefore Emotiv Epoc or Emotiv Insight might be a better option. In a later experiment we used Emotiv Insight to record the brainwaves while listening to a story read in different emotional tones, where we found that the brainwaves showed different patterns based on the emotions conveyed by the reader of the story. Emotiv Insight is quite fickle to use, as the electrodes are hard to position on the head of the wearer to collect a clear signal, and it can easily lose connectivity when the wearer moves their head.

To measure body movement, smartwatches provide built-in sensors such as an accelerometer, heartrate sensor, blood pressure sensor, microphone and light sensors. A smartphone will also include an accelerometer, microphone and webcam, however, the drawback is that the smartphone is not worn on the body most of the time, so it can only collect environmental variables such as GPS coordinates through the location sensor and movement when carried by the owner. Alternatively, body movement as well as facial expressions can be tracked through image recognition with webcams. As webcams are part of each laptop and smartphone, this is basically free technology, however, the challenge will be to first recognize the person, and then to calculate the features such as facial expression and body posture from the raw picture stream, particularly if there is more than one person in the room. Voice also delivers input to calculate emotions and microphones are readily available in smartphones, webcams and laptops. However, it is even more difficult than for video to assign a voice recording to the right person if there is more than one person in the room.

In our most recent research, we discovered that plants respond to human movement through electrical signals and leaf movement. This means that either image recognition to track leaf movement or highly sensitive electric current measurement devices such as the Backyard Brains plant SpikerBox can be used to measure the response of plants like Mimosa Pudica and Codariocalyx Motorius to humans (see Section 20.1).

Electronic communication archives such as email and Twitter provide convenient records of interhuman interaction. To construct social networks, communication records need a source or sender and a target or receiver, plus a timestamp indicating when the interaction happened. Senders and receivers can be Twitter users, email users, Reddit users, etc. As soon as there is content, such as the email body or a tweet, it will be possible to compute input features for machine learning using NLP.

12.2   CONVERTING RAW COMMUNICATION DATA TO DISCRETE MATHEMATICAL VALUES

The communication archives need to be converted into variables suitable as input for statistics and machine learning. These variables can be social network analysis metrics such as degree, betweenness centrality (see Chapter 13) or other signals extracted from content and body language. They can be single variables attached to an individual, such as the network position, for example the betweenness centrality of an individual in the network. They can also be variables computed from time series, for example the total number of oscillations in betweenness centrality in a time interval. Finally, they can also be time series attached to an individual, for example the betweenness value of the individual calculated for each day's email network.

The same is true for analyzing content, where word vectors can be calculated for instance through term frequency/inverse document frequency. This measures the frequency of a word within a document such as an email message, comparing it to the frequency of the word within the entire document collection (e.g., the entire email archive). For more sophisticated analyses, word embeddings, for example using word2vec, can be calculated that measure the probability distributions of n-grams in large document collections. N-grams are sequences of words, starting with the unigram representing single words, bigrams represent two words in sequence, trigrams representing three words in sequence, etc. This approach can be used to calculate word embeddings for the tribes of Tribefinder (see Chapter 19).

To convert electrical signals to time series, for instance from sound files, or from brainwave scans, or measuring the action potential of plants with the plant SpikerBox, various approaches can be used. The simplest method is to calculate average values per time interval, for example one value per second. Another option is to calculate the Euclidean distance between two time series to measure their similarity. A more differentiated approach is to compute Mel Frequency Cepstrum Coefficients by doing a Fourier transformation, mapping the spectrum to the mel scale of evenly distanced pitches and then doing a discrete cosine transformation, which will give a discrete value for each mel. This means that the sound wave or electrical signal is transformed into a series of discrete values per time unit.

12.3   OBTAINING "GROUND TRUTH" FOR HUMAN CHARACTERISTICS

To predict "soft" human characteristics such as emotions, morals, ethics, tribal affiliations, personality, risk-taking attitude, performance, stress and burnout, "ground truth" needs to be established. This is the "true" value as personally assessed by a human being, not the AI machine-learning system. Mathematically speaking, it is the "outcome" or "dependent" variable which will be predicted by the machine-learning system. For example, if the machine-learning system is predicting customer satisfaction based on the speed of answering emails of the customer, ground truth is the customer satisfaction directly reported by the customer. When measuring emotions through facial expression, ground truth is the emotion felt and reported by the user.

For personality characteristics, OCEAN ground truth can for example be measured with the FFI survey. Ground truth of ethics and morals can be measured with the Schwartz moral values survey and attitudes to risk with the DOSPERT survey (see Chapter 5). Ground truth for stress, burnout and emotions such as joy, happiness and sadness can be measured through experience-based sampling, by asking an individual to wear a smartwatch and querying the individual to enter these variables at random times by vibrating the smartwatch. Sometimes, ground truth can also be established through unsupervised learning, for example by training Tribefinder with the Twitter streams of all members of Congress to define a tribal embedding that contains the language of politicians. For "honest signals" computed from email analysis of the employees of a company, ground truth can be taken from business metrics such as the sales numbers of the company, or satisfaction surveys of the employees or the customers of the company. The later chapters in this part of the book will take you step by step through the process of how to set up such ground truth collection systems.

12.4   MACHINE LEARNING AND TIME SERIES ANALYSIS

Once independent variables, either as discrete values or as time series, are established (see Section 12.2), and dependent variables are available as ground truth (see Section 12.3), a machine-learning system can be built. Depending on the nature of the data, different machine-learning algorithms are most suitable. For discrete values such as actor-level betweenness values, machine-learning algorithms such as Bayesian classifiers, decision trees, random forests and support vector machines work well. Such a model can be used for example to predict customer satisfaction based on "honest signals" calculated from email for each employee of a company. For NLP, recurrent neural networks such as long short-term memory are well suited as they can handle word order in sentences. This is also well suited for time series analysis, for example predicting tomorrow's stock price based on a time series of the last seven days of the Twitter activity of the stock. Convolutional neural networks are multilayer neural networks that are well suited for recognizing images. They are thus predominantly used for analyzing emotions from facial expressions and body posture, be it of humans or animals. In the subsequent chapters we will look at all these use cases in more detail.

12.5   RESPECTING INDIVIDUAL PRIVACY IS KEY

> Better safe than sorry! (English proverb)

When I left industry and came back to MIT nearly 20 years ago to study social networks, my late mentor MIT professor Thomas J. Allen, who had been examining social networks for over 40 years, taught me two lessons: first, don't trust surveys, and second, never disclose the name of an individual employee in the network to management. Tom had been studying networks of engineers[2] and researchers at large firms well before social network analysis as a discipline emerged, drawing complex network maps by hand and authoring a seminal work in this area, *Managing the Flow of Technology*. He had collected all his networks through surveys, asking his users questions such as "Whom are you asking for advice?" or "How satisfied are you with your workplace?" He found that people forget very quickly, and that a network is only valid for the day when the question is asked. Already on the next day everything might have changed: the organizational structure, the office layout, the weather and the mood of the person being asked. He also taught me to use very short surveys, ideally not more than three to five questions, otherwise people will not answer them, particularly if they are asked to answer them repeatedly.

The second lesson, about respecting individual privacy, is even more important. Tom told me that in his 40-plus years of doing social network analysis he had never given any information about individual employees to management. If management insisted on getting individually recognizable networking information about a particular employee, Tom would refuse to do the project at their site. Tom was proud to tell me that he had never had any problem with his network research in his entire career while pursuing that approach. Only once did he break his own rule, and then by his own initiative to the advantage of both the company and the affected employee, when he noticed that management was about to fire the employee who – according to Tom's network analysis – was the key connector and knowledge expert to whom all other employees went for advice. This employee just was not high enough in the hierarchy and was too modest to be on the radar screen of management. Only Tom's network analysis had brought his invaluable contribution to the company to light.

In my own work I experienced this principle the hard way in my very first email social network analysis project. I was proposing an email network analysis to a large high-tech company, however, I had not built in safeguards regarding individual privacy. I was stopped cold in my tracks when presenting the project to the employees who were supposed to participate. I had previously introduced the project to management, who loved the idea. When I presented my slides to the employees, they told me that they would sabotage the project, as they did not trust their company to not use these insights for employee layoffs and demotions. The project was subsequently canceled on the spot.

In a project about ten years ago at a large teaching hospital, I applied Tom's privacy principle to the advantage of the participants. We were studying the communication among patients, nurses and anesthesiologists in the Post Anesthesia Care Unit of the hospital.[3] This was a beehive of over 20 patients waking up simultaneously from serious surgery, cared for by over 20 medical staff at any point in time. We promised participants absolute anonymity, however, each individual participant could get an early version of their virtual mirror, a chart of their social network interaction, on paper in a sealed envelope. We measured interaction between medical staff and patients using sociometric badges worn by the nurses and placed on the beds of the patients. We found that the more the nurses communicated with the patients, the faster and with fewer complications the patients would wake up. We also found that some doctors were surprisingly peripheral in this interaction network. When we presented the results to the nurses they loved it, and used their individual communication networks and insights for their annual performance reviews.

To reiterate, it is essential to treat all the data that are collected with the utmost confidentiality. The basic principle is to remove personally identifiable information in all interaction with management, and only present information about an individual to the affected individual with no way for management to eavesdrop. The manager and any other outside users will only get to see aggregated information about a team, department, business unit, etc. with no option to track down an affected individual. This means anonymizing all email, sensor and picture data and de-identifying it, storing the personal identifier and the data separately. Similarly, for instance when computing facial emotions, only the emotions should be stored, not the facial pictures, and these also should be de-identified. When calculating network variables from email, only the de-identified networking and content variables such as degree and betweenness centrality, and emotionality, tribes, moral values and risk attributes should be stored, but not the content.

I have been living by this principle since my big blunder in my very first (canceled) project, and it has served me well.

NOTES

1.   Przegalinska, A., Ciechanowski, L., Magnuski, M., & Gloor, P. (2018). Muse headband: Measuring tool or a collaborative gadget? Collaborative Innovation Networks Conference of Digital Transformation of Collaboration. Springer, pp. 93–101.
2.   https://en.wikipedia.org/wiki/Allen_curve.
3.   Olguın, D. O., Gloor, P. A., & Pentland, A. S. (2009, September). Capturing individual and group behavior with wearable sensors. *Proceedings of the 2009 AAAI Spring Symposium on Human Behavior Modeling*, 9.

13. Measuring social network structure

Other people are the greatest source of pleasure, and they are the main cause of misery. Only by connecting with others in meaningful ways in social networks are we sentient productive creatures. Skillfully navigating social networks is the key ingredient for success and happiness. "Social network analysis" or SNA is the science that makes "networking" measurable. SNA tracks relations between different people through the structure of their network. SNA applies graph theory to determine the strength of interactions between individuals. The more somebody connects groups of otherwise unconnected people, the more social capital this person has. The strength of these interactions between people has been traditionally measured through surveys, asking an individual questions such as "Name all the people to whom you went for advice last month" to generate a list of this individual's interactions in the last month. However, this way of data collection is prone to bias, as people might not remember who they asked. Human memories are short and skewed towards the most recent past. Therefore, using archives of electronic communication offers a more robust way of collecting these interaction records between individuals. Our team at MIT has been at the forefront of using email and other communication archives to analyze social networks for the last 20 years.

SNA applies graph theory and measures communication in the network by analyzing the structure of the network. Key network metrics are degree centrality and betweenness centrality. The degree centrality of a person is the number of direct contacts a person has, for example by exchanging email with others. The betweenness centrality of a person measures how much information flows through the person, in other words, how much the person is on all the shortest paths through the network. The more somebody is a gatekeeper connecting disparate communities, the higher her betweenness centrality.

Figure 13.1 illustrates the difference between degree centrality and betweenness centrality. It shows an email communication network of 39 students in my course working in seven teams, collaborating on seven different projects. Each network node is a student and each connecting line is at least one email exchanged between the two students. The shorter the connecting line and the closer two students are together, the more emails the two students have exchanged. In the network visualization on the right, the nodes representing the students are sized by degree centrality, and in the picture on the left, by betweenness centrality. We see that Mary and Max have the highest degree centrality, each exchanging emails with seven other students. However, Mary's betweenness centrality is much higher than Max's as she is the gatekeeper of the network, connecting to all the other teams, while Max is central only for his own team, with links to just two students outside his team. Compare this to Beth, who only connects with one person outside of her team, Joe. Her degree centrality is five, as she connects to her four teammates plus Joe. Beth's betweenness is higher than Max's, however, as she is the exclusive gatekeeper for her team members to the other teams through Joe, while in Max's team there are two other connectors to the other teams.

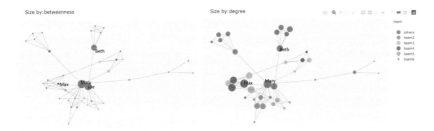

Figure 13.1   The difference between betweenness and degree centrality in a network

A second useful metric is a contribution index, which measures how active as a sender of emails and other messages somebody is. Figure 13.2 illustrates the contribution index of the same group of 39 students as shown in Figure 13.1.

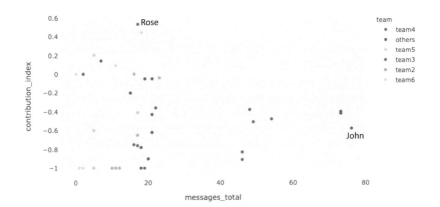

Figure 13.2   Example of a contribution index

In Figure 13.2, the x-axis shows the numbers of messages a student exchanged, i.e., sent and received, while the y-axis shows the contribution index of the student, which is defined as +1 if the student only sends emails without receiving any and −1 if the student only receives emails without sending any. If the contribution index of a student is 0, she has perfectly balanced communication behavior, sending and receiving the same number of messages. In the example in Figure 13.2, as John exchanges the most emails, close to 80, he shows a passive emailing behavior, with a negative contribution index of −0.6. Rose on the other hand exchanges fewer emails, slightly less than 20. However, she shows proactive behavior, with a contribution index of about 0.5, sending far more emails than she receives.

Figure 13.3 shows the same network as Figure 13.1, but with the teacher (myself) added. Note how the density of the network increases, as I am connected to almost all the students directly. This also means that as the hub in the network, I am connecting a lot of otherwise unconnected people. This is called "closing the transitive triad," meaning that if I have links to two people, for example Sam and Sara, I can introduce them to each other to connect them, thus completing the triangle or triad. The more triads there are in a network, and the higher the density of the network, the more cohesive is the community.

Size by:betweenness

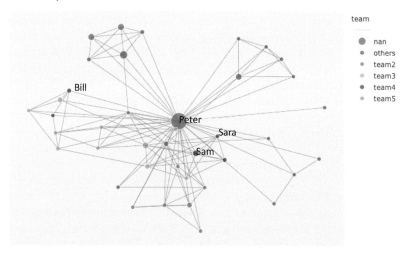

Figure 13.3   *Same class network including instructor, illustrating density and clustering of network*

The length of the link from me to Sara is proportional to the number of emails Sara and I have exchanged; the shorter the link, the more emails we have exchanged. The more emails we exchange, the "stronger" is the tie. As the link from me to Bill is much longer, the tie between Bill and I is called a "weak tie." In social network theory, strong ties represent social capital and trust, while weak ties are useful for information exchange.

Another metric that measures cohesion is the degrees of separation between any two people in the network. For instance, the degree of separation between Bill and Sara is two, meaning that it takes two hops in the network for Sara to reach Bill. This is also called the path length from Sara to Bill. The shorter the average path length in a network is for any two people to reach each other, the more connected and cohesive the community is. A network with short average path length will also be more suited for spreading new ideas quickly, as new ideas will quickly flow to all network members.

13.1   CREATING A VIRTUAL MIRROR OF MY OWN MAILBOX

Doing an SNA of my own mailbox is an excellent way to learn about myself. Figure 13.4 illustrates an email network constructed from my mailbox. Obviously I am the most influential person for myself, which is not surprising. The network nodes are sized by influence (see Chapter 17 for how influence is calculated). The nodes representing the people are colored based on the words they use, applying the tribe definitions described in Table 19.1. As shown by the coloring of the nodes, I am a member of the nerd tribe, and most of my contacts are either nerds, treehuggers or spiritualists. There are very few fatherlanders in the network.

To better understand the network relationships among my friends and collaborators in my own network, the best way is to take myself out of the picture and remove the node representing myself from the network. This is what was done in Figure 13.5.

In Figure 13.5 the nodes representing people are sized by betweenness centrality and colored by interest emotions computed from the text in the emails sent by them. Seven subgroups are now clearly recognizable, with two being distinctively larger than the other five. These two larger groups represent my two lives working in business and as an academic, teaching the COINs course at the Universities of Cologne and Bamberg. The COINs community is shown as the upper cluster, with the two large red nodes representing the two local instructors in Cologne and Bamberg. The business cluster is below, with the large red and green nodes representing my closest collaborators.

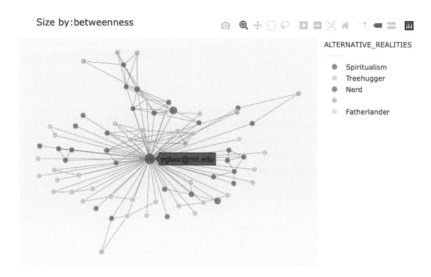

Figure 13.4   Sample email network of my mailbox (size of nodes by influence; nodes colored by tribes)

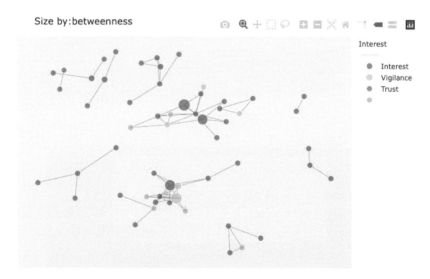

Figure 13.5   Sample email network of my mailbox (with myself removed; nodes colored by interest emotions)

13.2   SAMPLE NETWORK ANALYSIS IN A CORPORATE EMAIL ARCHIVE WITH GRIFFIN

To further illustrate how SNA can be used with email archives, this section briefly describes a sample organizational network analysis using the Griffin SNA tool. Griffin is a web-based, easy-to-use SNA tool that allows users to do all sorts of communication archive-based social network, emotions, tribe and contents-based analysis both for static and dynamic exploration. A free version of Griffin can be accessed at www.griffin.galaxyadvisors.com. As the email archive for this analysis the well-known public-domain Enron email archive is used. Enron was a Texan energy company that went bankrupt in 2002 because of systemic accounting fraud. During the investigations, the emails of 158

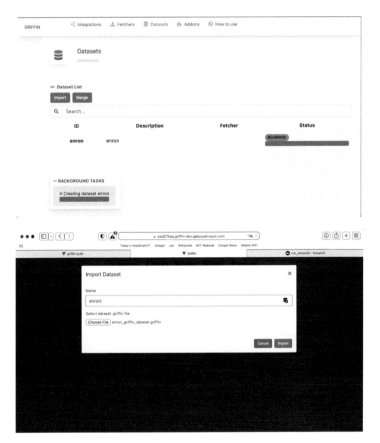

Figure 13.6   Opening Griffin and loading the Enron dataset

former employees of Enron were collected for analysis by law enforcement officials. These emails were later cleaned and are now in the public domain. They are frequently used for all sorts of email analysis experiments.

A cleaned subset of the Enron email archive in Griffin format can be downloaded from www.ickn.org/sociometrics/enron_griffin_dataset.griffin.

After having started Griffin from www.griffin.galaxyadvisors.com, click on the tab "Datasets" at the top. Then click on "Import" to import "enron_griffin_dataset.griffin," select the Griffin data file and give the newly created dataset a name. Here it is called "Enron" (Figure 13.6).

Afterwards, click on "processing" to go the Phoenix visualizer. You can annotate the nodes and edges, however, note that in this example the initial annotations have already been computed (Figure 13.7). If you delete nodes, you will have to recalculate the annotations.

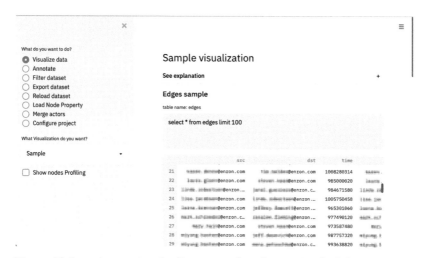

Figure 13.7   Annotating the Enron email archive in Griffin/Phoenix

You can visualize activity over time, showing that the most active time was from March to August 2001 (Figure 13.8).

Figure 13.9 shows the most central actors, sized by betweenness. It also shows who uses language representing predominantly "fairness" colored in red, "injustice" colored in green, "unfairness" in violet and "appreciation" in orange.

The scatter plot in Figure 13.10 shows each individual as a dot. Any "honest signal" annotation can be chosen for display in the x- and y-axes. In the example in Figure 13.10 the x-axis is "messages total" while the y-axis is contribution index. The dots are colored by "aggression" word usage. We see that Pete Davis is the most active emailer with 600 emails exchanged. His contribution index is 0, meaning it is well balanced. He sends and receives about 300 emails and his writing style is mostly "serene."

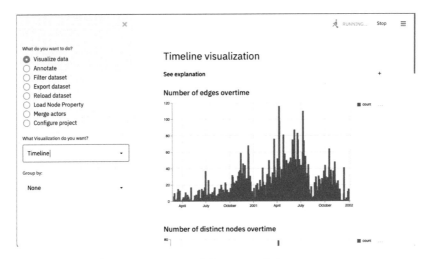

Figure 13.8   Activity over time of Enron email dataset

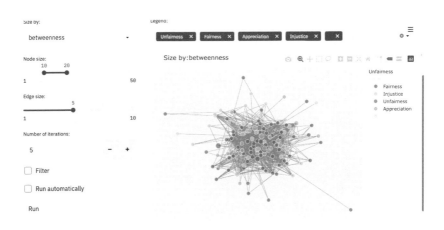

*Figure 13.9   Most influential actors in Enron dataset by betweenness,
colored by "unfairness" emotions*

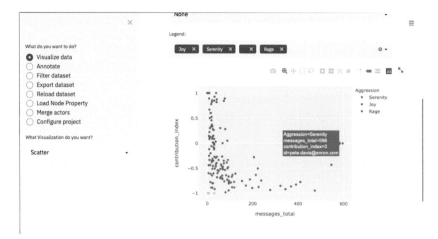

Figure 13.10   Contribution index plot of Enron dataset, nodes colored by "aggression" emotions

The view in Figure 13.11 shows the communication view. It illustrates (not shown here) how much two particular subgroups communicate with each other and it also shows the word cloud with the most used words in the entire Enron email archive.

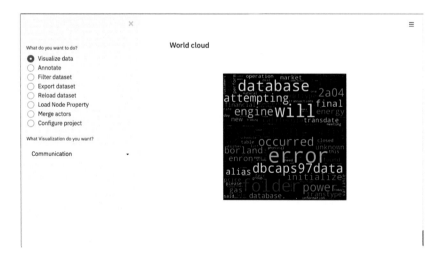

Figure 13.11   Communication view of Enron dataset

The radar chart in Figure 13.12 shows a comparison of "honest signal" annotations between different tribes based on their word usage. We can see that "risk takers" are most influential and on average send the most messages, however, the messages they get from others are not influential at all. "Politicians" on the other hand get influential messages from others but do not have much respect, as others on average take the most time (slowest average response time (alter_ART)) to send them emails back. The "stock traders" have the most respect as others respond to them the fastest (they have the lowest alter_ART).

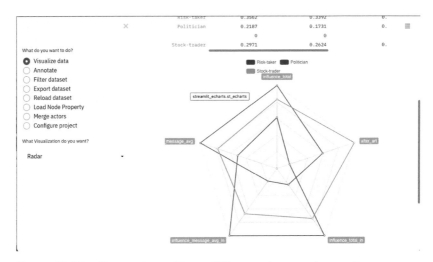

Figure 13.12   Comparison of three different subgroups by word usage

Further examples of Griffin's emotion calculation functions illustrated by the Enron email archive will be shown in the subsequent sections on measuring dynamics and emotions.

13.3   MEASURING NETWORKING DYNAMICS

The dynamics of changes in network position of an individual are excellent predictors of the passion, respect and creativity of that individual within the community. Figure 13.13 shows the full network of my mailbox for four months. Figure 13.14 illustrates three snapshots of the movie showing the network changes over time.

As can be clearly seen, the dynamic information in the movie conveys valuable additional information not available in a static picture showing the aggregated networking structure of the entire time period.

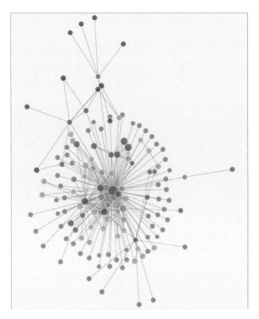

Figure 13.13   Network of my mailbox from November 1, 2020 to March 19, 2021

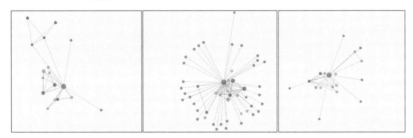

Figure 13.14   Three snapshots at the beginning, middle and end of the movie of my mailbox from November 1, 2020 to March 19, 2021

Figure 13.15 illustrates the same changes in the network structure over time, showing that group betweenness centrality reached a peak beginning in March. This means that at that time the network was strongly centralized (high group betweenness centrality) with somebody – most likely me – being a strong leader in the center. In mid-January and the end of February the network was highly decentralized (low group betweenness centrality), meaning that multiple people contributed similar numbers of messages to the conversation.

betweenness avg over time

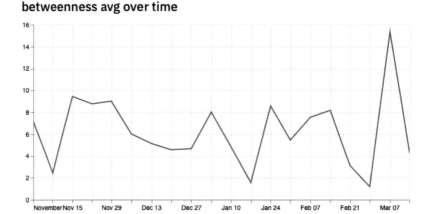

Figure 13.15   Betweenness over time of my mailbox

Figure 13.16 illustrates another dynamic property of a person, namely responsiveness. Each dot is a person, the x-axis shows the total number of messages, the y-axis shows average response time (ego_ART). As is shown in Figure 13.16, I am quite responsive, with an ego_ART of 1.58 hours, and a total of 2183 sent and received messages.

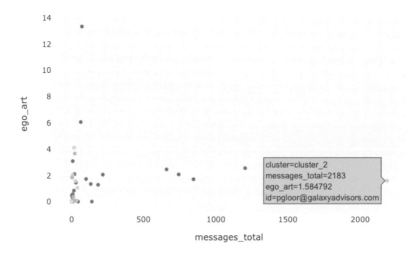

Figure 13.16   Average response time of all people in my mailbox

As has been shown with these examples, analyzing networking dynamics adds valuable information not available from static network structure.

14. Measuring emotions

Emotions are a window to the soul. How somebody responds to an external trigger is indicative of personality, ethical values and risk attitudes. Understanding emotions better also opens the door to improved collaboration. Emotions can be measured in many different ways, looking at facial expressions, body signals, voice patterns such as tone of voice and the choice of words somebody uses when communicating with others.

14.1   MEASURING EMOTIONS FROM BODY SIGNALS

In our work we have recognized emotions based on body signals collected with sociometric badges and smartwatches. We started with custom-built sociometric badges developed by the team of Sandy Pentland at the MIT Media Lab in 2006. The badges were then further developed by a startup founded by a group of graduate students of Sandy. The badges were worn around the neck and captured body movement through an accelerometer, physical proximity through triangulating the wearer's position with a Bluetooth sensor and tracked who was facing whom with an infrared sensor and who was speaking with a microphone.

We used these badges (see Figure 14.1) to measure personality characteristics, and to study interaction in hospitals among nurses in a post-anesthesia care unit (PACU) and surgeons, teamwork among employees in a bank, creative project work in a graduate student seminar, flow among jazz musicians and among teams of software developers, to name a few cases. We found that the way nurses moved around in the PACU predicted the speed of recovery of their patients, it also predicted the quality of the output of the bank employees and the grades of the graduate students. For instance, surprisingly, the more time nurses spent close to a recovering patient, the faster was the recovery. This is quite unexpected, as being close to a patient could just be an indicator of the surgery patient's need for special care. However, it seems patients get well faster simply by having more direct interpersonal interaction with PACU nurses.

Figure 14.1   Sociometric badge used in some of our projects

More recently, when smartwatches became widely available, we built the Happimeter (see Section 9.4), a body signal-collecting app where the data were collected from the sensors of a smartwatch and then processed on a server in the cloud using predictive machine-learning models, with the results being visualized on the smartphone. The system constructed a generic model pretrained with hundreds of users that made predictions about the emotions of the wearer of the smartwatch based on accelerometer, heartrate, light sensor, temperature, time of day, speech energy and GPS location (Figure 14.2). The emotion prediction can be corrected by the wearer of the smartwatch and if the prediction is wrong, the system learns from its mistakes to create a personalized emotion-tracking system. This is an extension of experience-based sampling, pioneered by Mihaly Csikszentmihalyi, who had participants in his study wear a device that would beep at random times, whereupon they had to write down their emotion. Our system extends his concept, as the smartwatch can not only remind the participant at random times, but even present an automatic prediction and allow the candidate to correct it directly on the smartwatch if it is wrong.

On a side note, when measuring happiness, we were quite surprised to find that about 50 percent of the happiness of a person is based on the weather. We integrated this into our model by including the current weather forecast based on the GPS coordinates of the smartwatch.

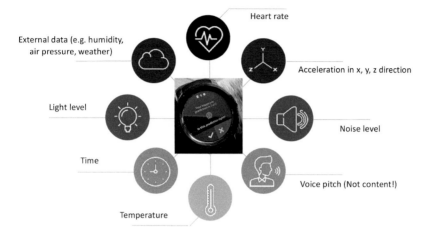

Figure 14.2   Sensor data input for smartwatch emotion tracking

We used the smartwatch emotion-tracking system to predict happiness and stress, training the machine-learning system with hundreds of students wearing the watches in different courses and entering their happiness repeatedly. The system was then used among others to measure emotions of actors and the audience in a theater play, to measure the emotions of jazz musicians during rehearsals, to track the performance of surgeons in training, to predict the sales success of bank employees when interacting with customers, to analyze the satisfaction of visitors in a museum, to measure the mood and performance of logistics workers in a warehouse and to measure the happiness of employees in the innovation center of a bank.

When teaching a Happimeter workshop with 20 to 40 participants, I found that just making the participants jump and dance around at the beginning of the workshop increased their happiness.

Figure 14.3 illustrates evolution of happiness at the executive committee meeting of an IT company, where 12 participants were wearing the smartwatch during the meeting. We can clearly see that the food quality at lunch was poor, after lunch in the first presentation by an external speaker happiness was rising and in the second presentation in the afternoon right after 14:00 happiness went down.

In another project, in a two-day creativity workshop with 15 participants, we found that going running in the morning increased creativity later in the day. At another event, where small teams of participants had to develop business

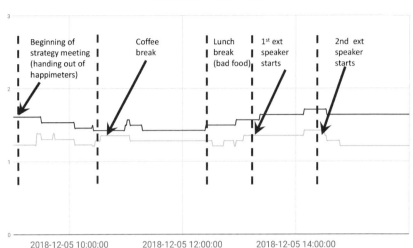

*Figure 14.3   Evolution of happiness at an executive meeting with 12
               participants*

plans and then present them in the plenary, which voted on the best business
plans, we found that the single most predictive predictor of a highly rated
presentation was participative presentation. In other words, if the entire team
went on stage and presented its result together, the collective energy of all
presenters assembled on the stage together got the audience to rate the quality
of the presentation significantly higher.

14.2   MEASURING EMOTIONS FROM FACIAL
           EXPRESSIONS

AI is giving us powerful tools to recognize emotions from facial images
in five lines of Python programming code, thanks to deep-learning and
machine-learning libraries. After first recognizing faces in a larger picture and
putting a bounding box around it, these libraries use deep-learning models
using convolutional neural networks. In the final step, the emotion of the face
is recognized based on a model being trained with thousands of face pictures
that have been prelabeled with the emotion being shown on the face.

Figure 14.4 describes the steps necessary to compute the emotions. In the
first step, once the picture is taken, the face must be detected in the picture.
This is frequently done using Haar-Cascades, basically sums of rectangles in
the image. In the next step the face has to be rotated to align the eyes horizon-

tally and the face is then cropped to the minimal face area necessary to express and recognize an emotion. Afterwards the image is downsampled to reduce unnecessary information and speed up processing, and the picture intensity is normalized to better recognize the edges in the picture. In the end a classifier is built using convolutional neural networks of face images with manually added labels. Mostly we use the six emotions defined by Paul Ekman, namely happy, sad, anger, fear, disgust and surprise. Additionally, a seventh emotion, neutral, is added, as we found that this increases emotion recognition accuracy. There are many publicly available face datasets with thousands of faces which are already prelabelled, for instance, the Cohn-Kanade Dataset. Instead of building a single classifier for predicting seven different emotional states, it can be better to build seven classifiers where each is able to predict exactly one emotional state (e.g., happy or not, surprised or not, etc.). In the end, only the likelihood that a particular emotion is recognized is stored, which also fully respects individual privacy, as it is not possible to reconstruct a face from an emotion likelihood. It should be possible with such a system to reach an accuracy of 70 to 80 percent based on a prelabeled test dataset.

Figure 14.4   Steps of facial emotion recognition

We have used our face emotion recognition system to recognize emotions of the audience in a theater play, emotions of musicians and the audience in a concert, of participants in Zoom meetings and for analyzing the emotions of participants in face-to-face meetings.

14.3   MEASURING EMOTIONS FROM VOICE

The tone of the human voice is a primary carrier of emotion. To recognize emotions from voice, the voice audio files first must be broken into segments and preprocessed. Towards that goal, voice activity has to be detected, which for instance can be done using the WebRTC Voice Activity Detector API from Google. In this step also, phases of silence are recognized and removed. As a last preprocessing step, the audio is converted to a standardized 22.050 Hz sample rate with 16 bits per sample. To find emotions in human speech, mostly spectral or prosodic features – relating to rhythm and intonation – are

used. The most popular spectral feature set for voice emotion recognition is
the Mel Frequency Cepstral Coefficient (MFCC), which can be interpreted
as the representation of the short-term power spectrum of the speech signal.
For instance, the popular Librosa Python library includes MFCC, applying
a Fourier transform to decompose a speech signal into its individual frequencies and the frequency's amplitude, thus converting the signal from the
time domain into the frequency domain. The result of this Fourier transform
is called a spectrum. The y-axis of the spectrogram is finally mapped to
MFCC, which splits the pitch into equal distances that sound equally distant
to a human listener.

MFCC is particularly well suited for voice emotion recognition, as it takes
human sensitivity towards frequencies into consideration. Figure 14.5 illustrates the process of how the waveplots are converted into spectrograms, which
are then mapped to emotion using a machine-learning model that has been
trained with prelabeled voice emotion datasets.

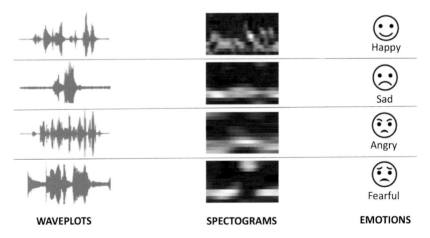

WAVEPLOTS   **SPECTOGRAMS**   **EMOTIONS**

Figure 14.5   Voice emotion recognition process

Good results have been reached with 26 MFCC features calculated with
a time window of 30 ms. To train the model, datasets like RAVDESS are
used. RAVDESS contains prelabeled speech segments where actors speak
a sentence in any of the six emotions happy, sad, angry, fear, disgust and surprise. The RAVDESS segments can then be used for both training and testing
a convolutional neural network or a long short-term memory recurrent neural
network, recognizing a particular emotion with about 70 percent accuracy.

We have used our voice emotion system for instance to recognize emotions
in face-to-face, in-person meetings and in a theater play.

14.4 MEASURING EMOTIONS FROM WORDS

Spoken and written words are a key source for recognizing emotions. NLP has long been the primary technology for automatically recognizing emotions in text. Before the rapid growth and availability of machine learning- and AI-based approaches, simpler bag-of-words systems were used to locate emotions in text. Such a bag of words for happiness would include words like "happy," "joy," "great," "good," etc. while a bag of words for sadness would include words like "sad," "bad," "horrible," etc. The more words of the happy bag of words a text will include, the happier the NLP system would rate it. The problem is that such a system would missclassify "Not bad at all" as an answer to "How are you?" as negative. Many extensions of these initial simple systems have been proposed. Today NLP is mostly done with variants of recurrent neural networks that are suited for sentences of text, such as long short-term memory.

The Griffin system also includes the capability to compute emotions using the Tribefinder function described in Chapter 19. The content visualization view of Griffin shown in Figure 14.6 illustrates the emotions injustice, unfairness, fairness and appreciation in the individual messages that two individuals exchange – alternatively all the messages an individual sends can be displayed. It also lists the words that make the individual a member of an emotion tribe. In the example below, the word "tahnks" indicates Steven Kean's fairness, while the word "mail" indicates injustice.

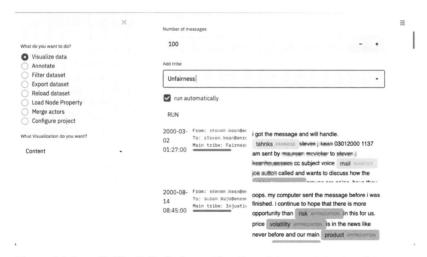

Figure 14.6   Griffin Tribefinder to identify unfairness, injustice, fairness and appreciation

We have done many projects where we use the sentiment of email users to predict their business results. For instance, if an employee becomes emotionally "flat," s/he is highly likely to leave the company in the next three months. We have also found that frequently more emotional people are more creative, although we have encountered significant exceptions to this rule.

14.5   MEASURING EMOTIONS IN MEETINGS

In large companies, employees spend up to 75 percent of their time in meetings. It is therefore highly relevant to make the time employees spend in meetings as productive as possible. Until now, measuring meeting efficiency and productivity has been mostly done through surveys of meeting participants or by placing observers in the meetings. A third line of research is based on analyzing videotaped recordings of meetings. These videos have then to be manually coded for later analysis. All three approaches involve a lot of manual questioning and video coding. A more automated and scalable approach to study meeting quality, efficiency and productivity is thus desirable. In our work we analyze the efficiency of meetings through measuring the emotions of participants, as measuring and mirroring the emotions of meeting participants back to them will increase the efficiency of meetings.

We created an AI-based system that measures the emotions of meeting participants by automatically recognizing the emotions of their faces and voices and their happiness and stress with the smartwatches. Their meeting satisfaction is measured using the Happimeter (see Section 9.4), and by asking them about their perceived efficiency and productivity during the meeting at the end of the meeting. Using webcams, the emotion of the faces can be tracked using machine learning. Using prelabeled test data, we found that our system achieved an accuracy of 63 to 80 percent using facial emotion recognition. Using microphones, a voice emotion recognition system was also integrated, which, again using publicly available test data, was shown to be 62 to 78 percent accurate.

This system has been tested in a series of meetings in a company setting and the emotions measured through face and voice emotion recognition have been correlated with subjective meeting outcomes rated through a survey among meeting participants. We found that happier and less angry faces and happy speech were positively correlated with self-rated meeting outcomes. This means that, other than in a jazz concert and theater performance, participants do not want a rollercoaster, but prefer a harmonious office meeting.

We also used the smartwatch-based Happimeter system to predict meeting outcomes through the body signals of the meeting participants wearing the Happimeter. Meeting participants trained the system using experience-based sampling entering their meeting satisfaction at random times during the meeting. We then trained a machine-learning system to automatically predict meeting satisfaction from the body signals, reaching 60 percent accuracy. In this project we found that the lower the variance in arm movement, the higher was the productivity of the meeting scored. That means either keeping arms still or moving them steadily is an indicator of better meetings; fidgeting around indicates unproductive meetings.

15. Measuring moral values from facial expressions

Facial expressions not only give away your emotions, but they also show your personality characteristics and ethical and moral values. Facial emotion recognition combined with machine learning will automate that process. Based on the insights that emotional responses predict tribal affiliation introduced earlier (Section 5.1), the emotional response shown on your face to an external event also depends on your personality characteristics and moral values. For instance, if you are open to new things, you might smile approvingly when seeing a new tech gadget, whereas if you don't like technology, you might frown critically when seeing the same gadget.

Figure 15.1   Predicting personality and morals from emotional reactions watching a video

Figure 15.1 shows the system we developed, that computes your FFI personality characteristics, your moral foundations, your Schwartz personal values and your risk-taking attitudes while watching a series of provocative video snippets.[1] The video snippets have been chosen to elicit strong emotional responses and to be politically divisive. They include a toddler throwing a tantrum, a cute puppy, a man killing a racoon, somebody riding a mountain bike over two skyscrapers, marching soldiers and Donald Trump giving a speech. Your facial emotions are captured by a webcam while watching the video and then fed into a machine-learning system.

Figure 15.2 illustrates the architecture of the personality- and morals-prediction system. The users can voluntarily start by entering their FFI personality characteristics, their Schwartz values, their moral foundations and their risk preferences by taking four online surveys. This will enable them to compare their manually-entered morals and personality characteristics with the automatic predictions of the AI system. Users can then watch 15 short videos with the topics as described above, while the webcam on their computer records their facial responses. Note that no pictures of the face of the user are recorded – the emotional response shown in the face is computed on your local computer in the web browser and only the recognized emotion is stored on a cloud server as a number.

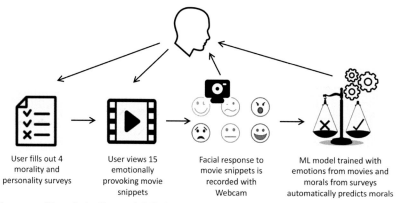

| User fills out 4 morality and personality surveys | User views 15 emotionally provoking movie snippets | Facial response to movie snippets is recorded with Webcam | ML model trained with emotions from movies and morals from surveys automatically predicts morals |

Source: Gloor, P. A., Fronzetti Colladon, A., Altuntas, E., Cetinkaya, C., Kaiser, M. F., Ripperger, L., & Schaefer, T. (2022). Your face mirrors your deepest beliefs: Predicting personality and morals through facial emotion recognition. *Future Internet*, 14(1), 5.

Figure 15.2   *Process to develop an automatic personality and morals prediction system from watching a video*

Afterwards, the machine-learning model predicts the morals and personality of the viewer.

The machine-learning model was trained by a large group of people taking the personality and morals surveys, who then also watched the videos. This is based on the big data principle, that a large collection of approximately accurate information will be made more accurate by aggregating this information. As has been shown in real-world experiments, personality characteristics and morals are recognized more accurately by the friends of a person than by the person answering these survey questions her or himself, because the person might have an overly positive or overly harsh view of herself or himself. In this system, the trained machine-learning model assumes the role of the friends, giving honest and unbiased feedback to the viewers about their personality characteristics and morals by showing them the differences between their self-assessment entered through the surveys and the predictions from their facial responses while viewing the videos.

NOTE

1.   Gloor, P. A., Fronzetti Colladon, A., Altuntas, E., Cetinkaya, C., Kaiser, M. F., Ripperger, L., & Schaefer, T. (2022). Your face mirrors your deepest beliefs: Predicting personality and morals through facial emotion recognition. *Future Internet*, 14(1), 5.

16. Measuring moral values from email

Moral values and personality characteristics can not only be computed from facial responses to video, but also from honest signals in emails and other interaction archives. Based on a combination of structural and dynamic social network metrics such as degree and betweenness centralities, and oscillation in betweenness centrality, a machine-learning model will predict with 65 to 90 percent accuracy FFI personality characteristics, moral foundations, Schwartz values and risk-taking attitudes (see Section 3.4). To further increase accuracy, content metrics such as positivity in sentiment and emotionality can be included if email contents are available. The prediction accuracy of most moral and personality attributes is quite high already when simply using structural and dynamic network metrics, as frequently email content is not available because of company policy and privacy concerns.

Figures 16.1–16.4 illustrate the email interaction network of a class of students collaborating in small teams, including the instructors, exchanging emails during a semester.

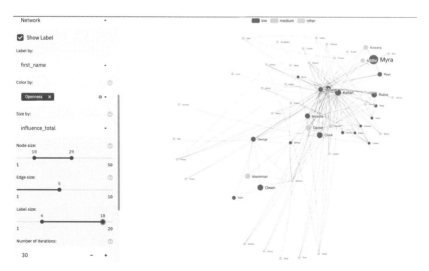

Figure 16.1   *Sample group network showing the openness to experience of the actors (blue = low; yellow = medium)*

Figure 16.1 shows the network of course participants, with the participants colored by their FFI personality characteristic "openness to experience." Blue persons have low openness, while green nodes have medium openness to experience. For the yellow actors there were not enough data available to make a prediction. Nodes are sized by influence on all four network charts (see Chapter 17). Myra is the most influential person in this network, measured by the influence algorithm described in Chapter 17, and she is of low openness to experience as indicated by the blue color of the node.

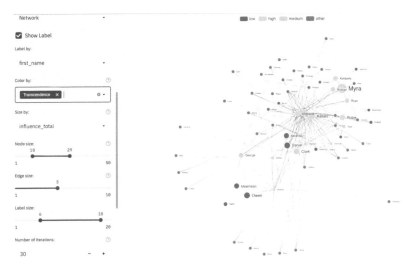

Figure 16.2   *Sample group network showing transcendence of the actors (blue = low; yellow = medium; green = high)*

Figure 16.2 shows the degree of transcendence as part of the Schwartz value system (see Section 3.4). Green people have high transcendence, meaning they show high transcendence and benevolence, nodes in yellow denote people with medium transcendence, people in blue have low transcendence, while nodes in red mark people where there is not enough information to make an analysis. For instance, Kellan and Clark are people of high transcendence, while Daniel has low transcendence based on the words he uses in his emails.

Figure 16.3 shows the level of caring as measured by the moral foundations framework introduced in Section 3.4. According to the color code, Kellan and Clark care a lot about others as indicated by the green color of their corresponding nodes, which aligns well with their high transcendence and benevolence demonstrated in Figure 16.2.

Figure 16.4 shows the risk-taking attitude of the course participants; the risk-taking framework is also introduced in Section 3.4. There are no high-risk takers in the course, for instance Myra and Kellan are medium-level risk takers, as indicated by their green node color.

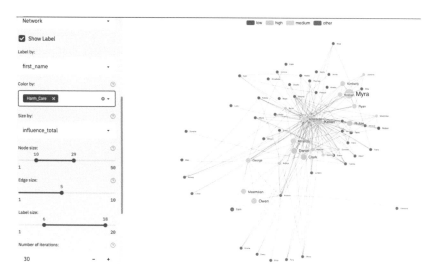

Figure 16.3   *Sample group network showing the degree of caring for others of the actors (blue = low; yellow = medium; green = high)*

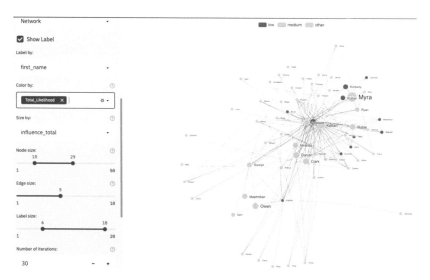

Figure 16.4   *Sample group network showing the likelihood of taking risks (blue = low; green = medium)*

This means that just measuring the interaction among a group of people through their network position and interaction dynamics will indicate their moral values, personality characteristics and risk-taking attitude. The accuracy of these predictions can be further improved if the content of the interaction is also available. Additionally, knowing the words that a person used when communicating with others will indicate the degree of influence that person has within the entire group.

17. Measuring influence through quoting novel words

How quickly inventors of new words get others to use their newly created words is an excellent measure for the persuasive power of the inventor. When I am giving talks about "COINs," the "Happimeter," "entanglement" and "virtual mirroring," the best metric of how well the audience liked my talk is if they start using these new words not only during the questions after my talk, but also during the coffee break afterwards. More generally, the speed with which new concepts are picked up is an excellent metric for the influence that the inventor of the new concept has within a community. Using NLP, this influence can easily be measured. We developed an algorithm that tracks the originality of new words using the well-established term frequency/inverse document frequency metric. It counts how popular a word is within a message compared to all the messages circulating in the community. The more frequent a novel word is in a single message, and infrequent in all others, the more distinctive and original the word is. The more somebody introduces distinctive words, the more creative that person is. The faster these novel distinctive words are picked up by others, the more influential the introducer of these new words is. We have implemented this influence algorithm in the Griffin SNA tool.

Figures 17.1 and 17.2 show how counting the quoting of new words can be used to measure the influence of the word inventor. Figure 17.1 illustrates the influence network of the Enron dataset. The nodes in the network are sized by influence and colored by ideology tribe membership. The picture below shows for example that Tana Jones is a highly influential member of the "capitalist" tribe.

A second way to show how influence in a community is distributed is the 3D histogram view. Here the x-axis lists all people in the network, the y-axis lists time and the z-axis is influence (or any other honest signal available in Griffin). Figure 17.2 illustrates the histogram view showing in one chart when a particular person was most influential for the Enron dataset. We see that Jeff Dasovich was most influential in February 2001. Note that any other "honest signal" can be chosen for display in the z-axis.

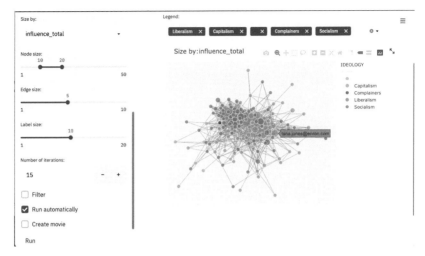

Figure 17.1   Influence calculation of the Enron network

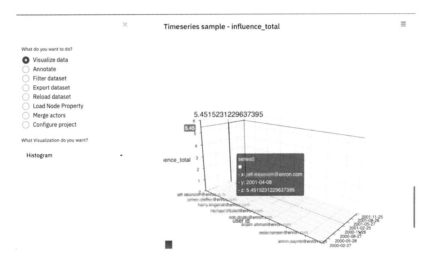

Figure 17.2   Influence 3D histogram of the Enron email archive

18. Measuring entanglement

Synchronization is a basic property of life. It appears everywhere, from oscillating fireflies to the natural behavior of humans. It takes place so invisibly that we usually do not notice it. For humans it is triggered by audio-visual stimuli, haptic perception or simply by the presence of other people. Synchronization can be analyzed as neuromuscular coordination, by tracking of body, hand and head movements, arousal or electroencephalogram readings. For example, it was found[1] that the audience of a concert synchronized its applause after an asynchronous start, while other researchers[2, 3] discovered that people synchronize their finger tapping to improve coordination. While these studies only look at synchronization as neuromuscular coordination and task coordination, other research efforts are uncovering connections between synchronization in cognition, task structure and performance outcomes in teams.[4] A team in groupflow is highly synchronized with entanglement being the enabler of creating the flow state among team members.

In our research we have been looking at synchronization and entanglement among members of small teams and large organizations. Studying online communication and face-to-face interaction we have found that teams which are well synchronized perform better. We have studied the flow state of jazz musicians jamming together, and of large orchestras, where we found that if the musicians are moving their bodies in synch – an indication of being in flow – they perform better, as measured by the applause of their audience and the emotions expressed through the faces of the musicians and the audience.

In one of our first studies, we put sociometric badges around the necks of two jazz bands performing at a concert. The two bands were playing in the same concert. At first there was a band of amateurs, warming up the audience, and then the main concert with a professional band, fully entangled after years and years of playing together multiple times per week. The sociometric badges showed us the different degrees of entanglement of the two bands. The amateur band was constantly coordinating by looking at each other and their bodies were moving independently. The professional band synchronized their playing together very differently. They never looked at each other, and their bodies were swinging in perfect synchrony, as measured by the accelerometers of the sociometric badges, which the band members were wearing in their pants. In other words, they were fully in groupflow.

The same behavior of multiple people synchronizing their communication behavior can also be observed using online social media and email. To measure the flow state in office teams, we have defined an entanglement metric[5] for email logs of an organization, looking at how synchronized the email exchange between two people is. The more they exchange messages in a similar rhythm, the more entangled they are. We validated the metric in different organizations, finding that selective, focused entanglement of employees is a strong predictor of team creativity, employee satisfaction, employee performance and customer satisfaction.

The idea of the entanglement measure is to determine how a person A is in sync or shares the same flow with another person B with regards to communication. Intuitively, the "more similar the communication" of two persons A and B is, the more person A is in sync or shares the same flow of communication with person B over time. Individuals that share the same rhythm might have higher abilities to productively channel their cooperative spirit.

Our approach for the team entanglement metric is to construct it from social network analysis metrics like betweenness and degree centrality (see Chapter 13) and communication activity between each pair of members in a team.

To illustrate the idea, Figure 18.1 illustrates entanglement in my mailbox containing the emails of people that worked with me on several projects. First, I calculated network measures such as degree and betweenness centrality, etc. and activity measures such as messages sent, messages received, etc., over time. The blue line shows the mailbox owner's rhythm (me), the other lines correspond to the people I am exchanging emails with most frequently. The more correlated the two curves between me and another person are, that means the more I have a spike in the curve and the other person also has a spike at the same time, the more we share the same flow or rhythm, are in sync and are thus "entangled." In other words, we measure the email pulse of teams based on shared activity and network position. Entanglement tracks if people exchange email in the same rhythm, meaning that they are sending a similar number of emails at the same time. Additionally, entanglement also measures if they have the same network position in the social network created by their email exchange at the same time. To compute the network, a connection between two people is constructed if they exchange at least one email. Adding all these connections together leads to a social network of email exchanges. To calculate the network position, we then assess if somebody at a given point in time is central or peripheral in this email network. Two people are entangled if they are both either central or both peripheral in this network at the same time.

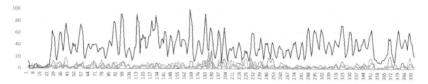

Figure 18.1   Activity entanglement in my mailbox

Among others we studied the "entanglement" of medical innovation teams to predict team performance and learning behavior. Applying the entanglement metrics to different email archives, we found for instance that innovation teams in healthcare were more creative if they had a highly entangled core team, with a more peripheral group of occasional collaborators (the "outgroup") who were weakly entangled with the core team members.

We also looked at a group of executives at a professional services firm, studying the email communication among hundreds of the most senior executives of the international services firm, where we found that the least entangled executives were most likely to subsequently leave the firm. We found that people who were similarly but weakly entangled to many people showed a higher likelihood of leaving the firm compared to their peers who were closely entangled with a core group of collaborators and weakly entangled with the rest. The more executives at this firm showed this behavior – being strongly entangled in networking behavior – the higher was their performance as assessed by their managers. High-performing managers were highly entangled with their core team and weakly entangled with the rest of their organization. This means it is good to have a few good friends with strong ties and a wider network of occasional acquaintances to rely on for information exchange. The highly entangled core group provides the crucial support managers can rely on in times of need, while the weakly entangled peripheral group is useful for information gathering and dissemination.

The same entanglement behavior also created happier customers, as measured by Net Promoter Score, a metric that asks customers of a firm how likely they are to recommend the firm to their friends. We found that the more entangled a core team of customer-dedicated employees caring about a particular customer was, the happier were their customers. The more the employees at the firm that the customers were interacting with had been communicating as a closely knit, fully entangled team, the higher was the satisfaction of the customers with the firm. This means that if people synchronize their email-sending activity and have similar network positions in the social email network – without knowing it – they are more entangled, which leads to more creative teamwork, happier team members and happier customers.

NOTES

1. Néda, Z., Ravasz, E., Brechet, Y., Vicsek, T., & Barabási, A.-L. (2000). The sound of many hands clapping. *Nature*, 403(6772), 849–850.
2. Yun, K., Watanabe, K., & Shimojo, S. (2012). Interpersonal body and neural synchronization as a marker of implicit social interaction. *Scientific Reports*, 2(1), 959.
3. Fairhurst, M. T., Janata, P., & Keller, P. E. (2013). Being and feeling in sync with an adaptive virtual partner: Brain mechanisms underlying dynamic cooperativity. *Cerebral Cortex*, 23(11), 2592–2600.
4. Gipson, C. L., Gorman, J. C., & Hessler, E. E. (2016). Top-down (prior knowledge) and bottom-up (perceptual modality) influences on spontaneous interpersonal synchronization. *Nonlinear Dynamics, Psychology, and Life Sciences*, 20(2), 193–222.
5. Gloor, P. A., Zylka, M. P., Colladon, A. F., & Makai, M. (2022). "Entanglement": A new dynamic metric to measure team flow. *Social Networks*, 70, 100–111.

19. Measuring tribes

We have built a system called "Tribefinder" that recognizes digital virtual tribes on social media by shared language. It is based on the assumption that members of the same virtual tribe use the same words, coined and promoted by the other members of the virtual tribe, such as #MakeAmericaGreatAgain. Tribefinder flags the use of similar words in similar contexts through applying deep learning. It assigns tribal membership based on word usage of individual tribe members on social media. The vocabulary has been defined by identifying tribal leaders for each category of a tribal dimension on Twitter, for example for the "politician" tribe in the "personality" dimension the Twitter streams of all US members of congress, US senators and living US presidents have been used to train the system, while the tweets of all journalists of the *New York Times*, *Washington Post* and *Guardian* define the vocabulary of the journalists. The idea is that politicians do not necessarily say the truth, but rather what they think their constituency wants to hear. Journalists of mainstream media, on the other hand, are paid to stick to the facts and thus mostly say the truth.

Based on an in-depth analysis of Wikipedia categories, we have created five different dimensions of tribal affiliations. The central dimension is "alternative realities" consisting of the four tribes "fatherlanders," "nerds," "treehuggers" and "spiritualist" (Figure 19.1).

Figure 19.1   The four tribal categories of "alternative realities"

In addition, we have identified four additional tribal dimensions, "ideologies," "lifestyle," "recreation" and "personality." The dimension "ideologies" includes the tribes for "socialism," "liberalism," "complainers" and "capitalists." The dimension "lifestyle" consists of the tribes for "fitness," "veganism," "sedentary" and "yolo"(you only live once). The dimension "recreation" includes the tribes "arts," "sport," "fashion" and "travel." The dimension "personality" consists of "journalist," "politician," "risk taker" and "stock trader." See Table 19.1 for a description of all tribal dimensions.

Table 19.1   Tribal dimensions of Tribefinder

Dimension	Tribe	Language characteristics
Alternate reality	Fatherlander	God, country and tradition
	Nerd	Technology, science, social inclusion and globalization
	Spiritualist	Contemplation and search for meaning
	Treehugger	Protection of nature and sustainable growth
Ideology	Liberalism	Individual freedom
	Capitalism	Minimal government intervention
	Socialism	Greater government influence
	Complainer	Constantly complains about everything
Personality	Stock trader	Emphasis on short-term profit at the expense of long-term investment
	Politician	Complex and evasive language rather than plain speaking
	Journalist	Descriptive and generally more honest language
	Risk taker	Language reflects daring decisions and behavior
Lifestyle	Fitness	Significant physical activity
	Sedentary	Low physical activity
	Vegan	No animal foods or use of animal products
	Yolo	Focus on the present with greater risk taking
Recreation	Art	Art forms stimulate appreciation for beauty and passion
	Fashion	Focus on popular trends and latest styles
	Sport	Watching, attending and playing sports
	Travel	Experiencing different cultures and environments

How did we come up with those 20 tribes? Initially we set out with hundreds of categorizations of beliefs and cultures listed in Wikipedia, and then started mining hundreds of millions of tweets, to identify through AI and deep learning cohesive subgroups who were using a similar vocabulary and had clearly recognizable tribal leaders. This led to the elimination of most tribe candidates and left us with the 20 tribes grouped into the four categories listed in Table 19.1.

Table 19.1 lists all predefined tribes of Tribefinder. They are shown calculated for my Twitter profile in Figure 19.2. There is an additional "emotion tribe" that assists in identifying the emotions of a person. It is also useful for identifying the emotions a person shows towards a particular tribe.

Figure 19.2   All predefined tribes of the Tribefinder system

Figure 19.3 illustrates the tribal affiliations of Donald Trump based on his tweets in 2020 (he has been banned from Twitter since February 2021). The Tribefinder system allows organizations to identify their different corporate cultures by analyzing their email archives, as well as customer demographics of brands and products on social media. For individuals, it tells them for instance if others perceive them as ultrapatriots (fatherlanders), as science and technology minded (nerds), as environmentally conscious (treehuggers) or as spiritualists.

We have for instance used Tribefinder to find virtual tribes in organizations through their email. To test the validity of the system, we analyzed Hillary Clinton's publicly released emails as part of the 2015 investigation into her use of a personal email server during her time as the US Secretary of State. We found that Hillary's ideology tribes are mostly "complainers" and "liberals." In their direct communication, she and her immediate collaborators also speak more in the matter-of-fact language of journalists than in the "politically

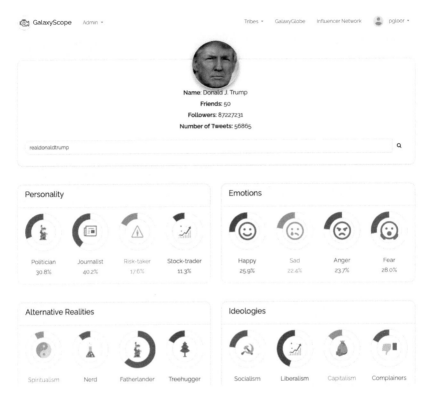

Figure 19.3   Tribefinder applied to the tweets of Donald Trump

correct" language of politicians – very different from her official communication with potential voters. Surprisingly, in the "alternative reality" dimension
Hillary mostly uses the language of "spiritualists" rather than the nationalistic
language of "fatherlanders." We also looked at the publicly available Enron
email archive of the now defunct energy trading firm, which includes 120
mailboxes of the employees who were indicted when the company went bankrupt in 2002,[1] and found them to be fatherlanders and nerds. We also found that
liberal and fashion-aware Enron employees sent the most emails.

In another project we looked at the email archive of a class of 120 students
from Germany, Switzerland and China, who were collaborating over long
distance in a one-semester course on COINs. The students worked together
in 12 different teams. Within a team, members mostly used either "spiritual,"
"nerdish" or "treehugger" language styles and there was no representative of
the fatherlander tribe among the students. Students also mostly used "journalist" language and not "political" language. This means that students within one

team tend to become entangled exhibiting a shared culture by using similar language.

The Tribefinder system allows users to create new tribes about any topic, brand, value or emotion. The new tribe creation process is illustrated in Figure 19.4. To create a new tribe, hundreds of thousands of tweets from hundreds of "tribal leaders" tweeting about the core values of their tribe must be collected from their Twitter profiles.

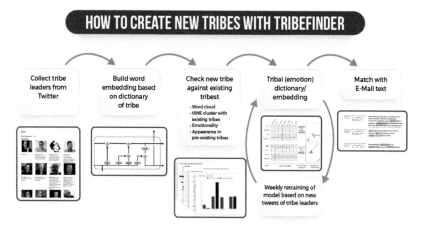

Figure 19.4   How to create new tribes with Tribefinder

Using this huge body of tribal language, an AI system will compute a dictionary of tribal words and how they are distributed in the text. This probabilistic distribution of a dictionary of millions of words is called a "word embedding." Once a tribe is created, the tribe members are plotted in proximity to each other, based on word usage and how they fit in with the predefined 24 tribes using the tSNE algorithm (see Figure 19.11 for an example and explanation of tSNE). This allows the tribe creator to conduct a consistency check, because the tribe members should all be close together in one cluster compared to members of the other tribes and belong to contextually similar predefined tribes. For instance, members of a "gun owner tribe" should be more fatherlanders than treehuggers. After the consistency check, the tribe dictionary (word embedding) is finalized, and any text, be it from Twitter, email, blogs or elsewhere, can be checked for how similar the text is to the language of other members of the same tribe, for example how much their language resembles the language of gun owners.

19.1   MEASURING THE TRIBES OF BEES, ANTS AND LEECHES

Chapter 6 introduced the bees, ants and leeches. Swarms of bees are motivated by creating something radically new, to draw satisfaction from inventing something that has not been there before, pollinating others and creating honey to be enjoyed by them and others in the process. Ants are social insects, too, who show loyalty to their swarm, but they are highly competitive, motivated primarily by trying to win at all costs, be it in sports or in their professional life. They also consume what they collect by themselves. Leeches are more solitary creatures, living off the blood they suck from others, motivated by money and try to get rich as quickly as possible through whatever means available.

I created these three tribes in Tribecreator, training the machine-learning system for the bee tribe with the Twitter feeds of Tim Berners-Lee, Jimmy Wales, J. K. Rowling and the profiles of an additional 150+ other creatives such as designers, musicians and artists. The ant tribe was trained with the Twitter feeds of 150+ athletes such as Rafael Nadal, Lance Armstrong, Tiger Woods, plus NASCAR racers, boxers and wrestlers, football coaches and professional computer gamers. The leech tribe was trained with the tweets of activist investors such as Bill Ackman and Steven A. Cohen, hedge fund managers, venture capitalists and peddlers of "get rich quick" schemes.

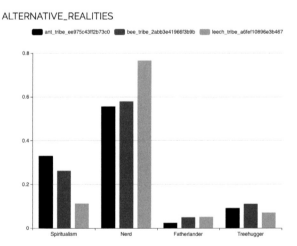

Figure 19.5   Alternative reality tribes for bees, ants and leeches

Figure 19.5 shows the alternative reality tribal affiliations for the bee, ant and leech tribes. We find that none of the three tribes are big fatherlanders, they all have other priorities. Leech tribe members are the biggest nerds, most likely because venture capitalists and hedge fund managers talk about the startups they are investing in. Surprisingly, ants are the bigger spiritualists than bees, while leeches don't care much about spiritualism. Bees are the biggest treehuggers, but this is a comparatively small dimension for all three tribes.

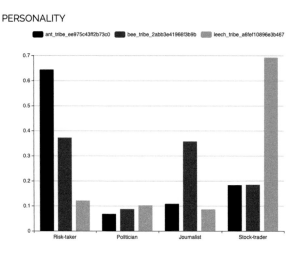

Figure 19.6   Personality tribes for bees, ants and leeches

Figure 19.6 illustrates the personalities of the three tribes. Ants are the biggest risk takers, followed by the bees who also take risks. Leeches, as expected, are huge stock traders, i.e., predominantly interested in money. On the other hand, bees talk mostly like journalists, i.e., using honest, matter-of-fact language.

Figure 19.7 shows the ideological tribal affiliations. Leeches are the biggest capitalists, while bees are more inclined towards liberalism. Ants are complainers.

Figure 19.8 shows the lifestyle tribes of bees, ants and leeches. Not surprisingly, the ants are huge fitness buffs, while the leeches are the most sedentary, followed by the bees. The bee tribe has the largest proportion of vegan tribe members.

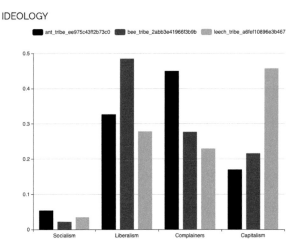

Figure 19.7   Ideology tribes for bees, ants and leeches

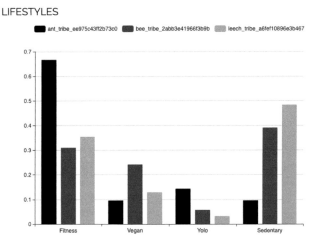

Figure 19.8   Lifestyle tribes for bees, ants and leeches

Figure 19.9 shows the recreation tribes. Not surprisingly, ants dominate in sport, while bees and leeches are prevalent in art, with the bees producing it and the leeches trading it as an investment or as part of their philanthropic activities.

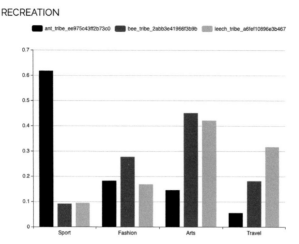

Figure 19.9   Recreation tribes for bees, ants and leeches

Figure 19.10 is the most interesting, showing the emotions of bees, ants and leeches. Bees are the happiest tribe, followed by ants, while leeches are the least happy! Leeches are angry, while ants are fearful. Bees show little anger or fear.

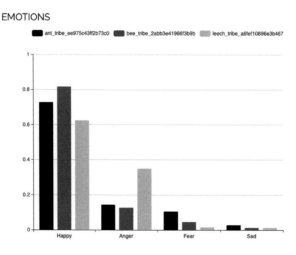

Figure 19.10   Emotions of bees, ants and leeches

Figure 19.11 illustrates the clustering by tribe of the hundreds of tribe leaders who have been used to train the machine-learning system to create the word embeddings for the three tribes. Each dot represents a person. Dots representing people who use similar language are shown together using a layout algorithm called tSNE that reduces the multidimensional word vector to two dimensions and can thus be plotted in a two-dimensional space. As the picture illustrates, members of the same tribe are close together, illustrating that each tribe forms a cohesive community based on common word usage.

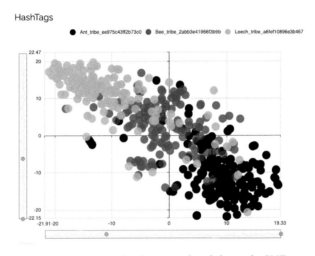

Figure 19.11   Cohesiveness of tribes visualized through tSNE

This word embedding can now be used to identify the tribal affiliation of any person based on their word usage. Figure 19.12 shows six months of my mailbox, with the people colored by groupflow tribe. As the picture illustrates, there are many bees in my community, with smaller groups of ants and leeches. The red dots show the people who did not have enough words in their email for the machine learning to make a tribal assignment with sufficiently high confidence.

Figure 19.13 shows what percentage of the messages in my mailbox included content related to beeflow, antflow and leechflow over time. Most of the time, beeflow was dominant, as we were mostly discussing new features of our software and other creative endeavors. Occasionally, for instance on February 11 and March 4, leechflow takes over, meaning that we talked about money, most likely negotiating the price of our software and services with customers. This chart illustrates that reality is not white or black, but somewhere in the middle, spanning all facets of daily life. What we can do, however, is decide where to put the emphasis.

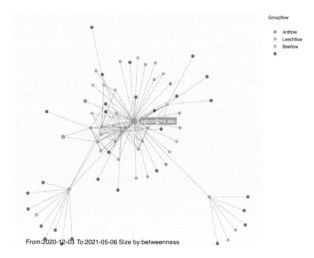

Figure 19.12   My mailbox, with people colored by tribe

Groupflow avg over time

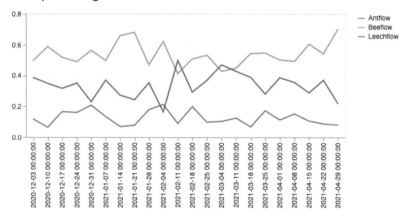

Figure 19.13   Beeflow, antflow and leechflow over time in my mailbox

19.2   BEES ARE GREAT FOR THE TEAM; ANTS AND LEECHES REAP THE REWARDS

Which mix of bees, ants and (phew!) leeches makes a perfect team? At first glance, for a creative team you want the bees, for a team involved in a strenuous task you want ants and if you want to optimize profits, leeches might come handy. However, it is not that simple. This section illustrates how to combine the measurement tools introduced in Part II to build and nurture creative, productive and happy individuals, teams and organizations. We will analyze three organizational email networks, in very different professions, with very different shares of bees, ants and leeches among their members, comparing their emotion and groupflow variables with the performance of the organizations. The first organization to be analyzed is the students in my COIN course, the second organization is members of healthcare innovation teams and the third analysis looks at employees of a professional services firm. These organizations cover a wide spectrum of activities, from highly research oriented to very production and process focused.

To better understand the characteristics of the bee, ant and leechflow tribes I measured the groupflow tribal properties of three cohorts of my COINs course, where small student teams of two to five students work together for a semester on a topic of their choice in the field of happimetrics, groupflow and SNA, basically learning and researching what is described in this book. The students come from many different study backgrounds, they are a mix of computer science, management science, psychology, sociology, political science and geography students from Germany, Switzerland and other countries in Europe, the Americas and Asia. I loaded the anonymized email communication of the students into the Griffin tool and ran the tribe analysis system. Out of 65 students, 39 were mostly bees, 16 mostly leeches and 10 mostly ants (Figure 19.14). As the network picture shows, the most central students are all predominantly bees. The number of people in the network is bigger than 65, as the students also communicated with university administrators and other students during the course.

Figure 19.14   Assignment of the 65 students to their main tribe

Note that all students showed to some degree characteristics of all three tribes, even the strongest bees showed a small percentage of leech attributes, meaning that the bees speak occasionally in ant and leech language. The x-axis in Figure 19.15 shows the three tribes, with each row showing one tribe, i.e., the antflow, the beeflow and the leechflow tribe. The y-axis shows the summed-up percentages of how much an ant is also leech or bee, how much a bee is also ant and leech and how much a leech is also bee and ant. As the grey bars in Figure 19.15 illustrate, leeches still use quite a high amount of bee language in their emails, as, to a lesser extent, do ants.

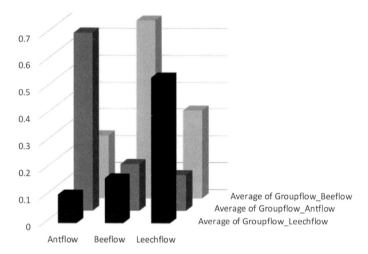

Figure 19.15   Distribution of other tribes among bees, ants and leeches

Next, the final grades of each student team were correlated with their tribal properties, aggregating the percentages of bee, ant and leech language for each team. The expectation was that the more bees there were in a team, the better the final grade of the team would be. However, it turned out that the number of bees had no significant influence, rather it is the number of hard-working ants who positively influence the final grade. The more ant-like students there are in a team, the better is the final grade.

We found that leeches are mostly angry, fearful and unhappy. Ants are not angry, and are somewhat happy. Bees have no fear and are even happier. Leeches are yolo, non-vegan, sedentary, stock traders, anti-politicians, anti-journalists and anti-risk takers. Ants are not yolo, vegan, not sedentary, politicians and risk takers. Bees are not sedentary, non-stock-traders and journalists. Bees are also the most popular, as their in-degree is the highest, meaning that they get more emails from many different people.

Figure 19.16 illustrates the aggregated emotions of the three groupflow tribes. Ants and bees are the happiest, while leeches are the angriest and the most fearful. Again, the x-axis shows the three tribes, while the y-axis shows how angry, fearful and happy the bees, ants and leeches are. It seems that being a leech makes you angry and unhappy!

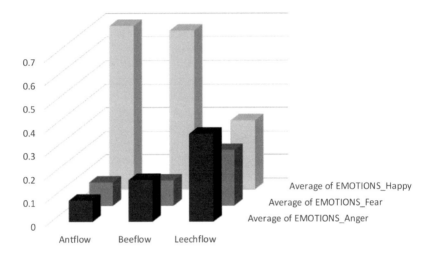

Figure 19.16   Emotions of the three groupflow tribes

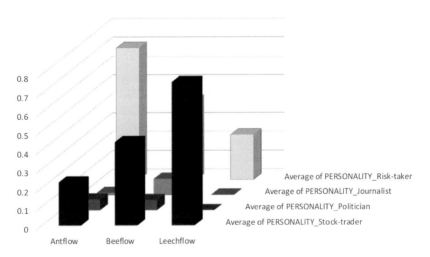

Figure 19.17   Personality of the groupflow tribes

Figure 19.17 shows the personality characteristics of bees, ants and leeches. Leeches are mostly interested in money as stock traders, while ants are the biggest risk takers. Bees speak the most like a journalist, in matter-of-fact language, of the three tribes. Remember that the premise of the journalist tribe is to speak more honestly than the members of the politician tribe.

We also analyzed the relationship between moral values of the students and their bee, ant and leech characteristics. A subgroup of the students had answered the moral values survey, thus providing ground truth for their moral values. We found that leeches score high on respect for authority. Ants score high on appreciation for purity and sanctity. Bees on the other hand show disdain for purity and sanctity.

We also found that people who have high moral values are all anti-journalists, or in other words, the more they care about moral values, the less they speak like a journalist. This illustrates that journalists, while pretending to have high moral values, frequently act the opposite way. People who worry about harming others are anti-yolo, they are vegan and they also send more emails. People high on the fairness score are less angry; they are also anti-yolo and they exchange emails with relatively fewer people. People who show high loyalty to their friends are less angry and they are happier. People who respect authority are anti-yolo and they are also stock traders.

In a second analysis, one year of email exchanged between 400 participants in 13 medical innovation teams was analyzed with Griffin. Figure 19.18 shows this social network of the participants, with the nodes sized by importance of the people (betweenness) and colored by their predominant tribe.

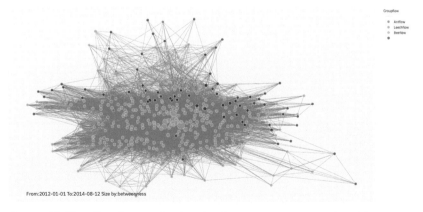

Figure 19.18   Email network of medical innovation teams colored by groupflow tribes

As Figure 19.18 shows, the most important team members (the largest nodes) are all bees. When measuring their networking behavior through their honest signals, we found that the more leech-like somebody is, the slower they are in answering their email. On the opposite side, the more bee-like a person is, the faster are they in answering their email. We also compared the performance of a team, as rated by a panel of managers, with their groupflow tribe membership. The higher the sum of all beeflow characteristics of all members of a team, the better is the team's performance. The same also seems to be true for the leech-like properties, as the higher the sum of all leech characteristics of the team's members, the higher is its performance, although this effect is quite small. This might illustrate the fact that also in academia behaving like a leech is sometimes rewarded.

In the third analysis we looked at 90 employees of a professional services firm, who were working for different large customers. The performance of the employees was measured by their performance rating by their superiors, as well as through the satisfaction of their customers measured through a Net Promoter Score.

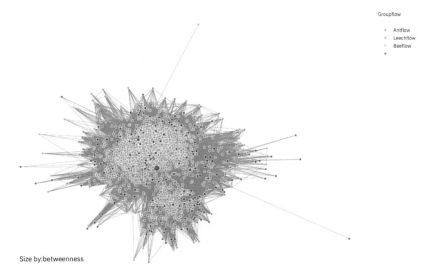

Groupflow

· Antflow
· Leechflow
· Beeflow
·

Size by:betweenness

*Figure 19.19   Email network of the professional services firm colored by
              groupflow tribes*

Figure 19.19 shows the full email network of all active employees of the professional services firm. Employees have been colored by their most prominent tribe. Compared to the medical innovation teams and the COIN course students described above, there are many more leeches among the employees of the professional services firm. While all employees have some ant characteristics, they are mostly either bees or leeches. When looking at the performance of the individual employees, in this professional services firm there is no correlation between being a bee, ant or leech, and individual performance as measured through customer satisfaction. However, the more bees a team working for a customer included, the more satisfied was the customer. There was also correlation between individual emotions and net promoter score, in that the less amazed and the less disgusted the members of a customer services team at the professional services firm were, the more satisfied were their customers.

Based on this analysis of bee, ant and leech behavior computed from email archives from very different organizations, there are four main insights:

1. *Being a bee makes happy!* The bee-like students were the happiest. There is an intrinsic reward in creating new things, giving huge satisfaction when the product has been created, independent of any monetary or other compensation, be it in the form of grades or more generally as power and glory. Bees are also fairer and they are more modest.
2. *Ants are good at winning!* While the creative student teams were mostly made up of bees, the best predictor of team success measured by grade was the number of ants who were complementing the bees. This is not so surprising, because the diligence of the ants is very helpful to complete a class project on time and at high quality. Creative ideas are great, but in the end also stamina and the capability to execute are needed. Compared to bees, ants and leeches were also more arrogant. This leads to the main insight.
3. *While bees are great for the team, ants and leeches reap the rewards!* In our analysis we found that when looking at group performance, having more bees in the team was a predictor of success. The more bees a health-care team included, the higher was its performance rated. However, when looking at individual performance evaluation of the managers in the service company, it was ants who were rated the highest by their managers. Leeches were bad for the satisfaction of the customers of the service provider, however, they were not punished but rather rewarded for their leechy behavior by their managers. Similarly, students who were ants were getting higher grades. The conclusion is obvious: *blessed is the team that includes bees, they will make the team happy and increase team performance, but woe unto the bee*. The outlook is bleak for individual bees, as they will get lower grades as students and worse performance ratings as managers. To get recognition, bees need to be recognized as such! Virtual mirroring enables you to do precisely that: if you are a bee, use your virtual mirror to point out your invaluable contributions to your team.

I consider myself a bee, and in my professional life as a manager at UBS, and a partner at PwC and Deloitte, I discovered what I call the "three-year rule of creative individuals." Creative individuals are agents of change at their organization, instigating fundamental change, but in this process, they hit their head against the ceiling so many times that after three years they have enough, and switch jobs. This was certainly true for me, as I worked for three years at UBS, three years at PwC and three years at Deloitte. Then I had had enough, and for the last 20 years I have been a happy bee as a research scientist at the MIT Center for Collective Intelligence. Similar insights have been found in a survey of creative professionals,[2] where 96 percent of those surveyed reported that they had switched jobs within less than five years. In fact, in this survey, half of the surveyed people said that they had left their job within two years.

Additionally, besides these three main insights, there is a fourth corollary: there might a place for bees, ants and leeches! While it is good to have many bees in a creative team, a small number of ants and leeches will make the overall team more successful. The resilience of ants, and the selfishness of leeches, when carefully channeled, will help the whole team deliver a better product. While the bees in the medical innovation teams were helping to develop creative solutions, in the professional services firm ant- and leech-like behavior was needed to provide efficient processes and get satisfied customers. To support collaboration in these teams, virtual mirroring of their communication will help bees, ants and leeches to keep their interaction and ethical behavior in check. It will also help identify the contributions of all three, bees, ants and leeches to organizational success, thus greatly increasing the self-motivation of individuals.

A key requirement for happily entangled teams is for team members to share the same values, culture and goals, in other words, to be members of the same virtual tribe. To measure the degree of happy entanglement, we have developed the Social Compass, a system automating virtual mirroring for the individual, that combines email analysis with sensing body signals with smartwatches, running on the web and on smartphones. The Social Compass will be described in Chapter 20.

NOTES

1. Morgan, L., & Gloor, P. A. (2019, October). Identifying virtual tribes by their language in enterprise email archives. Collaborative Innovation Networks Conference of Digital Transformation of Collaboration. Springer, pp. 95–110.
2. www.designweek.co.uk/issues/18-24-june-2018/creatives-do-not-stay-in-a-job-longer-than-five-years-research-shows/.

20. Building a social compass

Working remotely in the home office has been around for a long time for a small part of the workforce, however, most recently the Covid-19 pandemic has forced the majority of workers to work distantly from home. While some are energized by working in the privacy of the home office, using the quiet time at home to do productive work without being bothered by their colleagues, others respond with depression, feeling lonely and isolated. To help individuals navigate their emotional world to overcome isolation, loneliness and stress by entangling virtually with others, we have developed a "Social Compass" combining all the pieces described in the previous sections. Just like Google Maps shows where somebody is in the physical world, where they can go and where the bottlenecks and traffic jams are, the Social Compass helps individuals navigate the social landscape of their emotions and the emotions of others to become a member of a unified virtual team (Figure 20.1). It tells individuals how they see others, how others see them and what they can do to be happier and more collaborative and productive. The Social Compass connects knowledge workers in their home offices by creating COINs. COINs are self-organizing teams of intrinsically motivated innovators, collaborating over the internet to create new things (see Chapter 8).

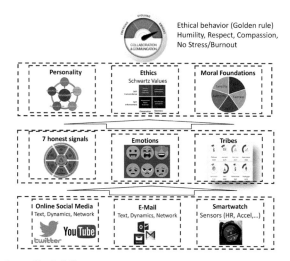

Figure 20.1   Social Compass components

In a workshop where I was presenting our approach, a participant asked if tools like the Social Compass would ensure that "Human resources knows you better than you know yourself." I told him that the opposite is true, that the Social Compass *helps you to know yourself better – without telling human resources* (except if you want to, see Section 12.5).

The Social Compass shows an individual's communication behavior *to the individual*. It is calculated based on an individual's communication behavior, by analyzing their interaction with others through email, social media and individual body signals measured with a smartwatch. The Social Compass takes full care of individual privacy, running on an individual smartphone and only aggregated anonymized data can be voluntarily shared with others on a server in the cloud. Based on communication archives from online social media, email and body signals from a smartwatch, the honest signals of collaboration, emotions and digital virtual tribes are calculated using machine learning, in turn giving input for computing the FFI personality characteristics, Schwarz ethical values and moral foundations. Comparing these AI-predicted values based on thousands of records with survey-based self-assessment provides the user with a virtual mirror to compare her own view of self with the view others have about her personality, morals and ethics.

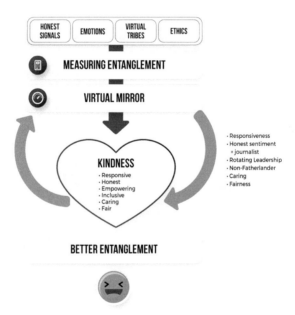

Figure 20.2   The impact of the Social Compass

The Social Compass is used to provide a virtual mirror to users, as shown in Figure 20.2, helping individuals and organizations to measure and improve their level of entanglement. It starts by analyzing communication logs and calculating interaction metrics such as "honest signals," "emotions," "tribes" and "ethics." These metrics are calculated for the individual using machine learning and shown to them in their virtual mirror. In particular, the metrics measure the "kindness" of the users by calculating their responsiveness, honesty, empowering of others, inclusiveness, caring and fairness. They also measure how much of a bee, ant or leech somebody is, and how much a nerd, treehugger, spiritualist or fatherlander. At the same time, based on these metrics, their entanglement with others is measured using the entanglement metric. If the entanglement of users is low, their virtual mirror gives immediate suggestions as to how to change their behavior for increasing entanglement in their team. A well-entangled person is a happy person, and an entangled team is a high-functioning team.

The Social Compass might occasionally give you pain for later gain, making you suffer in the short term for your own good. It shows the areas where you are deficient, exposing your weaknesses to change for the better. The crucial point is that this feedback is given only to you, in the privacy of your own smartphone; no other human being knows about it, only your smartphone. It shows how you can improve and how you can alter your behavior to achieve your goals, be it in your private life or in interaction with your colleagues at work (Figures 20.3 and 20.4).

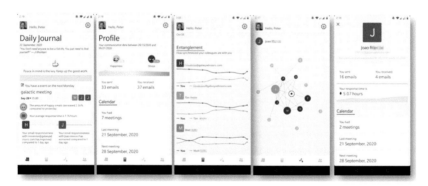

Figure 20.3   Social Compass smartphone snapshots

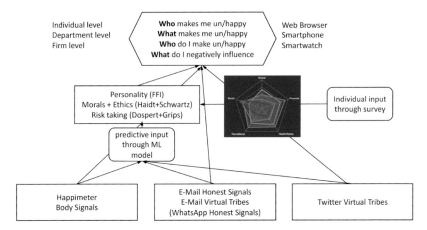

Figure 20.4   IT architecture of the Social Compass

To give an example, in an early test scenario we observed immediate behavioral change through using the Social Compass. Fred was part of a close-knit team of half a dozen software developers working frantically to build a new product. Fred was doing his part writing code, but his communication style was very different from the rest of the team. While the other team members constantly interacted using online chat and responded within minutes to questions from others, Fred used the privacy of his home office to take multiple days to answer a question sent to him by email. He usually only answered after multiple reminders and rarely interacted with the rest of the team. His big awakening came when the Social Compass on his smartphone showed to Fred that he was totally peripheral to the team, while the rest of the team had formed a close-knit highly entangled group. Fred was shocked. This shock got him to radically change his communication behavior, to reach out and contact others and turn him into a proactive team member.

This process of showing one's own communication behavior to an individual in the privacy of their own smartphone or web browser – we call this virtual mirroring – can thus lead to fundamental behavioral changes.

20.1   FINDING THE RIGHT TEAM MEMBERS WITH THE SOCIAL COMPASS

The Social Compass can be used to find the ideal team members, based on their moral and ethical values, their personality and their tribe.

Figure 20.5 illustrates the sequence of screens on a smartphone using the Social Compass, from left to right, to find new team members, based on the attributes of preferred team members. The second screen from the left shows that I chose Matt and Joao as poster team members. The Social Compass then gives me other members similar to them, based on their tribes. It proposes to add Joao Gabriel and Erkin to my dream team, as their tribal properties are most similar to Matt and Joao's among all the people with whom I have exchanged sufficient emails for the Social Compass to compute their tribes. The third screen from the right shows the current communication statistics of my aggregated dream team, showing for example that the team members on average respond in 49 minutes to an email and send most emails at 5pm. The second screen from the right shows the tribal characteristics of my team, aggregated from all team members. I see, for instance, that they are happy nerds willing to take risks. The rightmost screen shows the social network of my dream team, with the two team members in the center.

Figure 20.6 illustrates the sequence of smartphone screens, again from left to right, needed to find my ideal team members based on their tribal affiliations.

Figure 20.5   Find your team based on the profiles of your favorite team members

On the second screen from the left I can specify which tribes I want to include (green buttons) or explicitly exclude (red buttons) from my dream team. On the middle screen, the Social Compass shows me the list of people in my mailbox, sorted by fit to my tribal search criteria. I choose Joao Gabriel, Joao Marcos, Matt, Erkin, Harry and Tim as members of my dream team. The rightmost two screens show again the team statistics and the social network of the team.

Figure 20.6   Finding team members based on preferred tribes

20.2   ANIMALS AND PLANTS PROVIDE A SOCIAL COMPASS

If trees provided Wi-Fi, we would be planting them everywhere. But they only give us the air that we breathe. (Bear LeVangie, Massachusetts arborist[1])

In our most recent research, we have been analyzing the interaction of humans with other species, such as plants, dogs and horses. While we humans have a hard time communicating among ourselves, we find it even more difficult to communicate with individuals of other species. The main interaction between species consists of eating members of other species or being eaten. We humans consume huge amounts of pig, cow and chicken meat, we drink milk and eat eggs, bread, rice, corn and other veggies. However, when we are not eating plants and animals, we also like to talk to them. Some people even talk to their houseplants. And owners of dogs, cats and horses of course talk to their pets all the time, maybe even considering them their soulmates. But do the plants and animals really understand what we are trying to say to them? And even more importantly, can we understand what the dog, horse, cat or a mimosa or basil plant is trying to say to us?

Before we can start talking to others, we need to listen to what they have to say and try to make sense of their output. Computers and AI have made huge progress over the last 20 years helping us both to listen and talk to each other. Combining machine learning and AI with functional magnetic resonance imaging, computers are finally able to read the human brain. Computers are capable of knowing what we are thinking by tracking the activation of combinations of brain cells indicative of certain words. In the best implementations[2] at the moment computers can read up to 250 different words at 90 percent accuracy by looking at our neurons. In genetically engineered mice, computers have also spoken to the mice, telling them when to drink water by turning on their neurons, "playing them like a piano."[3] Google Translate and Deepl have become language geniuses, dynamically translating from English to Chinese, with me talking to my phone in English in the hotel in Beijing and the phone repeating my sentence to the hotel receptionist in Chinese.

What if we could do the same when talking to a horse, a dog or a mimosa, with the computer telling the animal or plant what I would like to say, and then the animal or plant talking back to me? Our research group has been studying how humans communicate online and face to face for the last two decades. In our work we have been building many tools for happier, more creative and more productive collaboration among humans, leveraging the computer and AI to read the "honest signals" and emotions of what a human really wants to say beyond the literal meaning of words. Only recently, in the last two years, have we been starting to do the same for animals and plants.

In our research, we have been applying these algorithms and technologies to interspecies communication. We have used body-sensing technology to better understand communication with horses and facial emotion recognition to understand the emotions of dogs and horses. Figure 20.7 illustrates the dog and horse emotion-tracking systems. The dog-tracking system[4] includes both the body posture and facial expressions of dogs to identify happiness, anger, fear and relaxation. The horse emotion-tracking system[5] has been trained with hundreds of pictures of horse faces labeled by an expert horse trainer with the four emotions relevant for horses, "alarmed," "curious," "relaxed" and "annoyed."

Source: Corujo, L. A., Kieson, E., Schloesser, T., & Gloor, P. A. (2021). Emotion recognition in horses with convolutional neural networks. *Future Internet*, 13(10), 250.

Figure 20.7   *Emotion recognition of dogs (left) and horses (right)*

In other projects we are trying to listen to plants. We have put "brain sensors" on mimosas, as they talk back to the outside world quite visibly: when their leaves are touched, they fold them. We found that they seem to sense the electrostatic discharge of human bodies and the rhythm of body movement near them (Figure 20.8). When putting our sensors on other plants such as basil they show the same response.

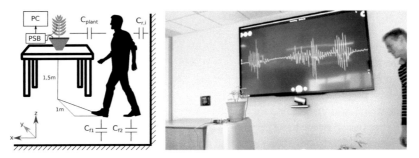

Figure 20.8   Experimental setting for measuring human emotions through electrostatic body discharge through Mimosa pudica

In a new series of experiments, we found that plants are at least as good as custom-built hardware in measuring body movements.[6] Mimosas and other plants act as biosensors, tracking the way somebody moves their body, and will thus deduce the same information as can be gleaned from wearing a smartwatch at least as good as the sensors of the smartwatch. The main difference is that there will be a little plant pot on the table to collect emotion data instead of the user having to wear a smartwatch. By measuring the pattern of electrostatic discharge of human bodies together with Mimosa pudica and other plants in response to the human movement we have been able to recognize individuals based on their distinctive pattern of body movements with 66 percent accuracy as well as the positive or negative mood of people based on their gait characteristics as perceived by the plant with 85 percent accuracy. As a measuring device we use the plant SpikerBox,[7] a device that measures the electrical action potential while also measuring the electrostatic discharge between the electrode on the leaves of a plant and the capacitively coupled human body.

We also recorded the leaf movement of the "dancing plant" (Codariocalyx motorius) in response to human voices and music. Using automatic image recognition, we found that its leaf movement was different in reaction to male and female voices talking nearby.[8]

This means that in the end we envision a scenario where interhuman interaction will be measured not only by computer hardware, but also by living growing sensors in the form of plants. This has the additional advantage of being surrounded by plants, as having plants on our desks and hallways will not just show us our own mood, but even make us happier and healthier. Being surrounded by plants is one of the best and proven ways of increasing happiness. In a groundbreaking experiment published in the journal *Science* in 1984,[9] Roger Ulrich found that patients who viewed trees from their hospital rooms recovered 15 percent faster compared to patients whose windows looked onto a brick wall. Tree-view patients also needed significantly fewer painkillers compared to brick-wall patients. As Oliver Sacks says in "The healing power of gardens,"[10] "even for people who are deeply disabled neurologically, nature can be more powerful than any medication." Sacks then continues: "Hortophilia, the desire to interact with, manage and tend nature, is also deeply instilled in us. The role that nature plays in health and healing becomes even more critical for people working long days in windowless offices." So, imagine a future where not just our web browser, smartphone and smartwatch measure and mirror us back our emotions, but our dog, cat, horse and even our houseplants do it too.

NOTES

1. www.nytimes.com/2020/10/07/climate/new-england-trees-forests.html?.
2. www.nytimes.com/2020/08/28/opinion/sunday/brain-machine-artificial -intelligence.html.
3. Carrillo-Reid, L., & Yuste, R. (2020). Playing the piano with the cortex: Role of neuronal ensembles and pattern completion in perception and behavior. *Current Opinion in Neurobiology*, 64, 89–95.
4. Ferres, K. (2021). *Predicting Dog Emotions Based on Posture Analysis Using Machine Learning Algorithms*. Master thesis, University of Cologne.
5. Corujo, L. A., Kieson, E., Schloesser, T., & Gloor, P. A. (2021). Emotion recognition in horses with convolutional neural networks. *Future Internet*, 13(10), 250.
6. Oezkaya, B., & Gloor, P. A. (2020). Recognizing individuals and their emotions using plants as bio-sensors through electro-static discharge. arXiv:2005.04591.
7. https://backyardbrains.com/products/plantspikerbox.
8. www.coinsconference.org/talks_pdf/Josephine_VBB.pdf.
9. Ulrich, R. S. (1984). View through a window may influence recovery from surgery. *Science*, 224(4647), 420–421.
10. Sacks, O. (2019). The healing power of gardens. *New York Times*, www.nytimes .com/2019/04/18/opinion/sunday/oliver-sacks-gardens.html.

Epilogue: from collective intelligence to collective wisdom

> We don't receive wisdom; we must discover it for ourselves after a journey that no one can take for us or spare us. (Marcel Proust)

There is a huge difference between intelligence and wisdom. Donald Trump is highly intelligent, but not wise. Intelligence focuses on interpretation of facts and knowledge; wisdom includes interpretation of feelings and emotions. Intelligence leads to behavior which is good for the intelligent person, while wisdom leads to behavior which is good for everybody. In other words, an intelligent person does what is good for her or him and a wise person does what is good for the world. Intelligence has nothing to do with morals and ethics. Highly intelligent people can be amoral and unethical; wise people have an ethical compass and adhere to moral principles.

Intelligent people recognize patterns and apply them again in similar situations. They might also adapt behavior that has helped them in the past to new or changed conditions, to gain a competitive advantage. Intelligence is not restricted to humans; animals and plants also show intelligent behavior. For instance, in a famous experiment Heidi Appel and Rex Cocroft showed that when Arabidopsis mustard plants hear a recording of the sound of cabbage butterfly caterpillars munching on the leaves of a plant, they produce an increased amount of mustard oil meant to deter the insects.[1] Plants are also collectively intelligent; acacia trees warn each other about herbivores. Trees whose leaves have been chomped on by giraffes emit ethylene into the air that triggers production of tannin in the leaves in nearby acacia trees, making them inedible to the giraffes. They also allow stinging ants to live in their thorns and feed them with their sap. In return ants defend the trees against herbivores. Social insects such as bees, ants and termites are also spectacularly successful by showing numerous examples of collective intelligence, with ants laying and following the most efficient pheromone trails, or Asian honeybees collectively cooking to death attacking murder hornets. It has even been shown that Indian meal moths become more altruistic and less selfish by eating less of their own kind – the larvae of meal moths are cannibals – when they live in close company with each other.[2] In other words, being closer with each other makes Indian meal moths more altruistic. In that sense, Asian honeybees and Indian meal moths are not just intelligent, but wise!

Wisdom is a much wider concept than intelligence. Wise people are intelligent, but they also show EQ and compassion and follow a moral compass. In the Schwartz theory of basic values, they have a universalist value system, which Schwartz defines as "understanding, appreciation, tolerance, and protection for the welfare of all people and for nature." They do not just focus on themselves or their immediate surrounding, but show benevolence and kindness in their interaction with others. Instead of self-focused ambition they show a concern for the welfare of everybody and think holistically. They live mostly by joy and sadness and try to evade fear and anger. They also rarely show disgust and surprise, as they accept everything the way it comes.

In the words of Nelson Mandela, wisdom combines the mind and the heart. A group showing collective wisdom extends these principles into the community. An early example of collective wisdom is the Ten Commandments, rules developed over millennia to enable peaceful coexistence for members of the community. Craving power is detrimental to happiness. According to the World Happiness Survey, the two most powerful countries, the US (number 14 on the 2021 World Happiness ranking) and China (number 52) are not particularly happy. It is thus not power, money or glory that makes people happy. In the top three spots are the rather insignificant and humble countries Finland, Iceland and Denmark. A clue to their happiness might come from the lowly cannibalistic Indian meal moths: living closely together makes them kinder to each other. Finland, Iceland and Denmark are small countries with a cohesive egalitarian culture, where people don't just pay lip service to the golden rule but live by "treating others as you want to be treated." Another unifying factor is the high trust that inhabitants of these three countries have for their government.

In the US I sometimes wonder if members of Gen Z are not wiser than Gen X and Millennials. In a course on happiness at Yale offered through Coursera that got 3.3 million participants during the Covid-19 lockdowns, participants in the age group of 34 and older found it life changing and revolutionary, while twentysomethings categorized it as good advice they already knew – they definitively did not find it revolutionary.[3]

So what are the steps towards collective wisdom? Be willing to learn wherever you can – be it from young people who prioritize a meaningful life over money, power and glory, or from Indian meal moths and Asian honeybees. And show trustworthy behavior, characterized by being conscientious, reliable, responsible, accountable and caring. Consistent behavior reinforces trust. Say what you mean, and do what you say.

In his international bestseller *The Swarm*, Frank Schaetzing describes a swarm made up of cellular organisms of superior collective intelligence, which, hidden from humanity, has been living in Earth's oceans for millions of years. Only now, as humans and their technology threaten to destroy life in the oceans, is the swarm emerging to stop humans from converting Earth into a wasteland. I hope that increasing awareness of who and what makes us *really* happy will help us humans to become a similar, more collectively intelligent, human swarm who will collaborate for a better future together!

NOTES

1. www.nationalgeographic.com/science/article/140709-plants-vibrations-insects -botany-science.
2. www.sciencedaily.com/releases/2021/03/210325115256.htm.
3. www.nytimes.com/2021/03/13/style/happiness-course.html.

References

Allen, T. J., Gloor, P. A., Colladon, A. F., Woerner, S. L., & Raz, O. (2016). The power of reciprocal knowledge sharing relationships for startup success. *Journal of Small Business and Enterprise Development*, 23(3), 636–651.

Alrajih, S., & Ward, J. (2014). Increased facial width-to-height ratio and perceived dominance in the faces of the UK's leading business leaders. *British Journal of Psychology*, 105(2), 153–161.

Babiak, P., Neumann, C. S., & Hare, R. D. (2010). Corporate psychopathy: Talking the walk. *Behavioral Sciences and the Law*, 28(2), 174–193.

Barnea, M. F., & Schwartz, S. H. (1998). Values and voting. *Political Psychology*, 19(1), 17–40.

Barrett, L. F. (2017). *How Emotions Are Made: The Secret Life of the Brain*. Houghton Mifflin Harcourt.

Benz, M., & Frey, B. S. (2008). Being independent is a great thing: Subjective evaluations of self-employment and hierarchy. *Economica*, 75(298), 362–383.

Bhattacharjee, A., & Dana, J. (2017). People think companies can't do good and make money: Can companies prove them wrong? *Harvard Business Review*, https://hbr.org/2017/11/people-think-companies-cant-do-good-and-make-money-can-companies-prove-them-wrong.

Boecker, H., Sprenger, T., Spilker, M. E., Henriksen, G., Koppenhoefer, M., Wagner, K. J., … & Tolle, T. R. (2008). The runner's high: Opioidergic mechanisms in the human brain. *Cerebral Cortex*, 18(11), 2523–2531.

Bohm, D., & Nichol, L. (2013). *On Dialogue*. Routledge.

Brom, C., Buchtová, M., Šisler, V., Děchtěrenko, F., Palme, R., & Glenk, L. M. (2014). Flow, social interaction anxiety and salivary cortisol responses in serious games: A quasi-experimental study. *Computers and Education*, 79, 69–100.

Carrillo-Reid, L., & Yuste, R. (2020). Playing the piano with the cortex: Role of neuronal ensembles and pattern completion in perception and behavior. *Current Opinion in Neurobiology*, 64, 89–95.

Caselli, M., Falco, P., & Mattera, G. (2021). When the mob goes silent: Uncovering the effects of racial harassment through a natural experiment. Dipartimento di Economia e Management, Universita degli Studi di Trento working papers.

Chapuisat, M., Bernasconi, C., Hoehn, S., & Reuter, M. (2005). Nestmate recognition in the unicolonial ant *Formica paralugubris*. *Behavioral Ecology*, 16(1), 15–19.

Chei, C.-L., Lee, J. M.-L., Ma, S., & Malhotra, R. (2018). Happy older people live longer. *Age and Ageing*, 47(6), 860–866.

Chou, T. J., & Ting, C. C. (2003). The role of flow experience in cyber-game addiction. *CyberPsychology and Behavior*, 6(6), 663–675.

Cohen, S., Alper, C. M., Doyle, W. J., Treanor, J. J., & Turner, R. B. (2006). Positive emotional style predicts resistance to illness after experimental exposure to rhinovirus or influenza A virus. *Psychosomatic Medicine*, 68(6), 809–815.

Colladon, A. F., Grippa, F., Battistoni, E., Gloor, P. A., & Bella, A. L. (2018). What makes you popular: Beauty, personality or intelligence? *International Journal of Entrepreneurship and Small Business*, 35(2), 162–186.

Corujo, L. A., Kieson, E., Schloesser, T., & Gloor, P. A. (2021). Emotion recognition in horses with convolutional neural networks. *Future Internet*, 13(10), 250.

Cowen, A. S., Keltner, D., Schroff, F., Jou, B., Adam, H., & Prasad, G. (2020). Sixteen facial expressions occur in similar contexts worldwide. *Nature*, 1–7.

Csikszentmihalyi, M. (1975), Play and intrinsic rewards. *Journal of Humanistic Psychology*, 15, 41–63.

Custodero, L. A. (2012). The call to create: Flow experience in music learning and teaching. In Hargreaves, D., Miell, D., & MacDonald, R. (Eds), *Musical Imaginations: Multidisciplinary Perspectives on Creativity, Performance, and Perception* (pp. 369–384). Oxford University Press.

Dave, D. M., Friedson, A. I., McNichols, D., & Sabia, J. J. (2020). The contagion externality of a superspreading event: The Sturgis Motorcycle Rally and Covid-19 (No. 13670). Institute of Labor Economics. http://ftp.iza.org/dp13670.pdf.

de Manzano, Ö., Cervenka, S., Jucaite, A., Hellenäs, O., Farde, L., & Ullén, F. (2013). Individual differences in the proneness to have flow experiences are linked to dopamine D2-receptor availability in the dorsal striatum. *Neuroimage*, 67, 1–6.

Denissen, J. J., Bleidorn, W., Hennecke, M., Luhmann, M., Orth, U., Specht, J., & Zimmermann, J. (2017). Uncovering the power of personality to shape income. *Psychological Science*. doi:10.1177/0956797617724435.

Dryer, D. C., & Horowitz, L. M. (1997). When do opposites attract? Interpersonal complementarity versus similarity. *Journal of Personality and Social Psychology*, 72(3), 592.

Easterlin, R. A., McVey, L. A., Switek, M., Sawangfa, O., & Zweig, J. S. (2010). The happiness–income paradox revisited. *Proceedings of the National Academy of Sciences*, 107(52), 22463–22468.

Fairhurst, M. T., Janata, P., & Keller, P. E. (2013). Being and feeling in sync with an adaptive virtual partner: Brain mechanisms underlying dynamic cooperativity. *Cerebral Cortex*, 23(11), 2592–2600.

Ferres, K. (2021). *Predicting Dog Emotions Based on Posture Analysis Using Machine Learning Algorithms*. Master's thesis, University of Cologne.

Frey, B. S. (2010). *Happiness: A Revolution in Economics*. MIT Press.

Frey, B. S., & Meier, S. (2003). Are political economists selfish and indoctrinated? Evidence from a natural experiment. *Economic Inquiry*, 41(3), 448–462.

Fritz, B. S., & Avsec, A. (2007). The experience of flow and subjective well-being of music students. *Horizons of Psychology*, 16(2), 5–17.

Gipson, C. L., Gorman, J. C., & Hessler, E. E. (2016). Top-down (prior knowledge) and bottom-up (perceptual modality) influences on spontaneous interpersonal synchronization. *Nonlinear Dynamics, Psychology, and Life Sciences*, 20(2), 193–222.

Gloor, P. A. (2006). *Swarm Creativity: Competitive Advantage through Collaborative Innovation Networks*. Oxford University Press.

Gloor, P. A., & Colladon, A. F. (2019, October). Heart beats brain: Measuring moral beliefs through email analysis. Collaborative Innovation Networks Conference of Digital Transformation of Collaboration. Springer, pp. 85–93.

Gloor, P. A., Fronzetti Colladon, A., Altuntas, E., Cetinkaya, C., Kaiser, M. F., Ripperger, L., & Schaefer, T. (2022). Your face mirrors your deepest beliefs: Predicting personality and morals through facial emotion recognition. *Future Internet*, 14(1), 5.

Gloor, P. A., Zylka, M. P., Colladon, A. F., & Makai, M. (2022). "Entanglement": A new dynamic metric to measure team flow. *Social Networks*, 70, 100–111.

Gordon, D. S., & Platek, S. M. (2009). Trustworthy? The brain knows: Implicit neural responses to faces that vary in dark triad personality characteristics and trustworthiness. *Journal of Social, Evolutionary, and Cultural Psychology*, 3(3), 182.

Graham, J., Haidt, J., Koleva, S., Motyl, M., Iyer, R., Wojcik, S. P., & Ditto, P. H. (2013). Moral foundations theory: The pragmatic validity of moral pluralism. In Gawronski, B. (Ed.), *Advances in Experimental Social Psychology* (Vol. 47, pp. 55–130). Academic Press.

Gray, J. R., Braver, T. S., & Raichle, M. E. (2002). Integration of emotion and cognition in the lateral prefrontal cortex. *Proceedings of the National Academy of Sciences*, 99(6), 4115–4120.

Gray, K. (2019). Moral transformation: Good and evil turn the weak into the mighty. *Social Psychological and Personality Science*, 1(3), 253–258.

Guo, T., Jelinewski, T., Mittermeier, G., & Veihelmann, T. (2019). Predicting the emotions and topics of Donald J. Trump based on Twitter data. Seminar Paper in 2019/20 COINs Seminar, www.dropbox.com/s/4olcg8qorwsvjzi/COINs1920_FinalPaper_Group2_final.pdf?dl=0.

Haidt, J. (2012). *The Righteous Mind: Why Good People Are Divided by Politics and Religion*. Pantheon Books.

Hare, B. (2017). Survival of the friendliest: Homo sapiens evolved via selection for prosociality. *Annual Review of Psychology*, 68, 155–186.

Hart, B., & Risley, T. R. (1995). *Meaningful Differences in the Everyday Experience of Young American Children*. P. H. Brookes.

Haselhuhn, M. P., Ormiston, M. E., & Wong, E. M. (2015). Men's facial width-to-height ratio predicts aggression: A meta-analysis. *PLoS One*, 10(4), e0122637.

Heyman, E., Gamelin, F. X., Goekint, M., Piscitelli, F., Roelands, B., Leclair, E., … & Meeusen, R. (2012). Intense exercise increases circulating endocannabinoid and BDNF levels in humans: Possible implications for reward and depression. *Psychoneuroendocrinology*, 37(6), 844–851.

Hosťovecký, M., & Babušiak, B. (2017). Brain activity: Beta wave analysis of 2D and 3D serious games using EEG. *Journal of Applied Mathematics, Statistics and Informatics*, 13(2), 39–53.

Jackson, J. J., Connolly, J. J., Garrison, S. M., Leveille, M. M., & Connolly, S. L. (2015). Your friends know how long you will live: A 75-year study of peer-rated personality traits. *Psychological Science*, 26(3), 335–340.

Jones, J. T., Pelham, B. W., Carvallo, M., & Mirenberg, M. C. (2004). How do I love thee? Let me count the Js: Implicit egotism and interpersonal attraction. *Journal of Personality and Social Psychology*, 87(5), 665–683.

Keeler, J. R., Roth, E. A., Neuser, B. L., Spitsbergen, J. M., Waters, D. J. M., & Vianney, J. M. (2015). The neurochemistry and social flow of singing: Bonding and oxytocin. *Frontiers in Human Neuroscience*, 9, 518.

Keller, A., Litzelman, K., Wisk, L. E., Maddox, T., Cheng, E. R., Creswell, P. D., & Witt, W. P. (2012). Does the perception that stress affects health matter? The association with health and mortality. *Health Psychology*, 31(5), 677–684.

Kelly, E. L. (1955). Consistency of the adult personality. *American Psychologist*, 10(11), 659.

King, D. D., Ott-Holland, C. J., Ryan, A. M., Huang, J. L., Wadlington, P. L., & Elizondo, F. (2016). Personality homogeneity in organizations and occupations: Considering similarity sources. *Journal of Business and Psychology*, 32(6), 641–653.

Knafo, A., & Sagiv, L. (2004). Values and work environment: Mapping 32 occupations. *European Journal of Psychology of Education*, 19(3), 255–273.

Konstan, D. (2008). Aristotle on love and friendship. *ΣΧΟΛΗ. Философское антиковедение и классическая традиция*, 2(2), 207–212.

Kreutz, G. (2014). Does singing facilitate social bonding? *Music and Medicine*, 6, 51–60.

Kristof-Brown, A., Barrick, M. R., & Kay Stevens, C. (2005). When opposites attract: A multi-sample demonstration of complementary person-team fit on extraversion. *Journal of Personality*, 73(4), 935–958.

Lazarus, R. S. (1993). Coping theory and research: Past, present, and future. *Psychosomatic Medicine*, 55(3), 234–247.

Lazarus, R. S., & Lazarus, B. N. (1994). *Passion and Reason: Making Sense of Our Emotions*. Oxford University Press.

Libby, E., & Ratcliff, W. C. (2014). Ratcheting the evolution of multicellularity. *Science*, 346(6208), 426–427.

Loehr, J., & O'Hara, R. B. (2013). Facial morphology predicts male fitness and rank but not survival in Second World War Finnish soldiers. *Biology Letters*, 9(4), 20130049.

Lyubomirsky, S., King, L., & Diener, E. (2005). The benefits of frequent positive affect: Does happiness lead to success? *Psychological Bulletin*, 131(6), 803.

Mattingly, J. E. (2017). Corporate social performance: A review of empirical research examining the corporation–society relationship using Kinder, Lydenberg, Domini social ratings data. *Business and Society*, 56(6), 796–839.

Mayer, D. M., Aquino, K., Greenbaum, R. L., & Kuenzi, M. (2012). Who displays ethical leadership, and why does it matter? An examination of antecedents and consequences of ethical leadership. *Academy of Management Journal*, 55(1), 151–171.

Morgan, L., & Gloor, P. A. (2019, October). Identifying virtual tribes by their language in enterprise email archives. Collaborative Innovation Networks Conference of Digital Transformation of Collaboration. Springer, pp. 95–110.

Néda, Z., Ravasz, E., Brechet, Y., Vicsek, T., & Barabási, A.-L. (2000). The sound of many hands clapping. *Nature*, 403(6772), 849–850.

Nussbaum, M. C. (2004). *Hiding from Humanity: Disgust, Shame, and the Law*. Princeton University Press.

Nuttin, J. M. (1987). Affective consequences of mere ownership: The name letter effect in twelve European languages. *European Journal of Social Psychology*, 17(4), 381–402.

O'Handley, B. M., Blair, K. L., & Hoskin, R. A. (2017). What do two men kissing and a bucket of maggots have in common? Heterosexual men's indistinguishable salivary α-amylase responses to photos of two men kissing and disgusting images. *Psychology and Sexuality*, 8(3), 173–188.

Oezkaya, B., & Gloor, P. A. (2020). Recognizing individuals and their emotions using plants as bio-sensors through electro-static discharge. arXiv:2005.04591.

Oh, Y., Chesebrough, C., Erickson, B., Zhang, F., & Kounios, J. (2020). An insight-related neural reward signal. *NeuroImage*, 116757.

Olguın, D. O., Gloor, P. A., & Pentland, A. S. (2009, September). Capturing individual and group behavior with wearable sensors. *Proceedings of the 2009 AAAI Spring Symposium on Human Behavior Modeling*, 9.

Oswald, A. J., Proto, E., & Sgroi, D. (2015). Happiness and productivity. *Journal of Labor Economics*, 33(4), 789–822.

Przegalinska, A., Ciechanowski, L., Magnuski, M., & Gloor, P. A. (2018). Muse head-band: Measuring tool or a collaborative gadget? Collaborative Innovation Networks Conference of Digital Transformation of Collaboration. Springer, pp. 93–101.

Quinn, R. W., & Dutton, J. E. (2005). Coordination as energy-in-conversation. *Academy of Management Review*, 30(1), 36–57.

Rößler, J., Sun, J., & Gloor, P. A. (2021). Reducing videoconferencing fatigue through facial emotion recognition. *Future Internet*, 13(5), 126.

Rotter, J. B. (1980). Interpersonal trust, trustworthiness, and gullibility. *American Psychologist*, 35(1), 1.

Sachser, D. (2009). *Theaterspielflow: über die Freude als Basis schöpferischen Theaterschaffens*. Alexander-Verlag.

Sacks, O. (2019). The healing power of gardens. *New York Times*, www.nytimes.com/2019/04/18/opinion/sunday/oliver-sacks-gardens.html.

Satyanath, S., Voigtländer, N., & Voth, H. J. (2017). Bowling for fascism: Social capital and the rise of the Nazi Party. *Journal of Political Economy*, 125(2), 478–526.

Schein, E. H., & Schein, P. A. (2018). *Humble Leadership: The Power of Relationships, Openness, and Trust*. Berrett-Koehler Publishers.

Schwartz, S. H. (2012). An overview of the Schwartz theory of basic values. *Online Readings in Psychology and Culture*, 2(1).

Schwitzgebel, E., Cokelet, B., & Singer, P. (2020). Do ethics classes influence student behavior? Case study: Teaching the ethics of eating meat. *Cognition*, 203, 104397.

Shank, C. A. (2018). Deconstructing the corporate psychopath: An examination of deceptive behavior. *Review of Behavioral Finance*, 10(2).

Sharfman, M. (1996). The construct validity of the Kinder, Lydenberg and Domini social performance ratings data. *Journal of Business Ethics*, 15(3), 287–296.

Spinoza, B. D., & Eisenberg, P. D. (1977). Treatise on the improvement of the under-standing. *Philosophy Research Archives*, 3, 553–679.

Stutzer, A., & Frey, B. S. (2008). Stress that doesn't pay: The commuting paradox. *Scandinavian Journal of Economics*, 110(2), 339–366.

Sun, J., & Gloor, P. A. (2020). "Towards re-inventing psychohistory": Predicting the popularity of tomorrow's news from yesterday's Twitter and news feeds. *Journal of Systems Science and Systems Engineering*, 1–20.

Sun, J., & Gloor, P. A. (2021). Assessing the predictive power of online social media to analyze Covid-19 outbreaks in the 50 US states. www.preprints.org/manuscript/202106.0105/download/final_file.

Sun, L., & Gloor, P. A. (2019, October). Measuring moral values with smartwatch-based body sensors. Collaborative Innovation Networks Conference of Digital Transformation of Collaboration. Springer, pp. 51–66.

Sun, L., Gloor, P. A., Stein, M., Eirich, J., & Wen, Q. (2019, October). "No pain no gain": Predicting creativity through body signals. Collaborative Innovation Networks Conference of Digital Transformation of Collaboration. Springer, pp. 3–15.

Todorov, A., Said, C. P., Engell, A. D., & Oosterhof, N. N. (2008). Understanding eval-uation of faces on social dimensions. *Trends in Cognitive Sciences*, 12(12), 455–460.

Ulrich, R. S. (1984). View through a window may influence recovery from surgery. *Science*, 224(4647), 420–421.

Vaillant, G. E. (2008). *Aging Well: Surprising Guideposts to a Happier Life from the Landmark Study of Adult Development*. Hachette UK.

Wei, W. (1999). *I Ching Wisdom: More Guidance from the Book of Changes*. Power Press.

Weston, S. J., Hill, P. L., & Jackson, J. J. (2015). Personality traits predict the onset of disease. *Social Psychological and Personality Science*, 6(3), 309–317.

Woolley, A. W., Chabris, C. F., Pentland, A., Hashmi, N., & Malone, T. W. (2010). Evidence for a collective intelligence factor in the performance of human groups. *Science*, 330(6004), 686–688.

Yang, Y., Tang, C., Qu, X., Wang, C., & Denson, T. F. (2018). Group facial width-to-height ratio predicts intergroup negotiation outcomes. *Frontiers in Psychology*, 9, 214.

Yang, Y., Wu, M., Vázquez-Guardado, A., Wegener, A. J., Grajales-Reyes, J. G., Deng, Y., … & Rogers, J. A. (2021). *Wireless Multilateral Devices for Optogenetic Studies of Individual and Social Behaviors*. Nature Publishing Group, pp. 1–11.

Yun, K., Watanabe, K., & Shimojo, S. (2012). Interpersonal body and neural synchronization as a marker of implicit social interaction. *Scientific Reports*, 2(1), 959.

Index

Ackman, B. 84, 184
actionable honest signals 135
agency 69
Aging Well 74
agreeability 50
AI-based interaction analysis between
humans 138–9
  data collection 139–40
  "ground truth" for human
    characteristics 141–2
  machine learning and time series
    analysis 142
  raw communication data conversion
    to discrete mathematical
    values
      betweenness centrality 140
      electrical signals to time series
        141
      word vectors 140–41
  respecting individual privacy 142–4
algorithm for happy employees 4–5
Allen, T. J. 142
alternative realities
  tribal affiliations 184–5
  from Varna castes to 59–62
anandamide 14
Andre the Giant 57, 58
Android Wear watch 111
anger 28, 31–2
antflow 70, 71
ants 71, 77–8, 184
  see also tribes
Apple 9, 102
Apple watch 111
Ärger 28
Aristotle 33, 43, 110
Armstrong, L. 184
artificial intelligence (AI) 131–2
  global networks 133
  and machine learning 3, 10
  measuring interactions 133–6

person's values and personality
    characteristics analysis 38
"reading the mind in the eye" test
    131
smartglasses, wearing 131–2
social map 132–3
Vuzix smartglasses, emotion
    recognition with 132
see also AI-based interaction
    analysis between humans
Asian honeybees 206–7
attraction pheromone 102
authority 36
autotelic experience 13

Barrett, L. F. 28
beeflow
  childhood, starting in 74–6
  described 70–71
bee in flow 76–8
bees 71, 77–8, 184
  see also tribes
benevolence 35
Berners-Lee, T. 102, 184
betweenness centrality oscillation 140,
    169
  degree centrality vs. 145–6
  people sized by 148–9
Biden, J. 66
#BlackLivesMatter 48, 134
body signal emotion recognition 159–60
Bohm, D. 121
Boston Symphony Orchestra musicians 2
brahmins 59–61
Brier, T. 88
Brown, M. 48
Brutus 41
Buffett, W. 61
Bush, G. W. 44
Buterin, V. 61